AF713084

The View of the Courts from the Hill

Constitutionalism and Democracy

GREGG IVERS AND
KEVIN T. MCGUIRE,
EDITORS

The View of the Courts from the Hill

INTERACTIONS BETWEEN CONGRESS AND THE FEDERAL JUDICIARY

Mark C. Miller

UNIVERSITY OF VIRGINIA PRESS CHARLOTTESVILLE AND LONDON

University of Virginia Press
© 2009 by the Rector and Visitors of the University of Virginia
All rights reserved
Printed in the United States of America on acid-free paper

First published 2009

9 8 7 6 5 4 3 2 1

Library of Congress Cataloging-in-Publication Data

Miller, Mark C. (Mark Carlton), 1958–
The view of the courts from the Hill : interactions between Congress and the federal judiciary / Mark C. Miller.
p. cm. — (Constitutionalism and democracy)
Includes bibliographical references and index.
ISBN 978-0-8139-2810-4 (cloth : alk. paper) — ISBN 978-0-8139-2821-0 (e-book)
1. Judicial power—United States. 2. Legislative power—United States. 3. Judicial independence—United States. 4. Political questions and judicial power—United States. I. Title.
KF5130.M55 2009
347.73'12—dc22

2008050478

CONTENTS

ACKNOWLEDGMENTS

This book was written in three very different places, and I want to acknowledge the assistance and encouragement I received in all three. All of the interviews for this book were conducted in Washington, D.C., while I was a visiting fellow at the Centennial Center for Political Science and Public Policy at the headquarters of the American Political Science Association (APSA) during the 2006–7 academic year (see the appendix for more details on the interviews). I also started writing the manuscript there. I would like to thank all of the staff at the APSA for making my stay so pleasant. They were extremely helpful and generous with their time. I would also like to thank the other fellows whom I met at the Centennial Center. Some were there for short periods, and others for many months. I appreciate their listening to my stories about scheduling interviews and other details of gathering interview-based data. Of course, I also want to thank all those individuals who agreed to talk to me during my interviews. Although I cannot name them, I am extremely grateful that they took the time to talk to me, and I must thank them for their frankness.

The first draft of the manuscript was completed in Worcester, Massachusetts. I thank my colleagues at Clark University for their encouragement and understanding. I also want to thank Cynthia Fenner, the former office manager of the Department of Government and International Relations, for all of her help. She provided enormous support to me in my continuing role as director of the Law and Society program at Clark, and she also put up with me for the five years that I served as the chair of the Government Department. Finally, I want to thank my students at Clark for raising interesting questions and challenging convention.

The final draft of the manuscript for this book was written in lovely Leiden, in the Netherlands. I never dreamed that I would be writing a book on the interactions between Congress and the federal courts in such a beautiful setting, where every evening I walked along the canals and windmills of Leiden. I finished the manuscript while holding the Thomas Jefferson Distinguished Fulbright Chair in the American Studies program at Leiden University. At Leiden University, I must thank Johanna "Joke" Kardux, the director of the American Studies program and a faculty member in the English department. Among many other things, Joke found me wonderful housing along a tiny canal just a ten-minute walk from my office in the history department and helped me navigate the bureaucracy of opening a bank account in Holland. Two other senior scholars at Leiden, both of whom teach American history, Eduard van der Bilt and Adam Fairclough, were excellent colleagues in the history department. Although I am not really a historian, they were quite willing to talk to me about a wide range of topics. I very much appreciate the friendship and support of these three senior faculty members. I also appreciate the friendship, humor, and generosity of three more junior scholars in the history department, Peter Tammes, Dennie Oude Nijhuis, and Jessica Roitman, who were very kind to me during my time in the Netherlands. I thank all of my colleagues in the history department, who asked me to lunch almost every day and put up with my inability to speak Dutch. I also thank my students in my two classes at Leiden, an undergraduate class on the government and politics of the United States and a graduate class on the Supreme Court in American history. The graduate students read a draft chapter of this book, and I appreciate all of their feedback. Finally, I am grateful to Marcel Oomen and Linda Pietersen, of the Fulbright Center in Amsterdam, who provided a great deal of support for my wonderful semester abroad.

Back in the United States, others assisted me with this project. Kevin McGuire and Gregg Ivers have been great in their role as the series editors at the University of Virginia Press, and I want to thank them for their support. Dick Holway, of the press, was very helpful in guiding this project through its various stages. I also want to thank the anonymous reviewers for their extremely useful comments and suggestions on the initial draft of the manuscript and on the revised version. Finally, I must thank my parents for all of their help and support over the years. I also want to thank all my friends in the greater Washington, D.C., area and beyond who read my many e-mails detailing my adventures in Holland. I could not have finished this book without the help and assistance of all of these very different groups of people in various locations around the world. Dank u wel.

Some of the arguments and interview quotations in this book also appear in my chapter "Interactions between the Federal Courts and the Other Branches," in the 2008 volume edited by me, *Exploring Judicial Politics,* published by Oxford University Press.

The View of the Courts from the Hill

INTRODUCTION

Governance as Dialogue

Scholars who study judicial politics in the United States have increasingly come to the view that the courts cannot be understood in isolation but must be seen as part of the larger system of government, since no governmental institution makes decisions in a vacuum. More and more, the popular press and interest groups have also discovered that courts and legislative bodies interact in a variety of ways and that these interactions have distinct political relevance. As Kevin Den Dulk and J. Mitchell Pickerill explain, "Treating the Court or Congress in isolation misconstrues the nature of inter-institutional lawmaking in the United States. The actions of each institution have important reciprocal effects; both contribute to the form and substance of laws" (2003, 420). And as Justice Robert Jackson argued more than fifty years ago with respect to the nation's highest court, "No sound assessment of our Supreme Court can treat it as an isolated, self-sustaining, or self-sufficient institution. It is a unit of a complex, interdependent scheme of government from which it cannot be severed" (1955, 2). This book explores congressional attitudes toward the federal courts in general and the U.S. Supreme Court in particular, concentrating on the period 1995–2006, when the Republicans mostly controlled both houses of Congress.

Given the importance of the relationship between Congress and the federal court system, this book examines the interactions between those two institutions, focusing mostly on congressional attitudes toward the federal courts and federal judges. Although scholars have traditionally tended to study these institutions in isolation, we must always remember that these institutions are part of a larger system of government. The interactions between Congress and the federal courts (and especially the Supreme Court) are essential to maintaining judicial independence so that the courts can assert their proper voice in the American system of government. As Charles Geyh has noted, "Viewing judicial independence and accountability through the eyes of Congress remains a largely untried exercise that is well worth the effort, given the profound influence that the legislative branch of government has exerted on the very nature of the judicial branch" (2006, 18).

Recently, there has been a fair amount of research on the interactions between Congress and the courts (see, e.g., Katzmann 1997, 1995, 1988; Campbell and Stack 2001; Den Dulk and Pickerill 2003; Lovell 2003; J. Barnes 2004a; Baum and Hausegger 2004; Burke 2004; Epstein, Knight, and Martin 2004; Pickerill 2004; Devins and Whittington 2005; and Geyh 2006). These works highlight the importance of understanding the complex, often strained relationship between these institutions. The American governmental system of separation of powers is the foundation for the study of the interactions between the institutions of government. Rejecting the metaphor of the three separate branches of government, Edward Rubin refers to the U.S. government as a "network of interconnected institutions" (2002, 61). Andrew Martin describes the relationship between Congress and the courts as "institutional interdependence" because "the Founders created a separation-of-powers system whereby no single institution could enact policy unilaterally" (2006, 4). Some would argue, as Patricia Wald and Neil Kinkopf do, that Congress and the courts have "a mutually dependent relationship" (2007, 69). Along these same lines, Pickerill argues that "lawmaking in our separated system is continuous, iterative, speculative, sequential, and declarative" (2004, 4). Or put more simply, as Richard Neustadt has argued, in reality the U.S. system of government features "separated institutions sharing powers" (1980, 26).

Some commentators argue that the American practice of having separate governmental institutions share power inevitably leads to conflicts between Congress and the federal courts (see, e.g., Fisher 1988; Jones 1995; Davidson and Oleszek 2004; and Pickerill 2004). Sometimes the federal courts work in harmony with Congress and/or the president; at other times they are the sole voice of their position in the inter-institutional conversation. At times, Congress or the president or both may try to weaken the courts in order to gain some advantage in the ongoing constitutional dialogue. On the other hand, sometimes Congress or the president will seek to increase the power of the courts in order to preserve a certain political agenda in the long term (see, e.g., Klarman 1997; and Gillman 2002). Sometimes the other branches will purposely defer issues to the courts for a variety of reasons, including to preserve fragile coalitions on certain pieces of legislation (see, e.g., Graber 1993; Lovell 2003; and Pickerill, 2004).

Although members of Congress and presidents throughout America's history have criticized judges and their decisions (see chapter 1), very few restrictions on the power of courts as institutions have ever been enacted into law. Writing in 1891, James Bryce observed that the courts in general, and particularly the Supreme Court, were held in high esteem by the American people, and even though many judicial decisions had provoked intense opposition, nevertheless "the credit and dignity of the Supreme Court stand very high" (264). Agreeing with this analysis, William L. Ransom observed in 1912, "The people believe in their courts, they admire their judges" (36). Building on this notion and their analysis of how the courts had survived strong rhetorical attacks throughout their history, scholars in the 1950s and 1960s arrived at the conventional wisdom that the courts were protected from institutional attacks by a popular reverence for the judicial branch. Walter Murphy, among others, refers to this phenomenon as "the cult of the robe" (1962). Jeffrey Segal, Harold Spaeth, and Sara Benesh use the term *judicial mythology,* which includes reverence, respect, secrecy, and mystery, to explain why courts are protected from many political attacks in America (2005, 17). In a similar sense, John Brigham refers to the "cult of the court" (1987), while David O'Brien prefers "the myth of the cult of the robe" (2003, 86). Combined, these myths demonstrate that the courts are seen as a special institution of government, one that is clearly more revered than the rough-and-tumble elected branches. This reverence is due in part to the fact that although they are a political institution of government, appellate courts explain their decisions in writing using legal analysis and legal reasoning.

Some have written that judicial prestige and professionalism protect the courts from attack (see, e.g., Murphy 1964, 19). C. Herman Pritchett believes that courts are protected by a general sense of respect for the institution of the judiciary (1961, 119). Murphy has also written that the "magic and mythology" surrounding the Constitution itself spills over to the popular perception of the courts as interpreters of the Constitution. As Murphy explains this phenomenon, "The sacred, mysterious character of the Constitution has been caught by the Justices in the performance of their priestly duty of expounding the meaning of that holy writ" (1964, 16). Further explaining this claim, Neal Devins contends that "median voters have historically backed judicial independence" because of a "reservoir of support for the power of the Court to independently interpret the Constitution" (2006, 1359). Stuart Nagel (1965) also asserted that the judiciary was protected from the most severe institutional attacks, although he did argue that the mere threat of retaliation from Congress could cause the Court to retreat on key hot-button issues. Glendon Schubert (1960) and I (Miller 1995) have maintained that the presence of so many lawyers in Congress protected the courts from serious institutional harm.

Many scholars argue that the courts are protected from attack because of the institutional loyalty they enjoy, meaning that the general public finds the courts to be legitimate decision- and policymakers (see, e.g., Gibson, Caldeira, and Spence 2003, 535–38). The legitimacy of the courts has grown as American history has unfolded. As Lawrence Friedman notes, "Over time, the aura of the high courts has gotten thicker and more mystical. The Supreme Court in particular seems to be protected by a kind of magic barrier of myth and mystery" (2006, 147). Robert McCloskey argues that the Supreme Court in particular is protected by a strong pool of supporters within the general public who believe that the courts, especially the Supreme Court, are a necessary part of the rule of law. These supporters protect the Court because they "venerate it and are prepared to defend it as the symbol of continuity and fairness" (McCloskey 1994, 47). "The legitimacy of the Court is its most important resource," writes Richard Pacelle. "As long as the Court is perceived to be fulfilling its role, it will retain its authority" (2002, 168). Although he is referring to the U.S. Supreme Court in particular, Pacelle could be writing about the entire federal court system.

This concept of respect for the courts and for judges is often phrased as diffuse support for the courts, as opposed to support for the outcomes of specific court decisions (see, e.g., Easton 1965, 1975; and Benesh 2006). Mostly, there is broad public support in the United States for the federal courts, especially the U.S. Supreme Court (see, e.g., Caldeira and Gibson 1992; Mondak and Smithey 1997; Gibson and Baird 1997; and Kritzer 2001). According to Lauren Bell, "Public opinion polls routinely reveal that the public holds the judicial branch in higher esteem than it holds either the legislative or the executive branches of government" (2008, 39). This reservoir of diffuse support protects the judicial institution from attack even when the general public disagrees with specific court decisions.

Geyh (2006) argues that the courts are protected from the most virulent institutional attacks from Congress because over the years these two institutions have reached a "dynamic equilibrium" that favors judicial independence. However, Geyh cautions, "every cycle of court-directed hostility has featured serious and substantial congressional factions intent on curbing the courts in significant ways. It would be a mistake to assume that independence norms have been so deeply entrenched as to render either these episodic challenges inconsequential or the vigilant defense of these norms unnecessary to their preservation" (260). Lawrence Baum goes even farther, arguing that the most serious forms of attack against the courts, that is, impeachment and court-stripping legislation, are seen as strongly illegitimate by many Americans (2004, 216).

This book examines the interactions between Congress and the federal courts in their many facets. It concentrates mostly on the current relationship between these two branches, in large part because there is more conflict today between Congress and the courts than there has been in a very long time. In order to gauge recent congressional attitudes toward the federal courts, I supplement the research for this book with more than forty interviews conducted by me over the 2006–7 academic year with members of Congress, key congressional staff, federal judges, interest-group representatives, employees of the judicial branch, and others interested in the courts. As is quite common in research on the interactions between Congress and the courts (see, e.g., Murphy 1962, viii; and Baker 2007), my interviews were all "not for attribution" and thus the quotations from those interviews I use in this book are not attributed to the specific individuals who made the statements (see the appendix for more information on the interviews).

The Governance as Dialogue Movement

This work is clearly rooted in what one could label the "governance as dialogue movement." Among academics in the United States, Alexander Bickel, in his famous book *The Least Dangerous Branch* (1962), was one of the first voices in this movement. Bickel said that the courts must engage in a "continuing colloquy" with the more political branches of government and with other political actors, refuting the judicial-supremacy approach then so common in U.S. law schools and among political scientists and other judicial scholars. Louis Fisher has argued in his *Constitutional Dialogues* (1988) and in many of his other writings that the courts, and especially the U.S. Supreme Court, are not solely responsible for interpreting the U.S. Constitution but that constitutional interpretation involves a very complicated conversation among various political and institutional actors. At times Fisher refers to this notion as "coordinate construction," meaning "the opportunity for all three branches to interpret and shape the Constitution" (Fisher and Adler 2007, 22). Elsewhere Fisher has cautioned that the independence of the courts and thus their ability to participate in the constitutional dialogue is fragile. Focusing specifically on the Supreme Court, Fisher has written, "Throughout its history, the Supreme Court has understood that its 'independence' relies on an astute appreciation of how dependent the judiciary is on the political system for understanding, supporting, and implementing judicial rulings" (2004, 153).

Other scholars also refer to constitutional interpretation as a form of inter-institutional dialogue or conversation. Although using the term *departmentalism* instead of the governance as dialogue metaphor, Walter Murphy has also written that constitutional interpretation in the United States is a complex process in which the key question is how much "deference one institution owes another under varying circumstances" (1986, 417). "It is a fact of American political life," writes Murphy, "that all public officials, from presidents to local police, often have to interpret the Constitution" (401). Robert McKeever (2006) and Fisher (2008) note that over a period of several years President George W. Bush and the Supreme Court were involved in a constitutional conversation over the rights of enemy combatants (see chapter 5). In the majority decision on this question in *Boumediene v. Bush* (2008) Justice Anthony Kennedy even described the back and forth among the branches of government on this issue as "this ongoing dialogue between and among the branches of Government" (128 S.Ct. 2229, 2243). Justice Ruth Bader Ginsburg has also stated that constitutional interpretation often requires courts to enter into "a continuing dialogue with other branches of government, the States, or the private sector" (1995, 2125). Stressing that courts can bring legal analysis and counter-majoritarian decisions to the inter-institutional constitutional conversation, Michael Comiskey concludes that "in a constitutional *democracy,* democratic and undemocratic elements interact in a 'constitutional dialogue' over the Constitution's meaning" (2004, 27, emphasis in original). For Comiskey, the undemocratic elements are of course the nonelected federal courts exercising their power of judicial review.

Thus the governance as dialogue movement acknowledges that all of the governmental actors plus other political voices must all participate in the constitutional conversation. As Roger Davidson and Walter Oleszek conclude, "All three branches of government constantly interact to shape and influence the laws Americans live under" (2004, 364). William Ross made a similar point when he observed that "although the Court may be the ultimate arbiter of the Constitution, the Court both influences and is influenced by the other two branches of government and the people. . . . Despite perennial tensions arising from the exercise of judicial power, this dialogue generally has ensured that judicial decisions and public opinion have remained relatively harmonious" (1994, 7).

In the United States, the governance as dialogue movement is thus reacting against the notion of judicial supremacy often taught in U.S. law schools, which roughly states that only the Supreme Court has the ultimate final word on constitutional issues (see, e.g., Johnsen 2004, 105; and Peretti 2005, 134–35). In refuting this conventional wisdom, Fisher explains his competing governance as dialogue view: "Instead of a hierarchical system, with the Court sitting supremely at the top, the process of making constitutional law and shaping constitutional values is decidedly polyarchic" (2004, 153). Barry Friedman generally agrees with Fisher but adds that courts "facilitate and mold the national dialogue concerning the meaning of the Constitution" (B. Friedman 1993, 581), especially in the area of fundamental rights. Friedman quickly notes that the dialogue certainly includes all three branches of the government but adds that "all segments of society participate in this constitutional interpretive dialogue" (581; see also B. Friedman 1990, 1991). Murphy concludes that the departmentalism, or governance as dialogue, as I term it, does not give the courts the last word on issues of constitutional interpretation: the courts must persuade other political actors to accept their pronouncements. Therefore the complex conversation among the branches of government requires the courts especially to use their highly refined skills of persuasion to convince the other institutions of the value of decision making rooted in the law and legal analysis (Murphy 1986, 417).

Others have argued that the interactions between the courts, the executive, and Congress are a highly complex multiple-player game, as, for example, William Eskridge (1991a, 1991b) claimed in two highly influential articles from the early 1990s (see also Ferejohn and Shipan 1990; Ferejohn and Weingast 1992; A. Martin 2006; and Zorn 2006). The rules of the game require that each institution recognize and respect the institutional perspective and institutional will of the others as much as possible. Moving beyond judicial interpretations to the general relationship among the institutions of government, Robert Katzmann has argued that "governance . . . is premised on each institution's respect for and knowledge of the others and on a continuing dialogue that produces shared understanding and comity" (1997, 1).

The interactions between Congress and the federal courts clearly fit this dialogue phenomenon (see, e.g., Paschal 1991). Davidson notes that Congress plays a clear role in interpreting constitutional provisions: "The increasing interaction between Congress and the judiciary is now an established phenomenon. Congress is an active partner in shaping the operational meaning of the constitutional text" (1993, 100). Den Dulk and Pickerill explain this complex conversation between Congress and the courts as follows: "Lawmaking in a separated system is sequential and iterative: lawmaking occurs through stages of development across institutions, and policy ideas change as they pass through these stages. In terms of Court-Congress interaction, this means that neither the judicial decision nor the statute is definitive—law is shaped and reshaped at both institutional sites at different points in time" (2003, 420). As one member of Congress told me in an interview, "The relationship between Congress and the courts involves a continuous back and forth between us and the courts. In other words, it is a complex dialogue among equal branches always jockeying for power."

Although they generally do not use the governance as dialogue metaphor, advocates of the strategic approach to judicial decision making in the United States share many of the concepts of the governance as dialogue movement. The various advocates of this approach generally believe that the Supreme Court and other federal courts in the United States do or should anticipate the reactions of the political branches, including Congress, when interpreting statutes and making constitutionally based decisions. Some of the publications advocating the strategic model of judicial decision making include those by Murphy (1964); Marks (1989); Gely and Spiller (1990); Epstein and Knight (1998); Maltzman, Spriggs, and Wahlbeck (2000); Bergara, Richman, and Spiller (2003); Epstein, Knight, and Martin (2004); and A. Martin (2006). Thus the "conversations" among the branches include both actual communication between Congress and the courts and "silent conversation," one branch merely anticipating the reactions of the other. This second kind of conversation could theoretically be as important for the governance as dialogue movement as the actual interactions between and among the institutions.

The governance as dialogue movement is now popular among many institutional and legal scholars in Canada as well, but the Canadians are reacting against the premise of *legislative supremacy* instead of the

American notion of judicial supremacy. In Canada, law-school dean Peter Hogg and Allison Bushell (1997) probably coined the term *governance as dialogue* in the Canadian context with their highly influential article in the *Osgoode Hall Law Journal.* Kent Roach has written a variety of works using the governance as dialogue metaphor (see, e.g., Roach 2001a, 2001b, 2005a, 2005b). Janet Hiebert's *Charter Conflicts: What Is Parliament's Role?* (2002) appears to support the view that both Parliament and the courts have an important policymaking role in Canadian society. Sujit Choudhry and Claire Hunter published an article in the *McGill Law Journal* (2003) that supports this school of thought, building on an article in the *Dalhousie Law Journal* by A. Wayne MacKay (2001). In a volume edited by Richard Bauman and Tsvi Kahana (2006) the various authors examine the governance as dialogue movement in a variety of countries but focus mostly on the United States and Canada. In Canada, the governance as dialogue movement adds the courts to the list of policymakers in that society, stating that courts should and do play a key role in constitutional democracies that goes beyond mere adjudication of disputes. In fact, in a growing number of key opinions the Supreme Court of Canada has referred to their responsibility of judicial review as a dialogue with elected officials (see, e.g., Petter 2006, 524).

In both countries, the governance as dialogue movement argues that the various institutions of government are all involved in a complex and continuous conversation about the meaning of various constitutional provisions and practices. Although *governance as dialogue* is an umbrella term for many different specific approaches to the study of governmental institutions, most works from this movement reject the notion of either total legislative supremacy or total judicial supremacy in favor of a much more complicated and nuanced, continuous process of interaction among the institutions. As I have stated in another work, "As a matter of constitutional design, the United States simply does not feature a hierarchy of lawmakers or compartmentalized niches for each branch of government. Instead, the U.S. Constitution creates a system of overlapping and diversely representative branches of government, which share and compete for power" (Barnes and Miller 2004b, 202).

In Canada, the governance as dialogue movement has been attacked by a variety of scholars (mostly political scientists) who prefer a more parliamentary supremacy and therefore a majoritarian approach to policymaking. It is interesting that in Canada many law professors favor the governance as dialogue approach, while many political scientists oppose it. Those who oppose the governance as dialogue metaphor in Canada view the Supreme Court of Canada as improperly activist in its interpretations of the Charter of Rights and Freedoms. Critics of the governance as dialogue school of thought in Canada include many judicial-politics scholars, such as Christopher Manfredi and James Kelly (1999); F. L. Morton and Rainer Knopff (Morton and Rainer 2000; Morton 2001); Ian Brodie (2002); Robert Martin (2003); and many of the authors in Patrick James, Donald E. Abelson, and Michael Lusztig's *Myth of the Sacred* (2002).

Today some right-wing critics of the governance as dialogue movement in the United States also seem to prefer a legislative-supremacy or at least a majoritarian model for constitutional interpretation. Social conservatives and others from the Religious Right have frequently attacked the U.S. courts for trampling on the will of the majority. For example, according to several of my interviewees, former Congressman John Hostettler (R-IN), a nonlawyer former member of the House Judiciary Committee and "a leading voice for social conservatives" (Barone, Cohen, and Ujifusa 2005, 643), apparently on several occasions told the committee that *Marbury v. Madison* (1803) had been wrongly decided and should be ignored. Hostettler is not alone in his belief in legislative supremacy. As one movement conservative congressional staffer told me, "Law schools teach the myth that there are three co-equal branches of government in the U.S. In reality, the courts are subservient to the will of the majority as expressed by the legislative branch."

Some conservatives have used a majoritarian model to encourage congressional oversight of the courts. For example, former House Speaker Newt Gingrich, at a conference on judicial independence held at the Georgetown Law Center in September 2006, argued, "To arrogate that a handful of lifetime appointees in the third branch are somehow superior to the first two branches is an explicit violation of Hamilton's writing in the Federalist Papers. . . . The danger you have is that a court which imposes elite values in variance with the country weakens its own believability and puts itself in a position to be repudiated by the legislative and executive branches" (see "Fair and Independent Courts" 2006).

There are also advocates of legislative supremacy in the American academy (see, e.g., Bickel 1962; and Wells 1991). Although he would probably describe himself as center-left, Stanford Law School Dean Larry D. Kramer articulated this concept of legislative supremacy, which has become the rallying cry of the Religious Right in the United States, when he wrote:

> We in the twenty-first century tend to divide the world into two distinct domains: a domain of politics and a domain of law. In politics, the people rule. But not in law. Law is set aside for a trained elite of judges and lawyers whose professional task is to implement the formal decision produced in and by politics. The Constitution, in this modern understanding, is a species of law—special only inasmuch as it sets the boundaries within which politics takes place. As law, the Constitution is set aside for this same elite to handle, subject to paramount supervision from the U.S. Supreme Court. . . . This modern understanding is . . . of surprisingly recent vintage. It reflects neither the original conception of constitutionalism nor its course over most of American history. (2004, 7–8)

In a call for more judicial restraint that may start to sound like legislative supremacy, the law professor Mark Tushnet even entitled one of his many books *Taking the Constitution Away from the Courts* (1999). Thus both Kramer and Tushnet (who probably see themselves as left of center) have articulated the notion of popular constitutionalism, which is one of the major themes of the Religious Right in discussions of their preferred role for the courts.

Academics on the left have been highly critical of Kramer and Tushnet's idea of popular constitutionalism, which is usually perceived by them as a right-wing theory of constitutional interpretation. For example, in response to Kramer and Tushnet's advocacy for popular constitutionalism, Erwin Chemerinsky wrote, "I kept thinking about what [this] theory would mean for civil rights and civil liberties litigation. The answer is chilling. Popular constitutionalism would mean that courts would be far less available to protect fundamental rights. The rights of minorities would be largely left to the whims of the political majority with severe consequences for racial, ethnic, sexual orientation, and language minorities as well as criminal defendants, public benefits recipients, and others" (2004, 1013).

Left-wing academics clearly see Kramer and Tushnet as making right-wing arguments in this instance. As Frederick Schauer explains the ideological paradox in these arguments from scholars like Kramer and Tushnet, although Kramer and others who attack, or at least question, judicial supremacy might loosely be thought of as lying to the left of center in contemporary American politics, the contemporary academic attack on judicial supremacy was in fact initiated by conservatives such as Michael Paulsen (1994) and Gary Lawson (1996). Moreover, the position espoused by Kramer and Paulsen, among others, was embraced in 1986 by Ronald Reagan's attorney general, Edwin Meese III (see Schauer 2004, 1049). As Schauer explains, "Challenges to judicial supremacy were Justice Department policy throughout the administrations of Ronald Reagan and George H. W. Bush, and were a central focus of conservative plans at the beginning of President George W. Bush's administration" (1050).

Thus in the United States the legislative-supremacy notion not only fueled the theory behind the work of the Radical Republicans in the Reconstruction period after the Civil War but also formed a foundation for some of the criticism of the Supreme Court in the 1950s. However, strong advocacy for legislative supremacy in the United States has been somewhat rare over the years. As Walter Murphy explained, "Systematic assertions of legislative supremacy in constitutional interpretation have been infrequent, though they have at times been vigorously pushed. . . . Constitutionalism is wary of arguments that allow popularly elected officials final authority to define substantive rights" (1986, 410–11). Thus the notion of legislative supremacy has negative connotations for many commentators, especially those on the left. As one liberal lobbyist whom I interviewed quipped, "Legislative supremacy in this context means 'Father Knows Best.'"

A New Institutionalist Approach

In addition to using the governance as dialogue foundation, I also utilize a "new institutionalist" approach to the study of judicial politics. While new institutionalism underlies my entire approach to the study of the interactions between Congress and the courts, its use is most evident in chapter 4, where I explore the changing institutional culture of the House Judiciary Committee.

The new institutionalist approach argues that a political actor's behavior is shaped by his or her institutional setting and institutional role. New institutionalist scholars explore how institutional realities constrain the behavior of political actors such as judges and legislators. Thus new institutionalism attempts to combine the traditionalist scholar's interest in understanding governmental bodies as institutions with the behavioralist's emphasis on empirical, individual-level research. Rogers Smith describes the new institutionalist approach as focusing on "the interrelationship between human 'institutions' or 'structures' and the decisions and actions of political actors" (1988, 91). As Howard Gillman and Cornell Clayton describe the approach, new institutionalism pays attention to institutional norms and traditions, while situating the institution in the larger political context (1999, 5). Christopher Banks and David O'Brien argue that new institutionalist analysis aims "to connect, from an interpretative and historical perspective, normative conceptions of law and courts with the contemporary analysis of legal institutions and their political roles" (2008, 303).

In judicial politics, the new institutionalist approach combines attributes from other conceptions of judicial decision making. Thus the new institutionalists agree that the legal model, according to which judging is based purely on legal reasoning and legal analysis, is important in understanding judicial decisions, as is the attitudinal model, which stresses the importance of the ideologies of individual judges in judicial decision making. The new institutionalist approach can also embrace most of the strategic model of judicial decision making. Thus new institutionalism combines and borrows from a large number of academic approaches to the study of judicial decision making. The key point is that institutional norms and cultures constrain the behavior of political actors; the institution almost takes on a life of its own. As Tom Ginsburg and Robert Kagan have noted, "Institutions are more than the sum of the individuals that make them up" (2005, 2). Thus John Rawls described a political institution as "an abstract object" realized in "thought and conduct" (1971, 11), and Howard Gillman entitled an essay on new institutionalism "The Court as an Idea, not a Building (or a Game)" (1999).

New institutionalist analysis is often interdisciplinary in nature, and the new institutionalist study of judicial politics draws on the disciplines of law, politics, history, sociology, and occasionally economics (see, e.g., Banks and O'Brien 2008, 303). While *new institutionalism* is an umbrella term for a variety of methodologies, my approach is most clearly within the historical-interpretive stream (see, e.g., Hall and Taylor 1996; and Pierson and Skocpol 2001), although I do borrow some concepts, such as institutional culture, from the sociological school. New institutionalism thus attempts to bring a new understanding of how political institutions actually operate in society. Thus Brigham notes, "One quality of a social institution is that we take it for granted" (1987, 14). He argues that institutional analysis works to "show how an institution is revealed through evolving traditions of possible action and in terms of the practices that constitute them" (6). New institutionalism thus looks at how institutional norms and cultures affect the behavior of individual political actors.

New institutionalist analysis can also focus on concepts such as institutional culture (see, e.g., Hall and Taylor 1996, 939) and the "institutional will" (see, e.g., Dodd 1981, 391). The notion of an institutional will dates back to *Federalist No. 51,* in which James Madison, in his discussion of the notion of the separation of powers, said that "to be essential to the preservation of liberty, it is evident that each department should have a will of its own." The will of a governmental institution is thus more than just the sum total of the individual preferences of those political actors who make up the institution. Treating the institution as an entity unto itself, new institutionalist scholars can examine the culture, the perspective, and the will that make that political institution unique. Scholars can also focus more easily on the interactions between institutions if they consider each institution as a unique entity with its own institutional will. Thus Brigham argues that "institutions are not simply robes and marble, nor are they contained in codes or documents. Meaningful action makes institutions" (1987, 21). New institutionalism has been especially useful in explaining the role of the courts in America's inter-institutional constitutional conversation. As Banks and O'Brien note, "Historical institutionalism contextualizes judicial decision making by situating it within the framework of institutional arrangements and practices, such as the structure of courts, judicial norms, and the makeup of law schools or bar associations, which are embedded in the legal culture" (2008, 303).

The interactions between institutions also form part of the institutional constraints for political actors, as Lee Epstein and Jack Knight articulated so well in their influential book about the strategic behavior of judges, *The Choices Justices Make* (1998). Epstein, Knight, and Andrew Martin (2004) argue that even constitutional interpretation by the Supreme Court is highly influenced by the Court's interactions with Congress and with other political actors. Examining the interactions between and among institutions helps us move beyond understanding political behavior as caused or produced by a single dominant variable such as the ideology of an individual political actor. The reality is much more complex and multifaceted. As Cornell Clayton has helped to clarify the new institutionalist approach, "At the heart of the new institutionalism is a challenge to the reductionist and instrumentalist conception of politics that characterized behavioralism" (1999, 30). In order to understand how political actors view their institutional role and the culture of the institution in which they serve, we must examine both their actions and their words. I believe that personal interviews with political actors such as judges and legislators are very useful for furthering our understanding of the institutional constraints facing political decision makers in both institutions.

New institutionalism examines institutional constraints on political behavior by using multiple levels of analysis, often simultaneously (see, e.g., Miller 1995). These levels of analysis include treating the political institution as a unique entity, as well as examining its component parts. A new institutionalist approach also assumes that the study of political institutions can get quite messy at times, because "institutional politics is comprised of multiple orders and patterns of intercurrence that often create unintended consequences, paradoxes, and disjunctions" (Gillman 2006a, 141). This book thus examines congressional attitudes toward the federal courts at the levels of the individual member of Congress, the congressional committee, the chamber, and Congress as a whole. Using different levels of analysis helps us better to understand the relationships between these two governmental institutions.

How Congress Can Attack the Courts

When Congress is angry with the courts, it potentially has a variety of tools at its disposal to attack the judiciary. Individual members of Congress can of course criticize various court decisions, and this has been quite common throughout American history. Talk is cheap, and many members of Congress routinely denounce judicial decisions with which they disagree. Nicholas Katzenbach, U.S. attorney general under President Lyndon Johnson, once observed that "legislators frequently have gone after the Supreme Court because it doesn't cost anything" (qtd. in O'Brien 2005, 346). If the courts issue an opinion on a statutory interpretation with which the majority in Congress disagrees, the legislature can merely enact a new statute to counteract the court's decision. Congress can also initiate constitutional amendments in an attempt to overturn judicial decisions based on the Constitution, although Congress has also been known to pass statutes with this intent. The Supreme Court has generally ruled such statutory attempts to be unconstitutional, congressional statutes on flag burning, the *Miranda* warnings, and the Religious Freedom Restoration Act being prime examples (see Miller 1995, 156–61; Kamisar 2006; and Bragaw and Miller 2004, respectively).

The legislature can also use its power of the purse in an attempt to force the courts to change their opinions. The Constitution gives federal judges life tenure, and it prevents Congress from reducing their salaries while they are on the bench. But nothing requires Congress to appropriate funds for annual cost-of-living adjustments, to provide adequate funding for courthouse construction and repair, or to provide staff, computers, or even air conditioning for federal judges. In theory Congress could also use its taxing powers to send clear signals to the courts when it is unhappy with judicial decisions (see Entin and Jensen 2006).

Congress can also use its powers to increase or decrease the number of federal judges serving on any particular court, as well to change the boundaries for the federal courts of appeals. President Roosevelt unsuccessfully attempted to pack the Supreme Court by significantly increasing the number of justices on the Court when it kept declaring his New Deal to be unconstitutional, although the Court eventually gave in to FDR's wishes in the famous "Switch in Time that Saved Nine" (see, e.g., O'Brien 2003). The Senate can also use its advice-and-consent function for judicial nominations to help shape the membership of the federal judiciary (see, e.g., Schumer 2007). Many of these possible actions are discussed in more detail in chapter 2.

Thus sometimes congressional attacks against the courts can turn into threats to judicial independence. It is important to distinguish between rhetorical criticisms of particular judicial decisions or even of particular judges and more dangerous institutional attacks on the foundational notion of judicial independence (see chapter 6). Historically, both the Right and the Left at various times have threatened the independence of the courts, although these threats have rarely been put into action. Generally, attacks on the courts as institutions and other court-curbing efforts can be divided into four main categories (see Culp 1929). With respect to the Supreme Court, these categories include (1) proposals for appeals of Court decisions, often to legislative committees of review; (2) proposals to require supermajorities on the Court before legislation can be declared unconstitutional; (3) proposals to change the methods for selecting and removing judges from the bench; and (4) proposals to strip the lower federal courts and often the Supreme Court of jurisdiction to hear certain types of cases or to hear litigation involving certain groups of litigants. All of these court-curbing efforts have the intent of changing the relationship among the institutions and weakening the voice of the courts in the inter-institutional conversation.

Some of the weapons available to Congress when it is upset with the federal courts can cause long-term harm to the judicial institution itself. Although it is highly controversial and the constitutional limits of such actions are unclear, Congress can prevent the federal courts and/or the U.S. Supreme Court from hearing certain classes of cases. These so-called court-stripping measures have been quite rare in U.S. history, although as explained in chapter 5, Congress has enacted quite a few of these measures in the last several years. Congress can also increase its oversight of the judicial branch through an inspector general or some similar mechanism. Finally, there have been increasing threats from various politicians and interest groups to push for the impeachment of federal judges who hand down decisions that these groups dislike. No federal judge has been removed from office for purely political reasons, and the last federal judge to be impeached (but not removed from office) for clearly partisan reasons was Justice Samuel Chase, in 1803 (see, e.g., Rehnquist 1992). But the threats of impeachment from an angry Congress have grown more severe lately.

Current Conflicts between Congress and the Courts

Now, in the first decade of the twenty-first century, we may be experiencing one of the greatest periods of conflict between Congress and the courts. Some legislative attacks on the courts even threaten the independence of the courts as certain elements in American society attempt to silence the voice of the judiciary in the inter-institutional constitutional dialogue. As Lyle Denniston, a journalist who has covered the Supreme Court for many years, stated recently, "In 56 years of journalism, most of which has been spent hanging around lawyers and courthouses, I have never experienced the depth of venom that now flows around the relationship between the branches of government, particularly around the judiciary" ("The Courts" 2004, 221). In interviews with this author during the fall of 2006, before the midterm elections held in that year, various members of Congress and congressional staff described the relationship between Congress and the federal courts as "venomous," "hostile," "tense," "deteriorating," "contentious," "animosity," and "strained." A conservative Republican described the relationship as "adversarial." One liberal U.S. representative lamented, "The relationship between the Congress and the federal courts is at an all time low." Another liberal representative said that "there is less respect for the independence of the courts today."

Others agree that the relationship between the legislative and judicial branches has clearly deteriorated. Recent criticisms of the federal courts have come from both the Right and the Left in American politics, as the Rehnquist Court handed down both liberal activist and conservative activist decisions simultaneously (see, e.g., Keck 2004). But as we shall see, the most serious attacks on the judiciary have come from social conservatives, who have little trust in the courts as an institution. Referring to these recent right-wing attacks on the courts, in 2005 *Newsweek* even ran a story entitled "The War on Judges," in which Debra Rosenberg argued that "concern over the rising tide of anti-judge rhetoric has rocked even the Supreme Court. Though judges have been dragged into the culture wars before, lately the animosity—and a range of new efforts to curb judicial power—have reached fever pitch" (D. Rosenberg 2005, 23). Many have noted the recent strained relationship between Congress and the federal courts. One journalist observed in 2004, "Relations between the legislative and judicial branches have deteriorated to a level not seen since the tumult over civil rights and busing in the 1960's and 1970's" (Perine 2004, 2148).

The relationship between Congress and the courts was so bad in 2005 that in May of that year more than two-thirds of the deans of U.S. law schools signed a letter addressed to the leaders of both houses of Congress asking them to take steps to protect the courts from congressional attacks. In part, the letter stated that the deans were writing in opposition to "the recent threats of retaliation against federal judges for decisions they have made on the bench" (Revesz et al. 2005, 1). In his recent book on the subject, Ross Baker described the relationship between Congress and the federal courts as one of "mutual wariness, suspicion, jealousy, and even a bit of spite" (2007, 116).

Many of the justices of the U.S. Supreme Court have also noted the deteriorating relationship between Congress and the federal courts. In 2004 Justice Sandra Day O'Connor said that the relationship between Congress and the federal courts was "more tense than at any time in my lifetime" (qtd. in Greenhouse 2005c). Justice Ginsburg stated that the judiciary was "under assault in a way that I haven't seen before" (qtd. in Mauro 2006a). Chief Justice John Roberts even called for conservatives to back off from attacking the courts (see Mauro 2006b). Even Justice Samuel Alito has said that the threats to judicial independence are at an all-time high (see Scholl 2006). As Chief Justice William Rehnquist stated in his 2004 annual report, "Criticism of judges has dramatically increased in recent years, exacerbating in some respects the strained relationship between the Congress and the federal judiciary" (2004, 4).

Many of the Supreme Court justices have begun to speak out publicly on the need to protect the independence of the courts from congressional attacks. Justice O'Connor even wrote an op-ed piece published in the *Wall Street Journal* in September 2006 entitled "The Threat to Judicial Independence." This piece ran a few days after Justices O'Connor and Stephen Breyer appeared on the *Charlie Rose Show* on PBS to defend the courts. After outlining many of the current attacks on the judiciary from Congress and the state legislatures, Justice O'Connor concluded in the op-ed piece: "The breadth and intensity of rage currently being leveled at the judiciary may be unmatched in American history. The ubiquitous 'activist judges' who 'legislate from the bench' have become central villains on today's domestic political landscape. . . . Though these attacks generally emit more heat than light, using judges as punching bags presents a grave threat to the independent judiciary."

Have the rhetorical attacks on the courts as an institution, especially from those on the right, placed the courts in new peril? Are the attacks in Congress today of a different magnitude than those of previous eras? Many seem to think that the relationship between the courts and Congress is reaching a dangerous tipping point. Stephen B. Burbank, of the University of Pennsylvania Law School, is quite concerned about the attacks on the courts: "I think that the current attacks on the courts, although of course not unprecedented, are unusual and potentially quite dangerous for two reasons. One, because they evidently reflect the strategies of some interest groups and even, alas, of some politicians to attack the courts. That's new. And two, those strategies themselves reflect the view of judges as policy agents, . . . or as a means to an end" ("Fair and Independent Courts" 2006). The former Senate majority leader Tom Daschle (D-SD) recently said, "I think this tension is different today; it's more insidious and I'm troubled by it. . . . The frequent and strident attack on the courts is an effort to persuade the public that the courts are really nothing more than ordinary politics and as such ought to be held accountable. What troubles me is that we would destroy 200 years of building these institutions for the sake of the next news cycle" ("Fair and Independent Courts" 2006).

Many see the current rhetorical attacks on the courts as an institution as harming judicial independence, an independence that allows the courts to be full participants in the inter-institutional constitutional dialogue. Justice O'Connor has become a leading spokesperson on the issue of judicial independence since her retirement from the Court. In September 2006 she and Justice Breyer hosted an influential conference on judicial independence at the Georgetown University Law Center entitled "Fair and Independent Courts: A Conference on the State of the Judiciary." The conference was attended by several of her colleagues on the Supreme Court, including Justices David Souter and Clarence Thomas and Chief Justice Roberts, as well as influential national leaders in business and politics. In her opening remarks Justice O'Connor stated: "We must not be deceived into overlooking or underrating the real and serious dissatisfaction with courts and lack of respect for the law, which exists in the United States today." At this same conference, after discussing the fact that politicians have long criticized the courts in the United States, Stanford law professor Kathleen Sullivan talked about how the current attacks on the courts as institutions differ from earlier attacks. In colorful language, she said, "The kind of ferocity of the attacks on judges that we see in single-issue legislation . . . is perhaps new in its intensity, although not in its nature. And that's the reason to have some alarm here, and to try to re-establish our basics and remember that judicial independence is part of our birthright. We shouldn't give it away for a mess of porridge." As Justice O'Connor concluded at the conference, "Judicial independence is for the benefit of all of society" ("Fair and Independent Courts" 2006).

Differences in Role Theory and the Decision-Making Styles of Judges and Politicians

Because judicial decision making is rooted in legal analysis and legal reasoning, federal judges view their roles very differently than do elected politicians. Thus a person is very likely to make different decisions as a judge than he or she would as a legislator or other type of politician (see, e.g., Graber 2006, 59). As C. Herman Pritchett explained many years ago, "Not even on the Supreme Court is the judicial function to be equated with that of the legislator" (1948, 20). These differences are due in part to differences in roles and decision-making styles, but they are also affected by the different institutional constraints and institutional norms in the two branches of government. To the question whether the different institutional cultures, different institutional norms, and different institutional wills of the courts and Congress would compel different results from the same individual depending upon the institution in which he or she was serving and his or her role, the answer seems clearly to be yes, because judges approach their decision-making duties differently than do politicians. While serving in a political institution, judges must explain their decisions using the law and legal reasoning (see, e.g., Richards and Kritzer 2002). Thus judges use the language of law and lawyers. Justice Kennedy, for example, noted that the Supreme Court was "set apart from other branches of government because it speaks a different language from the political branches" (qtd. in Perry 1999, 48). Judges have their own, unique way of understanding the world. As Lawrence Friedman argues, "Most of the time, as far as we can tell, judges of all political stripes, outlooks, backgrounds, and philosophies, tend to come to the same *legal* conclusions in ordinary cases" (2006, 149) (emphasis in original). While judicial decision making can certainly be political in nature, it most certainly must also be based on the law. The unique factor that the courts bring to the inter-institutional constitutional conversation is their legal analysis and explanations based on the rule of law.

Judge John M. Walker Jr., of the United States Court of Appeals for the Second Circuit, has written a great deal about the differences between the decision-making processes of judges and politicians. Walker refers to the concept of "judicial modesty." He says that judges must approach their job very differently than elected officials do theirs because judges must use a limited number of traditional sources of law, while politicians can use whatever sources they please to inform their decisions. Appellate judges must explain their decisions through their written public opinions, while in many circumstances politicians need not explain their decisions at all. Judges are passive decision makers, waiting for the parties to a lawsuit to bring the issues to the court; elected officials, especially legislators, are active decision makers who must wait for no one before acting. Although judges consult a variety of sources of law, writes Walker, "primacy [must] always be given to the language used by the people's representatives" (2007, 124). Thus there are very real restraints on judges' decision making, while politicians need not worry about such things. Walker concludes, "Respect for the authority of the law depends on judicial modesty—judges performing their proper role within the judiciary's institutional limitations. Yet judicial modesty does not engender respect for the rule of law unless the public is aware of that constraint and realizes its significance in shaping judicial behavior" (123).

A good example of the difference between the role orientations of judges and politicians is the decision of the Supreme Court in the first of the Legal Tender Cases, decided just after the Civil War. In *Hepburn v. Griswold* (1870) the Supreme Court by a vote of 4-3 declared unconstitutional a federal statute of 1862 requiring that creditors of the United States accept paper money not backed by gold or other precious metals in payment of debts owed by the United States. The Lincoln administration had considered this act necessary to maintain the war effort during the Civil War. The *Hepburn* decision was quickly overturned by *Knox v. Lee* (1871) by a vote of 5-4 after President Grant appointed two new justices to the Court. The irony of the *Hepburn* decision was that it was written by Chief Justice Chase, whom Lincoln had appointed to the Court in large part because Chase had been Lincoln's secretary of the treasury in 1862, and Chase had authored the Legal Tender Act in the first place. One can only assume that Chase had believed the act to be constitutional when he proposed it, even if his views changed after he was appointed to the Supreme Court. As Chief Justice Rehnquist has noted, "Chase's vote in the Legal Tender cases is a textbook example of the proposition that one may look at a legal question differently as a judge from the way one did as a member of the executive branch" (2001, 214).

Justices have often stated that they made different decisions as judges than they would have made as politicians. In *Texas v. Johnson* (1989), the case that declared that burning the American flag was protected political speech under the First Amendment, Justice Kennedy in his concurring opinion wrote about judges in general: "The hard fact is that sometimes we must make decisions we do not like. We make them because they are right, right in the sense that the law and the Constitution, as we see them, compel the result. And so great is our commitment to the process that, except in the rare case, we do not pause to express distaste for the result, perhaps for fear of undermining a valued principle that dictates the decision" (491 U.S. 397, 420–21). Justice O'Connor addressed this question in her dissent in *Roper v. Simmons* (2005), in which the majority ruled that the death penalty was unconstitutional for juveniles who had committed the crime in question before they were eighteen years old: "Were my office that of a legislator, rather than a judge, then I, too, would be inclined to support legislation setting a minimum age of 18 in this context" (543 U.S. 551, 607). Justice O'Connor made similar comments in her dissent in *Gonzales v. Raich* (2005), in which the majority of the Supreme Court said that the California law allowing the use of marijuana for medical purposes had to yield to federal drug laws outlawing the substance: "If I were a California citizen, I would not have voted for the medical marijuana ballot initiative; if I were a California legislator I would not have supported the Compassionate Use Act. But whatever the wisdom of California's experiment with medical marijuana, the federalism principles that have driven our Commerce Clause cases require that room for experiment be protected in this case" (545 U.S. 1, 57).

Thus sometimes judges wish that they could act like legislators but feel that their reading of the law requires a different result. Take Justice Potter Stewart's dissent in *Griswold v. Connecticut* (1965), in which the Court declared the state's statutory ban on the use or sale of contraceptives to be unconstitutional. Refusing to follow the liberal judicial activism of his colleagues, Justice Stewart wrote: "I think this is an uncommonly silly law. . . . As a philosophical matter, I believe the use of contraceptives in the relationship of marriage should be left to personal and private choice, based upon each individual's moral, ethical, and religious beliefs. . . . But we are not asked in this case to say whether we think this law is unwise, or even asinine. We are asked to hold that it violates the United States Constitution. And that I cannot do" (381 U.S. 479, 527). Justice Thomas made a similar claim in *Lawrence v. Texas* (2003), a case in which the majority declared the Texas ban on homosexual sodomy to be unconstitutional. After echoing Justice Stewart's claim in *Griswold* that the statute was "uncommonly silly," Justice Thomas wrote in his dissent in *Lawrence:* "If I were a member of the Texas Legislature, I would vote to repeal it. Punishing someone for expressing his sexual preference through noncommercial consensual conduct with another adult does not appear to be a worthy way to expend valuable law enforcement resources. Notwithstanding this, I recognize that as a member of this Court I am not empowered to help petitioners and others similarly situated. My duty, rather, is to decide cases agreeably to the Constitution and laws of the United States" (539 U.S. 558, 605).

Justice John Paul Stevens has also said that his decisions on a variety of issues would be different if he were in Congress rather than having to make the decisions from the bench. For example, in 2005 the Supreme Court handed down two highly controversial decisions. The first said that local governments could use their power of eminent domain to "take" private property in order to facilitate private economic development (*Kelo v. City of New London* [2005]); this decision is discussed in more detail in chapter 3. The second decision ruled that Congress could decide to use federal drug laws to overrule various state decisions that had allowed marijuana use for medical purposes (*Gonzales v. Raich* [2005]). In a public speech to a bar association meeting in Las Vegas, Justice Stevens said that from a policy point of view both outcomes were "unwise" but were required by his reading of the Constitution. Clearly illustrating the differences between decisions made by members of Congress and those made by judges, Justice Stevens stated that "in each [decision] I was convinced that the law compelled a result that I would have opposed if I were a legislator" (qtd. in Greenhouse 2005b). In a more recent discussion of the *Kelo* decision, Justice Stevens said that the strong negative reactions to the decision reflect the rough-and-tumble of interest-group politics, implying that legal analysis should not take such political realities into consideration: "As you know there are pressure groups that have very strong feelings about property rights. I sympathize with all that, but I thought that was a clear case of what the law compelled. It's part of the job to write unpopular decisions. No doubt about it" (qtd. in Rosen 2007, 78). Thus in areas where law and politics collide, judges tend to make decisions based on their reading of the law, while legislators have the luxury of basing their decisions on purely political considerations.

The Unwillingness of Judges to Speak Out on Their Own Behalf

Efforts to protect judicial independence are hampered by the professional and ethical requirements of judges. Professional norms and ethical rules often prevent judges from speaking out publicly when the courts are under assault. As one lobbyist told me, "Judges are restricted in their public communication, and they can't really defend themselves from political attacks." As mentioned previously, Judge John M. Walker Jr., of the United States Court of Appeals for the Second Circuit, refers to this refusal of judges to protect themselves in the political arena as "judicial modesty." This inability to speak out publicly hampers the ability of judges to respond to attacks against the judiciary as an institution. As John Ferejohn and Larry Kramer note, "Judges are, generally speaking, a cautious lot, which is hardly surprising for officials whose decisions deal with controversial public matters but who lack access to most normal channels for acquiring political capital" (2006, 167). Judges themselves have noted the apparent inability of federal judges to respond to attacks against them, in part because judges have little political clout. As Judge Harry T. Edwards puts it, "We [judges] have no natural constituency to lobby for us and we do not feel at ease ourselves in doing battle in the political arena" (2006, 234). Chief Justice Earl Warren also made this point when he stated, "We have no constituency. We serve no majority. We serve no minority. We serve only the public interest as we see it, guided by the Constitution and our own consciences" (qtd. in Simon 1973, 2).

Although judges often refrain from defending themselves, others often step in to protect them from attack. Robert McCloskey notes that lawyers are often strong defenders of an independent judiciary, in large part because they have been trained to understand the importance of the courts in promoting the rule of law (1994, 47). Since lawyers have been involved in American politics in a wide variety of positions since the founding of this country (see, e.g., Miller 1995), they can use their skills to protect judges and the courts from most institutional attacks. Academics are also able to defend judges when they cannot or will not defend themselves. Many judicial scholars and law professors have argued that threats to judicial independence must be turned back. In their May 2005 letter to the congressional leadership, the deans of more than two-thirds of the law schools in the United states observed, "Judges are expected to comport themselves in a reserved and dispassionate matter at all times, making it difficult for them to defend themselves effectively" (Revesz et al. 2005, 1).

Groups such as the American Bar Association (ABA), the American Judicature Society, and Justice at Stake also speak out in favor of judicial independence and against attacks on the federal judiciary, whether these attacks come from the Right or from the Left. For example, Ross (1994) discusses the role that the ABA has played in protecting the courts from the worst attacks. The ABA continues its efforts to protect the courts from institutional attacks. As its Web site recently declared, "Although robust criticism of judicial decisions is fully protected by the First Amendment and is indispensable to the well being of a democracy, misleading or intemperate judicial criticism misinforms the public, distorts their view of the judicial process, and may undermine public confidence in our courts" (American Bar Association 2008).

Sometimes even retired judges speak out in order to help protect the courts from attack. Since retiring from the bench, for example, Justice O'Connor has defended judicial independence in a variety of settings, including the fall 2006 conference at the Georgetown University Law Center (for a transcript of the proceedings see "Fair and Independent Courts" 2006). Justice O'Connor has also called for lawyers and others interested in protecting the courts from attacks to speak out. As she stated, "Statutes and constitutions do not protect judicial independence—people do" (qtd. in Lash 2006b).

One way in which judges can defend themselves is to speak out against anti-court legislation being considered by Congress. Instead of speaking for themselves, judges often allow the Administrative Office of the United States Courts or even the Judicial Conference to speak for them on legislative matters. The Administrative Office includes the Office of Legislative Affairs and the Office of Judicial Impact Assessment. The Federal Judges Association was established as a lobbying organization for judicial salaries and budgets. However, the Judicial Conference has a long-standing policy of not contacting Congress about pending legislation unless Congress requests its input. This policy is sometimes honored in the breach, because the Judicial Conference will sometimes seek invitations to comment on legislative proposals. On the rare occasions when federal judges do appear at congressional hearings, they do everything they can to appear differential to the legislative body (see Geyh 2006, 239–41).

Many judges do not want to be seen as pushing a political agenda in Congress. As Deborah Barrow and Thomas Walker explain, "The idea of judicial lobbying is anathema to many. It somehow seems inappropriate for federal judges, whose adjudicative role requires neutrality rather than advocacy, to urge the passage or defeat of proposed legislation" (1988, 258). Along these lines, Judge John Walker notes, "My concern was and remains that centuries-old observation that the authority of the law and its courts rests on principles, not politics" (2007, 124).

During my interviews, I asked members of Congress and congressional staff how often they heard from federal judges on legislation being considered by Congress. Some said that they heard from federal judges quite often, while others said they had never heard from federal judges themselves but had heard instead from the Administrative Office of the United States Courts or the Judicial Conference. Many legislators said that they would like to learn more about federal judges' views on pending legislation. For example, one member of the House Judiciary Committee told me: "I think there should be a helpful dialogue between the courts and Congress. I think it is good for us to share our perspectives with each other. I think we need more input from federal judges on a variety of questions, but we especially need judicial input on criminal sentencing issues." Others said that direct communication between legislators and judges was quite routine. Along these lines, a Senate staffer told me, "All Senators seem to want to hear from federal judges directly. It is a natural relationship that draws on the judicial confirmation process. My boss has a lot of former employees on the bench, so he likes to network with the judges."

A variety of members of Congress said they welcomed more input from federal judges on legislation that would affect their daily lives. One member of Congress told me, "I hear from attorneys more than I do from judges. I think we need more communication from judges on caseload and judicial salary issues especially." One Democratic congressman told me that he advocated having members of Congress and federal judges sit down with each other and talk at least three times a year, because he wanted a more formal mechanism for hearing the concerns of federal judges. Another congressman told me that he hears regularly from federal judges on many policy issues, such as the federal sentencing guidelines. "It is good to share our different perspectives," he told me. "I think it is a helpful dialogue when the judges share their views with me. We need a better process for judges to weigh in on appropriate issues of concern to them." Another member of Congress told me, "Nobody understands how Congress works very well, but most federal judges do as well as anyone at understanding how this place should work. But many Members of Congress don't understand how the courts work or understand the daily lives of federal judges."

Most of the federal judges to whom I spoke, however, said they felt quite uncomfortable contacting politicians about proposed legislation unless they knew the legislators personally. As one federal judge told me, "I have contacted my elected representatives when I felt that Congress was considering legislation that went against the interests of the judiciary, but they never seem to listen to me or even to acknowledge my communication." Others felt that judges should refrain from contacting elected officials on issues before Congress. As one Senate staffer told me, "There is a clear taboo for judges giving opinions in advance on issues that could come up in their future cases."

On the other hand, there are many who support greater communication between the courts and Congress (see, e.g., Katzmann, 1997). For example, Maeva Marcus and Emily Van Tassel (1988) argued that the founders did not intend to limit communication between federal judges and Congress. Others have called for more routine communication between Congress and the federal courts. As then political scientist and now federal judge Robert A. Katzmann has written, "If Congress and the courts are to interact intelligently, each has to understand the other's activities. And that understanding must involve communication, direct or indirect, necessary for reasoned decisionmaking" (1988, 10; for more on the infrequent lobbying efforts of federal judges, both institutionally and individually, see, e.g., Walker and Barrow 1985; and Resnik 2000a).

Many whom I interviewed thought that there should be better communication between Congress and the courts. The ABA, among others, has endorsed better communication between the branches. It has called on lawyers to "correct the record" when it comes to attacks on the judiciary. Even justices of the Supreme Court are calling for more communication with Congress. In a rare appearance before the Senate Judiciary Committee, Justice Kennedy told that body, "Separation of powers and checks and balances are not automatic mechanisms. They depend upon a commitment to civility, open communication, and good faith on all sides" (U.S. Senate 2007).

Prolonged political criticism of judges does seem to affect the decisions that judges hand down. Lawrence Friedman writes, "No judge likes to be criticized. No doubt many judges will hesitate before making a decision, or a statement, that is likely to end up in the newspapers and make them look bad" (2006, 145). And as Ferejohn and Kramer note, "The judiciary's capital is intellectual and reputational, limited to what it can acquire through effective job performance, and the sort of thing that quickly wears thin in the face of persistent criticism" (2006, 167).

The Importance of Judicial Independence

The federal courts in the United States are often considered among the most independent and powerful courts in the world (see, e.g., Bickel 1962, 1; and Kornhauser 2002, 49). As Gerald Rosenberg notes, "The independence of the federal judiciary from political control is a hallmark of the American legal system" (G. Rosenberg 1992, 369). Chief Justice Rehnquist has said that judicial independence "is one of the crown jewels of our system of government today. Change is the law of life, and the judiciary will have to change to meet the challenges which will face it in the future. But the independence of the federal judiciary is essential to its proper functioning and must be retained" (1996, 274). The U.S. Supreme Court in *United States v. Will* (1980) defined independent judges as "judges who are free from potential domination by other branches of government" (449 U.S. 200, 218). But that independence may be fragile, as I shall argue.

Federal courts in the United States enjoy both decisional and institutional independence. Their decisions are not dictated by another branch of government, and the institution of the judiciary is separate and independent from the other branches of government. Many argue that these two aspects of independence are foundational requirements and that both must be present for there to be true judicial independence in any democracy (see, e.g., Barak 2006, 77–78). Federal judges experience decisional independence because the federal courts are generally protected from political pressures; this is because federal judges enjoy life tenure and the U.S. Constitution prohibits Congress or the president from reducing their salaries while they are in office. According to Lawrence Friedman (2006), judges are expected to be impartial, independent, and autonomous; therefore, they should not receive political pressure to decide a case in a particular way. Decisional independence is critical in order to maintain public support for the courts. As Terri Peretti argues, "The public must believe that judges are deciding impartially, not out of bias or fear of political reprisal" (2002, 116). "Independent judges," notes Friedman, "are judges who are free from political interference as they go about their work. The government has no right to dictate decisions. Independent judges are the opposite of judges in a dictatorship, who could lose their jobs or their heads if they went against government policy" (L. Friedman 2006, 141).

The theory of separation of powers in the United States and American norms and traditions also provide a great deal of institutional independence for the federal judiciary (see, e.g., Geyh 2002, 2006). As Charles Franklin reminds us, "Proponents of judicial independence are particularly concerned with the problem of arbitrary judicial decisions based on the demands of other political actors" (2002, 149). Both institutional and decisional independence are essential if courts and judges are to carry out their duties in the U.S. system of government (see, e.g., Tarr 2007; cf. Zemans 1999, 628–33). Both forms of independence are also necessary if the courts are to remain an independent voice in the inter-institutional constitutional dialogue.

Geyh argues that much of the separation of powers in practice revolves around the notion of the "customary independence" of the courts. He breaks judicial independence down into three aspects: doctrinal independence, functional independence, and customary independence. As Geyh observes, "Customary independence embodies the constitutional balance struck by the political branches over time between judicial independence and accountability. The political branches have the power to alter that balance, just as the courts have the power to alter the scope of doctrinal independence" (2002, 163). For Geyh, the customary independence of the federal judiciary is part of the constantly evolving constitutional conversation among the branches of government.

The Role of the Courts in the Inter-Institutional Dialogue

Independent courts can and should be a key player in the inter-institutional dialogue about how the Constitution shapes American society. At times, Congress and/or the president can partners with the courts in this dialogue; at other times, the elected branches may attempt to limit the power of the courts, thus limiting their ability to contribute to the inter-institutional constitutional conversation. Of course, both the president and the Senate may try to change the nature of the judicial voice through the confirmation process (see chapter 2). Sometimes the courts may serve an anti-majoritarian function through their power of judicial review, while at other times they may serve to protect majoritarian interests. The constantly evolving place of the courts in the U.S. system of government is both fascinating and intriguing.

One of the differences between courts and the elected branches is that judges use both legal reasoning and political reasoning in their decision making, while the those in the other branches tend to consider only political factors. Martin Shapiro (1964a, 1964b) coined the term *political jurisprudence* for the notion that courts use both legal and political analysis when making decisions. The elected branches generally do not use legal reasoning in their decision making. For example, Pickerill (2004) found that Congress rarely deliberates over constitutional issues unless a court has declared one of its statutes to be unconstitutional. In other words, Congress does not usually debate constitutional considerations without prior prompting from a court. Likewise, presidents rarely are accused of using legal reasoning when making decisions (see, e.g., Fisher 2008). Thus legal reasoning is the unique factor that courts bring to the inter-institutional constitutional dialogue. Mark Richards and Herbert Kritzer concluded "that the courts, including the Supreme Court, are different [from legislative bodies], and that part of this difference is the role of *law* in decision making" (2002, 305, emphasis added).

The question of how judges make decisions has long dominated political scientists' thinking about courts, as well as some of the thinking from law professors. Political scientists continue to debate whether judicial decisions are based purely on the legal model and legal reasoning, purely on ideology and the political attitudes of judges, or on a strategic model according to which judges try to anticipate the reactions of their colleagues and of the other institutions of government before making final decisions. In general, legal academics have generally argued more for the legal model (on the legal literature, see Richards and Kritzer 2002, 306; and Keck 2007b, 511–12), while political scientists such as Segal and Spaeth (2002) have stressed the purely political nature of judicial decision making. Works such as those by Epstein and Knight (1998), Forrest Maltzman, James Spriggs, and Paul Wahlbeck (2000), and others stress the strategic model. These three approaches seem to be mutually exclusive explanations for judicial decision making. However, recent work by Bryan Marshall, Richard Pacelle, and Christine Ludowise (2008) finds that the Supreme Court often uses all three approaches, and these scholars advocate the use of an integrated model for understanding judicial decision making instead of relying solely on one explanatory approach. Richards and Kritzer reach similar conclusions: "We theorize and observe that both the justices' policy goals and legal considerations matter in Supreme Court decision making" (2002, 315). Therefore Marshall, Pacelle, and Ludowise (2008) and Richards and Kritzer (2002) specifically reject the notion that the Supreme Court is merely a superlegislature, making purely political decisions as legislative bodies do. Instead, they believe, judges combine political, legal, and strategic decision-making approaches.

Thus we should not forget the importance of legal reasoning in the decision making of Supreme Court justices and other federal judges. It is this legal reasoning that makes courts different from legislatures or presidents. As Richards and Kritzer remind us, "Courts and judges are certainly part of the political world, but they are also part of a distinctive legal culture" (2002, 305). These authors go on to conclude that "the Supreme Court is not simply a small legislature. Law matters in Supreme Court decision making in ways that are specifically jurisprudential" (315). Thus the law and legal analysis clearly matter for the courts. Emphasizing the importance of law in Supreme Court decision making, Shapiro observed, "[Even if] *stare decisis* does not dictate automatic results, . . . [that] does not mean that legal decision-making is a form of free play in which every judge can do exactly what he pleases" (1968, 71). Legal reasoning thus creates very real institutional constraints on judicial decision making. Gillman (1993) also emphasized the role that legal reasoning can play in the unique institutional culture and institutional approach of the Supreme Court. Keith Whittington emphasized the role law plays in judicial decision making when he stated, "The justices may adhere to the law because, in an important sense, that is what justices do" (2000, 624).

Another question that has dominated debates among judicial scholars is whether it makes any difference for political-theory purposes whether the courts make anti-majoritarian decisions. Since the courts use legal reasoning in their decision making, they may sometimes make decisions that are not supported by the majority of Americans or by the institutions, such as Congress and the presidency, that are designed to reflect more majoritarian views. Of course, Congress and the president may also promote anti-majoritarian policies at certain times (see, e.g., Klarman 1997; and J. Barnes 2004b). Legal academics have long been obsessed with what Bickel (1962) termed the *counter-majoritarian difficulty* created by the courts' unrestrained use of their power of judicial review. Numerous books and articles have been written about this issue, far too many to cite here. In many ways, this concern over the so-called counter-majoritarian difficulty seems misplaced. The better question is whether the constitutional conversation should exclude or include the legal analysis, whether majoritarian or anti-majoritarian, that the courts bring to the table. Stressing the advantages of having legal analysis as part of the constitutional dialogue, Comiskey argues: "To maintain a constitutional democracy, the democratic elements—principally Congress and the president in the federal government—and the constitutional elements—in particular, the unelected federal judiciary—must exist in some sort of balance. The Founders did not advocate a 'judgocracy' in which elected judges run amok any more than they favored majoritarian tyranny" (2004, 27).

While law professors have seemed to be obsessed with internal and purely legal explanations for judicial decision making, some political scientists seem overly concerned with purely external explanations. Many students of the courts now advocate a "regime politics" approach in order to explain the role of the courts in the separation of powers in the U.S. government (see, e.g., Clayton and May 1999; Peretti 1999; Gillman 2004; Clayton and Pickerill 2006; and Gillman 2006b). They generally view the courts as part of the broader governing coalition. Cornell Clayton and David May state that the core concern of this new approach is to "situate Supreme Court decision making within the broader political and legal system. The approach suggests that judicial attitudes and strategies in decision making are both constituted and constrained by the broader context with which the Court operates" (1999, 234). According to Gillman, "'Regime politics' refers to the various ways in which governing coalitions organize their power and advance their political agenda with a system of interrelated institutions" (2006b, 107).

The courts are thus seen as equal partners in the governing coalition of institutions; and parties, interest groups, and other political actors will attempt to influence their decision-making approaches just as they do those of the legislative and executive branches. "Scholars adopting this 'political regimes' approach," write Clayton and Pickerill, "have developed a large body of research that ties judicial decision making to specific patterns of party politics, group coalition building, critical elections, the policy agenda of the governing elites, and other features of the political regime" (2006, 1391).

The legislative- and executive-branch players in the constitutional dialogue will also attempt to influence the voice of the courts because they recognize the courts as full participants in the constitutional conversation. Gillman continues, "Because courts, like executive branch agencies, have policy-making authority, members of the governing coalition have an interest in influencing what might be called their decision-making bias, or the general political and ideological predispositions that they bring to their institutional responsibilities" (2006b, 108).

This regime politics approach has even been taken up by law professors such as Michael Klarman (2004), Jeffrey Rosen (2006), and Mark Tushnet (2006a), who rely heavily on political-science approaches in their new examinations of the role of the Supreme Court in the wider political system. Thomas Keck summarizes this approach as follows: "The leading proponents of a regime politics approach (in both [law and political science]) have generally relied on historical and interpretative methods to trace the connections between the Court's decisions and the demands of governing elites" (2007b, 513).

The regime politics approach is quite useful in explaining the role of the U.S. Supreme Court in the broader system of government, but only to a point. The courts are thus properly seen as part of the broader system of government and as full participants in the inter-institutional constitutional dialogue, yet the regime politics approach can be seen as underemphasizing the unique legal voice that the courts bring to the constitutional dialogue. We must always remember that courts differ from the legislative and executive branches because of the legal culture in which they operate. Instead of following the lead of Bickel (1962) and his concern with the counter-majoritarian difficulty, regime politics scholars trace their roots mostly to the works of Robert Dahl (1957), McCloskey (1960), and Shapiro (1964a, 1964b, 1968). Dahl argued that the Supreme Court was really part of the majority coalition and that it would rarely declare unconstitutional a policy supported by the current ruling coalition. A long list of studies now relate judicial decision making to the needs of the broader political elites, seeing the federal courts as a partner in the so-called governing coalition. For example, Gerald Rosenberg (1991) argued that the Supreme Court justices were unable to check the will of the majority even if they were inclined to do so, thus making broad social change through the courts "a hollow hope." Many other studies have observed that the courts have generally supported the needs of the governing coalition in America.

We should never forget that courts are legal as well as political institutions and that judges rely on both political and legal frameworks in their decision making. Thus Shapiro, using the term *political jurisprudence,* argued that the courts should be understood not only as part of the overall political and governmental structure but also as different from other political actors because of their reliance on legal reasoning and legal analysis. McCloskey also stressed that the Supreme Court was both a political and a legal body, blending its policymaking role "with orthodox judicial functions . . . in a complex mixture" (1960, 20). Sometimes it seems that scholars stress either the "political" side or the "jurisprudence" side but neglect Shapiro and McCloskey's idea that these two aspects of judicial decision making are inherently joined and cannot be separated. Thus law professors have tended to ignore the political side, while political scientists have tended to downplay the legal side. Law professors certainly need to pay more attention to the political-science literature, but political scientists need to remember that the decisions of courts are framed and communicated to the public through legal mechanisms, even if those decisions can be traced to the political-policy preferences of individual judges.

Law professors may have put too much stress on internal explanations for judicial decision making, while political scientists may have focused too much on external explanations. As Richards and Kritzer have argued, "Leaving jurisprudence out of the analytic framework fails to recognize both the distinctive nature of courts and the theoretical point that ideas and institutions matter" (2002, 306). Again, the institutional perspective and the institutional will of the courts are certainly shaped by judges' legal reasoning and analysis. As Gillman reminds us, "Like all power holders, judges must reconcile their world view with the norms, procedures, and missions of the institutions with which they are affiliated. The law professorate may, at times, overstate the constraints on ideology imposed by these institutional norms and processes, but political analysts sometimes make the opposite mistake by underestimating a judge's obligation to organize her or his decision making into a set of relatively stable rules, concepts, doctrines—in short into a jurisprudence" (2006b, 113).

The courts' legalistic approach to decision making may at times isolate them from the other branches in the inter-institutional constitutional conversation. The courts may not only serve the needs of the governing elites in the other branches but also function as an independent voice in the constitutional dialogue. Thus Keck (2007a) found in his analysis of instances when the Supreme Court has struck down federal statutes as unconstitutional that the Court sometimes acts in partisan terms and sometimes acts in ideological terms but most often acts to protect its own institutional interests. Keck follows the lead of Karen Orren and Stephen Skowronek (2004) in arguing that institutional contexts shape the behavior of political actors in a variety of ways: "The justices of the contemporary Court have sometimes acted on institutional motivations that are distinct from their own policy preferences. . . . The most significant line of conflict has pitted judges against legislators rather than liberals against conservatives, or Democrats against Republicans" (Keck 2007a, 321). Thus independent courts bring their own legal and institutional voice to the inter-institutional constitutional dialogue. The U.S. constitutional democracy demands independent federal courts that are free to use legal reasoning and legal analysis in order to protect their status as full participants in the constitutional conversations that shape American society in the long run. In examining the interactions between Congress and the federal courts, this book attempts to clarify how congressional attitudes toward the courts affect their ability to bring legal reasoning into the inter-institutional constitutional dialogue.

The following chapters examine the relationship between Congress and the federal courts as follows: Chapter 1 examines historical periods of conflict between the federal courts and Congress and between the federal courts and the president. For most of American history, liberal forces in the United States have complained that the federal courts were impeding progress in the society by protecting the powerful minority. However, since the 1950s it has been conservative critics of the courts who have complained that the federal courts have been protecting minority concerns within society at the expense of majoritarian democratic values. Anti-court rhetoric from congressional critics of the federal courts has been fierce at times, but institutional attacks on the courts have been few. Chapter 1 helps to put the recent anti-court actions of Congress into context.

Chapter 2 examines regular interactions between the federal courts and Congress. These interactions include the confirmation of judicial nominees by the Senate Judiciary Committee; annual appropriations for the federal courts, including judicial salaries; and decisions by Congress to increase the number of federal judges, including Supreme Court justices, or to change the boundaries of the United States Circuit Court of Appeals. The chapter ends with the ways in which Congress has reacted to statutory-interpretation decisions of the federal courts as well as to constitutionally based rulings from the courts. Some of these routine interactions between Congress and the courts inevitably produce friction between the two institutions.

Chapter 3 explores some of the contemporary tensions between Congress and the courts, due in large part to the views of the Religious Right about the role of judges and courts in America. As the culture wars have played out in American politics, the courts have often been caught in the middle. The Religious Right has followed a three-pronged approach to the courts. First, it has taken a keen interest in placing judges on the federal bench who follow its view of law. Second, it has increased the amount of its litigation before the courts in hopes of overturning what it perceives as liberal activist decisions from the federal courts. Third, it has greatly increased its criticisms of the federal courts and its attacks upon the institutional power of the courts in an attempt to reign in what it sees as the hopelessly liberal activist federal judges currently on the bench. Chapter 3 conclude by beginning to examine some of the differences between the ways the two political parties express their current understanding of the proper role of the courts in American society.

Chapter 4 explores how the House Judiciary Committee under Republican control evolved into an anti-court body, with its conservative lawyer members leading the charge in institutional attacks on the federal courts. Although the Senate Judiciary Committee usually receives more attention because of its role in the confirmation of federal judges, the House Judiciary Committee has taken the lead in the recent assaults on the courts. Chapter 4 examines how the institutional culture of the House committee has changed over the years. At one time the House Judiciary Committee, "the Committee of Lawyers," protected the courts and federal judges from most political attacks. Recently, however, the conservative members of the committee have been at the forefront of Religious Right attempts to reign in the power of the courts by increasing congressional oversight of the judiciary and its decisions. The chapter also examines the changes in the institutional culture and the institutional will of the committee from the time that Congressman Henry Hyde (R-IL) led the committee to the period when Congressman James Sensenbrenner (R-WI) served as its chair.

Chapter 5 explores three recent attacks on the institutional power of the federal courts, all initiated by the House Judiciary Committee under Chairman Sensenbrenner. These institutional attacks on the courts include the enactment of court-stripping legislation designed to prevent the federal courts from hearing certain types of cases, a proposal for an inspector general for the federal judiciary in order to give Congress more oversight of the judiciary in general and of judicial decisions in particular, and threats to impeach federal judges because the majority in Congress disagreed with their decisions. Chapter 5 thus discusses in some detail the recent institutional attacks on federal judges and on the federal courts.

The final chapter explores the need for judicial independence in the American system of separation of powers. Although Congress and the judiciary will probably always have different institutional perspectives and different institutional wills, chapter 6 calls for restraint in Congress in order to preserve judicial independence and maintain the judiciary as an independent third branch of government. For the separation of powers to work, the inter-institutional constitutional conversation must include legal analysis as well as political reasoning. It is the courts who add a component of law and legal reasoning to the constitutional dialogue.

ONE

Historical Periods of Conflict with the Courts

Strained interactions between Congress and the federal courts are not a new phenomenon. Throughout American history there have been periods of intense conflict between the courts and the other branches of government. While this book focuses mostly on the relationship between Congress and the courts, the president is also a key player in the constitutional dialogue (see, e.g., Jones 1994; McMahon 2004; Whittington 2007; and Comiskey 2008). Indeed, as James Simon reminds us, "History suggests that American presidents have been most attentive to the work and personnel of the Supreme Court in periods of extreme national tension" (1973, 17). This chapter explores some of the more tense moments in American history when the courts have been in conflict with the president, Congress, or both.

Scholars generally cite several periods in American history when the tensions between the courts and Congress and/or the president have been at their highest (see, e.g., Nagel 1965; G. Rosenberg 1992; and Geyh 2006). These include the Jeffersonian period; the Jacksonian period; the pre– and post–Civil War periods; the period of Progressive attacks on the courts, during the early twentieth century; the New Deal period; and the period of conservative attacks on the Warren Court, during the 1950s and 1960s. As Charles Geyh says, "Bouts of court-directed animus have come and gone at generational intervals since the founding of the nation" (2006, 2). Thus periods of severe tension between Congress and the courts serve to highlight the often strained dialogue between these two branches.

Throughout American history, Congress and the president have attempted to alter the voice of the federal courts in the inter-institutional constitutional conversation. Sometimes the other branches have succeeded in changing the direction of judicial rulings. Even the threat of attack from politicians can have profound effects on the decision making of the courts. Those who advocate the strategic approach to judicial decision making argue that the Supreme Court sometimes alters its decisions in order to take into account the potential reactions of the other branches of government, including Congress (see, e.g., Epstein and Knight 1998, 138–57; and Graber 2006). Among others, Lawrence Baum (2004, 216) has argued that when threatened with direct attacks, the Supreme Court may retreat in order to lessen congressional anger and thus Congress's determination to take action against the courts. In his study of various eras of political attacks on the courts, Gerald Rosenberg found that in many historical periods the mere threat of attack caused the Supreme Court to alter its decisions (see G. Rosenberg 1992; see also Peretti 2005, 134–45). For example, even though it took for itself the power of judicial review in *Marbury v. Madison* (1803) when it declared parts of the Judiciary Act of 1789 to be unconstitutional, the Supreme Court did not declare another major act of Congress to be unconstitutional until its ill-fated decision in *Dred Scott v. Sandford* (1857). As another example, it took the Court only two years to retreat from its decision in *Watkins v. United States* (1957), when it championed the rights of witnesses appearing before Congress in the McCarthy era. Many members of Congress were furious with this decision, and there was real fear that Congress would take steps to weaken the Supreme Court as an institution. The Court responded by running away from the fight. In *Barenblatt v. United States* (1959) it basically allowed Congress to abuse its investigatory powers without judicial interference. Lee Epstein and Jack Knight said of these two decisions, "The justices occasionally eschew policy to protect the legitimacy of the Court" (1998, 47).

These retreats may be necessary to protect the federal courts in general and the Supreme Court in particular against institutional attacks from the other branches. Thus sometimes the Court takes the long-term position of protecting the courts as an institution instead of making a decision that will obviously draw the fire of Congress or the president. "A wise judiciary knows its vulnerability well," Charles Franklin reminds us, "and must act to protect its autonomy even as it asserts that independence" (2002, 148).

How Did the Supreme Court Become Part of the Constitutional Conversation?

During the early history of America, the role and powers of the federal courts under the new Constitution were not at all clear. For example, the Constitution is silent on the structure of the federal courts, except that there must be a supreme court of the United States. This silence was due in part to disagreements at the Constitutional Convention over the structure and organization of the proposed federal courts (see Tarr 2006, 29). Thus the Constitution left the details of the lower federal court system to the new Congress. In the Judiciary Act of 1789 Congress created the now familiar three-tier federal court system. Under the provisions of this act, justices of the Supreme Court also served on the newly created federal circuit courts of appeals. The Judiciary Act also established the jurisdiction of the federal courts, with one notable aspect being that jurisdiction over federal questions was denied to the lower federal courts; they would not obtain this jurisdiction until 1875. Thus cases requiring interpretation of federal statutes or of the U.S. Constitution were initially heard in the state courts exclusively, with eventual appeal to the U.S. Supreme Court from states' highest courts. The Constitution also does not specify the number of Supreme Court justices, and this number has fluctuated over the years, as discussed in more detail below and again in chapter 2.

During the Constitutional Convention there was little discussion of the role of the federal courts in the new constitutional regime, although Alexander Hamilton did argue that the federal courts should have, and in fact did have, the right of judicial review, in other words, the right to declare the actions of other political actors unconstitutional. Hamilton repeated this argument in the *Federalist No. 78*, again strongly implying that the federal courts should have the power of judicial review. While ratification of the Constitution was being debated within the states, the Antifederalists offered a variety of amendments concerning the courts. Some of these amendments would have created a legislative-review committee to oversee decisions of the Supreme Court (see Culp 1929, 389). None of them were adopted, of course (see Ellis 1971, 9–11). Although the Federalists and Antifederalists disagreed about the proper role of the federal courts in the new system of government, that disagreement did not compare in importance to some of their other critical disagreements. The courts were regarded as the least dangerous branch.

Eventually, after ratification of the Constitution, the courts became both a partisan and an ideological issue in the new regime, with the Federalists generally supporting strong federal courts and the Democratic-Republicans (Jeffersonians) fearing that the federal courts would become too powerful. Ideologically, the Democratic-Republicans argued that the federal courts should defer to the elected branches and uphold majoritarian principles, while the Federalists believed that the courts should serve as a check on the power of Congress, hinting that they should play an anti-majoritarian role in the U.S. system of government. Both parties realized that life appointments to the federal courts could change the nature of both politics and the law in the new United States. In 1793, in the case of *Chisholm v. Georgia*, the Federalists on the Supreme Court did attempt to increase federal power by allowing states to be sued in federal courts. This Federalist judicial victory was short lived, however. Because the states were outraged by this judicial decision, the ruling was directly overturned by the passage of the Eleventh Amendment in 1795 (see, e.g., Murphy 1962, 7).

The Jeffersonian Period

Many commentators measure the true nature of a democracy by what happens when the party in power changes. The Jeffersonian period became an early test of the status of the Supreme Court and the lower federal courts in the new system of government. With the 1800 election, for the first time in the new constitutional democracy the party in power (the Federalists) lost and a new party (the Democratic-Republicans, or Jeffersonians) took control of the apparatus of government. Donald Stephenson argued that both the "victorious challengers" and the "vanquished incumbents" saw the election of 1800 as a "revolution" (1999, 30). Stephenson also noted that in that election, reactions to judicial decisions became important campaign issues for both parties (37). And as Geyh concludes, "The election of Thomas Jefferson ushered in the first sustained wave of national anger directed at federal judges" (2006, 53). After the election, the victorious Jeffersonians were especially upset that the federal courts had been packed with Federalists during the relatively short period after the election but before the Jeffersonians could claim power.

After the 1800 election, before the members of the new Democratic-Republican Congress could take their seats, the lame-duck Federalists enacted the Judiciary Act of 1801. This act made some useful reforms to the judicial system, including ending the practice of having justices of the Supreme Court ride circuit and sit on the U.S. Circuit Courts. The act also, however, had some provisions inserted into the legislation that were motivated primarily by extreme partisanship. For example, the 1801 act reduced the number of justices on the Supreme Court from six to five following the next vacancy on the Court, thus preventing the newly elected President Jefferson from appointing a new justice until two of the then current justices left the Court. It also created a new system for the U.S. circuit courts of appeals, allowing the Federalists to appoint sixteen new federal circuit judges. Because these appointments came so late in the term of President John Adams, they are often referred to as the "midnight appointments" or the "midnight judges." The 1801 act also gave the lower federal courts jurisdiction over federal issues, which had been denied them in the 1789 act. Congress also generally broadened federal jurisdiction over a host of potential federalism cases (see, e.g., Preyer 1992, 474–75).

The Jeffersonians were furious at what they perceived to be the court-packing efforts of the losers in the election, the Federalists. Obviously, the Federalists hoped that federal judges with life appointments would uphold the values of their party and protect their now anti-majoritarian interests. After taking office, the Democratic-Republicans in Congress quickly repealed the Judiciary Act of 1801 through the Judiciary Act of 1802. Thus the 1802 act abolished the new federal circuit courts, and Congress refused to appropriate money to pay the Federalist judges who had been appointed to these courts. By repealing the broad grant of federal jurisdiction to the federal courts, including jurisdiction over federal questions, the 1802 act severely restricted the ability of the lower federal courts to effect drastic change in American society. It also delayed the Federalist-dominated Supreme Court from meeting for more than a year (see Pritchett 1961, 6). However, the act did not restrict the jurisdiction of the U.S. Supreme Court. During the congressional debates on the 1802 act, some Jeffersonians expressed their distaste for the federal judiciary. Senator James Jackson of Georgia stated, "I am more afraid of an army of judges . . . than an army of soldiers" (qtd. in Murphy 1962, 9), while Senator Stevens Thompson Mason of Virginia stated that "he was in favor of an independent judiciary but not of judges who were 'independent of the nation itself'" (qtd. in Murphy et al. 2006, 9). President Jefferson was so infuriated by the Federalist-dominated federal courts that he privately referred to the Supreme Court as "that subtle corps of sappers and miners constantly working underground to undermine the foundations of our confederated fabric" (qtd. in Simon 1973, 10).

It was not at all clear that the Jeffersonians conceived of the federal courts as an independent branch of government that was an equal partner in the inevitable inter-institutional conversations about the real meaning of the Constitution. They probably saw the courts in much the same way as the British viewed them, not as policymakers and important players at the federal level but as bodies designed to serve the interests of justice only in specific cases and for the specific parties before them. Nevertheless, the Federalist-dominated Supreme Court continued to disappoint the new Democratic-Republican majority. Although President Jefferson did his best to appoint loyal Jeffersonians to the Supreme Court, Chief Justice John Marshall's intellect prevailed over the partisan tendencies of the new justices. Thus the Supreme Court remained a "Federalist judicial monopoly" until well after President Jefferson had left office, when Presidents Jackson, Van Buren, and Polk could make enough appointments to the Court to change its character forever (see Simon 1973, 10).

While the Supreme Court remained a Federalist bastion, the justices took care not to provoke the Jeffersonians any more than necessary. In fact, facing potential crippling attacks from the Democratic-Republicans in Congress and in the presidency, the Supreme Court mostly retreated from the fight. The constitutionality of the Judiciary Act of 1802, including its abolition of the new federal circuit courts and Congress's refusal to pay the midnight judges, was upheld by the Supreme Court in *Stuart v. Laird* (1803) (see, e.g., Ellis 1971, 36–68). Geyh describes the *Stuart v. Laird* opinion, coming only a few weeks after the Marshall Court's brilliant landmark opinion in *Marbury v. Madison* (1803), as "a short, timid opinion" that failed even to acknowledge that the issue of the constitutionality of the 1802 repeal act was before the Court. As Geyh concludes, "The 1802 repeal qualifies as an episode of court unpacking in which the Supreme Court was intimidated into acquiescence" (2006, 54). It appears that the Federalists on the Supreme Court, wary of continued attacks from the Jeffersonians, retreated from further confrontation with Congress on this issue. However, in another case that would become critically important in American history, *Marbury v. Madison* (1803), the Supreme Court permanently inserted itself into the inter-institutional dialogue about the future effects of the Constitution. The issue centered on the question of which institution had the right to interpret the still new Constitution.

Judicial review is today defined as the power of the courts to determine the constitutionality of the actions of other political actors, including Congress, the president, the permanent federal bureaucracy, and the states. The question of whether the Supreme Court had the power of judicial review was decided in *Marbury v. Madison* (1803), as supplemented by *Martin v. Hunter's Lessee* (1816), in which the U.S. Supreme Court took for itself the power to review decisions of the state supreme courts. Although there is continued academic debate about the courts' power of judicial review and the role of the *Marbury v. Madison* ruling in solidifying that right (see, e.g., Graber 1998; Levinson 2003; Tushnet 2005; and Whittington 2007), it is generally accepted that U.S. courts today do possess the power of judicial review. Almost all commentators would agree that this power is a result of the Supreme Court's decision in *Marbury v. Madison.*

The facts of the *Marbury* case present an interesting story. Among the many new judgeships created by Congress in 1801, President Adams appointed William Marbury to be a justice of the peace. Marbury was a fervent Federalist and an activist in Maryland politics. President Adams appointed Marbury to this judicial position, but his secretary of state, John Marshall, forgot to deliver the commission papers to Marbury before the newly elected President Jefferson took office. Marshall had just been appointed chief justice of the United States, and delivering these judicial commissions was one of his very last tasks before taking his seat on the Supreme Court. When the newly elected Jeffersonians took power, they discovered the undelivered commission for Marbury, and President Jefferson refused to allow his new secretary of state, James Madison, to deliver the commission papers to Marbury, thus preventing Marbury from taking his judicial seat. Marbury sued to get his appointment as justice of the peace. In a remarkably brilliant decision, the Supreme Court ruled that Marbury was entitled to his position but that the provision of the Judiciary Act of 1789 allowing the federal courts to force executive-branch officials to deliver the judicial commission papers to Marbury was unconstitutional. Although Marbury was entitled to be a judge, no court could force President Jefferson and his administration to honor the appointment. Marbury did not get the job. Thus in this landmark decision the Supreme Court took the power of judicial review for itself, but President Jefferson had one fewer Federalist judge to worry about. In the short term, the Jeffersonians won the case, but in the long term the courts were the real winners in this struggle.

In *Martin v. Hunter's Lessee* (1816) the Supreme Court solidified its judicial-review powers while at the same time advancing the notion of federal constitutional supremacy. The Court declared that it possessed the right to declare unconstitutional state laws and state court decisions as well as federal governmental actions. The facts of this case provide an interesting look into the practices of governments before and after the American Revolution. During the Revolutionary War, the state of Virginia enacted legislation that allowed it to confiscate the property of Loyalists (those who continued to support British rule over the colonies). Lord Fairfax owned land in Virginia, obtained by one of his ancestors from original land grants from the King of England. A Loyalist, Lord Fairfax fled to England during the Revolutionary War. He died in 1781, leaving the land to his nephew, Denny Martin, who was a British citizen. The following year, the Virginia legislature voided the original land grant to Lord Fairfax and transferred the land back to Virginia. The government of Virginia then gave a portion of this land to David Hunter. The 1783 Treaty of Paris, between the United States and Britain after the end of the Revolutionary War, seemed to make it clear that Lord Fairfax's heirs were entitled to the property. One of Lord Fairfax's heirs, Martin, became involved in a lawsuit in the Virginia courts, where he tried to get the land back. Eventually the U.S. Supreme Court declared that Lord Fairfax's heirs were entitled to the property and remanded the case back to the Virginia courts to settle the details of the case. But the Virginia courts refused to follow the Supreme Court's ruling. The Virginia Supreme Court asserted that the U.S. Supreme Court did not have authority over cases originating in state courts. In an opinion written by Justice Joseph Story, the U.S. Supreme Court declared that it did have the power to overrule the Virginia court, thus solidifying the notion of federal constitutional supremacy and enhancing the Court's power of judicial review. Chief Justice Marshall did not participate in this case because he and his brother had signed a contract with Martin to buy the property in question.

The *Marbury* ruling on judicial review, coupled with the Court's later decision in *Martin v. Hunter's Lessee,* made the Supreme Court and the other federal courts key players in the eventual interbranch dialogue about how the Constitution should shape the American system of governance. Although the benefits of having the federal courts have the power of judicial review are still widely debated today in many academic circles, apart from a very small number of right-wing politicians (see chapter 2), most American voters today clearly accept the idea that the courts have this power. The key question then becomes how activist or restraintist the courts should be in exercising it.

The Supreme Court forced its way into the constitutional conversation through its *Marbury* decision, but it was at first hesitant to demand equal treatment from the other branches of the federal government. Although the Supreme Court took for itself the power of judicial review in the *Marbury* case and declared portions of the Judiciary Act of 1789 to be unconstitutional as part of the decision, it did not strike down another major *federal* statute as unconstitutional until *Dred Scott v. Sandford* in 1857. Thus the Court did not seem willing to confront directly the new Democratic-Republican government that came to power with Jefferson (see, e.g., G. Rosenberg 1992). Perhaps the Marshall Court understood the potential danger for the courts as an institution if they angered the Jeffersonians even further.

Although they technically won the decision in *Marbury* and clearly had the Federalist Supreme Court in full retreat in *Stuart v. Laird,* the Jeffersonians nonetheless took a variety of actions against the federal courts in addition to the passage of the 1802 Judiciary Act. Although the Supreme Court had only struck down one federal statute with its new power of judicial review, it did strike down a number of state laws that it felt violated the needs of the federal government. The Court thus took steps to increase federal power at the expense of the states. Because the Jeffersonians had campaigned on a platform of stronger state powers and weaker federal ones, the Jeffersonians in Congress, seeing the courts as the leaders in the struggle for increased federal control, eventually attacked the courts as an institution. President Jefferson and his Democratic-Republican Congress were no friends of the federal courts, which were dominated by Federalists at the time, although Jefferson himself did not have "an undying enmity toward the concept of a strong and independent judiciary" (Ellis 1971, 26). As president, however, Jefferson did question the concept that only the Supreme Court could interpret the Constitution, thus anticipating the notion that the courts are part of an inter-institutional dialogue about the meaning of the Constitution (see, e.g., Whittington 2007, 32–33). Wanting to reduce the power of the Federalists on the bench, the Jeffersonians in Congress turned to impeachment as a tool to reduce Federalist influence and increase the presence of Democratic-Republican values in the federal courts.

The Democratic-Republican Congress first impeached and removed from office Judge John Pickering, of the U.S. District Court in New Hampshire, in large part because he was a severe alcoholic and probably insane. The Constitution provided no method for removing from the federal bench judges who were incapable of performing their judicial duties, except through impeachment. The House voted articles of impeachment, and after a highly partisan trial in the Senate, Judge Pickering was removed from office in 1804 (see Ellis 1971, 69–75). One could argue in this case that although the majority in Congress had some partisan motivations for this impeachment, they were using legitimate procedures to remove an incompetent judge.

After the successful impeachment of Judge Pickering, however, the Democratic-Republicans decided to use the impeachment process for purely partisan reasons in order to reduce the Federalist control of the federal judiciary. They moved to impeach Supreme Court Justice Samuel Chase because he was an outspoken partisan and a supporter of the Federalist cause (see Ellis 1971, 76). It was widely assumed at the time that if Justice Chase had been removed from office, the Democratic-Republicans would have then moved to impeach Chief Justice Marshall (see Pacelle 2002, 96). The House voted to bring articles of impeachment against Justice Chase in 1804, and the Senate held a trial against him in 1805. The Chase trial was a highly partisan affair, but the Democratic-Republicans in the Senate were not able to muster the necessary two-thirds vote to remove him from office (see, e.g., Murphy 1962, 14). The failure of the Chase impeachment had some long-term implications. As Geyh cautiously concludes, "Chase's acquittal . . . sucked the life out of the Jeffersonians' anti-judiciary campaign and set a precedent against removing judges for high-handed decision making" (2006, 54).

The Jeffersonians remained bitter about not having been able to wrest control of the judiciary away from the Federalists. Reflecting back on the failed Chase impeachment, Thomas Jefferson wrote almost fifteen years later, "Having found from experience that impeachment is an impracticable thing, a mere scarecrow, they [the judiciary] consider themselves secure for life" (qtd. in Stephenson 1999, 19). Because the Jeffersonians were unable to curb the courts through the means of impeachment, eventually the federal courts would evolve into a truly independent third branch of government. Because the concept of judicial independence was preserved in the Chase incident, the courts would become a real and important participant in the inter-institutional dialogue about the future of the nation. If the Chase impeachment had been successful, the courts might instead have become subject to the ever-changing whims of the political branches.

The Chase trial represents the last time a federal judge was impeached (and almost removed from office) purely because the majority in Congress disagreed with his or her judicial decisions (see Rehnquist 1992). This case is often cited in support of the idea that Congress must respect the independence of the judicial branch. As Chief Justice Rehnquist has written, "The framers were particularly concerned about the possibility of overreaching and bullying by the legislative branch—Congress—against the other branches" (1992, 9). For Rehnquist, even the threat of impeachment of federal judges merely because of their judicial opinions was improper behavior from Congress. Some scholars, such as Geyh (2006), doubt that the failure of the Chase impeachment has had such a long-term effect of discouraging other impeachment attempts based on disagreement with a judge's decisions from the bench. Geyh notes that threats of impeachment for purely political reasons have continued to this day, although to date Congress has not removed a judge merely because of his or her judicial decisions. Others believe that the Supreme Court and the other federal courts survived the attacks from the Democratic-Republicans in this period only because the Court retreated, as evidenced by decisions such as *Stuart v. Laird* (1803), and then became "subservient to the preferences of the Jeffersonians" (G. Rosenberg 1992, 380). Still other scholars believe that the Chase impeachment served as a final determination that judicial independence must be preserved at all costs in the U.S. system of separate institutions sharing powers. If the courts had not had the power of judicial review, and the ability to exercise this legal power without the constant fear of being removed from office because of their decisions, the judicial branch would have remained inferior to the political branches. But because of *Marbury* and the failed attempt to impeach Justice Chase, the federal courts could assert themselves as key and independent players in the constitutional conversation about the future of the United States. American society would be quite different today without an independent third branch of the federal government sometimes protecting minority interests against the wishes of the majoritarian political branches.

Clearly, the Supreme Court justices and the other federal judges were in grave danger from an angry majority in the Democratic-Republican Congress. The Jeffersonian period could have meant the destruction of the independence of the federal judiciary, but it did not. "Although it is clear that the founders of the United States were committed to judicial independence in principle," concludes Geyh, "it is equally clear that the Constitution—and the independent judiciary it established—were fragile innovations with uncertain futures. Judicial independence would survive only if the political branches responsible for its care and feeding took that responsibility seriously, because the Constitution gave the Congress in particular (and the political branches generally) ample latitude to obliterate the judiciary's autonomy if it was so inclined" (2006, 51). Because the courts survived the Jeffersonian assaults, the norm of judicial independence grew stronger. That Chief Justice Marshall remained on the Supreme Court for many years also helped to consolidate the power of the judiciary.

The Jacksonian Period

The Jacksonian period was another era in which the independence of the courts was in jeopardy. The election of Andrew Jackson as president in 1828 brought a new populist era to the country. Strong supporters of majoritarian democracy, the Jacksonians tried to eliminate any vestiges of elitism from the political system. The Jacksonians had inherited the Jeffersonians' distrust of the federal judiciary, which was augmented by the personal distain that President Jackson had for Chief Justice Marshall (see Murphy 1962, 26). The Jacksonians introduced many bills aimed at weakening the courts, but none were ever enacted (see, e.g., McCloskey 1994, 42). Some of these bills would have made the Senate a review committee to examine any decisions of the Supreme Court that declared a federal or state statute to be unconstitutional (see Culp 1929, 389). President Jackson did not weaken the judiciary as an institution in part because he eventually came to see federal judges as allies in his fights with the more extreme supporters of states' rights, often known as "nullifiers," who argued that the states were not bound by federal court decisions or other federal actions, such as statutes enacted by Congress (see Fisher and Adler 2007, 24). Although Andrew Jackson was certainly not a champion of the life-term federal judiciary, he and his supporters in Congress did not take any direct actions to weaken the independence of the courts, because those institutional attacks might have come with high costs for their short-term political agenda. Instead of preventing the courts from participating in the constitutional dialogue, Jackson merely refused to use the power of the executive branch to enforce judicial decisions with which he disagreed.

The two most important instances in which President Jackson refused to follow the decisions of the Supreme Court concerned *McCulloch v. Maryland* (1819) and *Worcester v. Georgia* (1832). *McCulloch* involved the legality of a national bank, known as the second Bank of the United States, chartered by Congress. The first central bank had been created in 1791, but its charter had been allowed to expire in 1811. Congress chartered the second national bank in 1816. States' rights supporters never supported the concept of a national central bank, and they felt that this latest congressional action was unconstitutional. In an effort to destroy the hated national bank, the state of Maryland placed a heavy tax on the federal institution. In *McCulloch,* the Supreme Court ruled that the states had no right to tax a federal entity, because the right to tax was the right to destroy. Federal supremacy would not permit the states to dismantle a federal institution. Thus the Court extended its ability to use its power of judicial review against the states. Chief Justice Marshall's opinion rested on an expansive reading of federal constitutional power, as well as on a broad reading of the powers of Congress under the Constitution.

Jacksonian Democrats had not supported the creation of the national bank in the first place, and they were not happy with the expansion of federal power inherent in this decision. In 1832, however, Congress passed an extension of the national bank charter, but President Jackson vetoed the bill. Thus the national bank and the role of the Supreme Court in this controversy became a key issue in the election of 1832 (see Stephenson 1999, 70). In his veto message of 10 July 1832 on the bank legislation, President Jackson clearly stated that he did not find the Supreme Court's *McCulloch* opinion on the constitutionality of the national bank to be controlling. In fact, he stated that the Supreme Court did not have the final authority to interpret the Constitution, because his notion of majoritarian democracy did not allow such a reading of the Constitution.

What is very interesting about Jackson's approach to this issue is his assertion that while he did not oppose an independent judiciary, he did oppose judicial supremacy. In his view, his actions were necessary to preserve the balance of power among the branches and thus to preserve the ability of all the institutions of government to participate fully in the constitutional conversation. Jackson's veto message attacking judicial supremacy is worth quoting at some length:

> Mere precedent is a dangerous source of authority, and should not be regarded as deciding questions of constitutional power except where the acquiescence of the people and the States can be considered as well settled. . . . If the opinion of the Supreme Court covered the whole ground of this act, it ought not to control the coordinate authorities of this Government. The Congress, the Executive, and the Court must each for itself be guided by its own opinion of the Constitution. . . . The opinion of the judges has no more authority over Congress than the opinion of Congress has over the judges, and on that point the President is independent of both. The authority of the Supreme Court must not, therefore, be permitted to control the Congress or the Executive when acting in their

> legislative capacities, but to have only such influence as the force of their reasoning may deserve. (qtd. in Murphy et al. 2006, 358–59)

Thus Jackson saw his veto of the bank legislation as a necessary step to protect the American system of separation of powers, and he believed that the veto was necessary to preserve the constitutional dialogue among the institutions of government.

Worcester v. Georgia, the second key instance in which President Jackson refused to follow the ruling of the U.S. Supreme Court, involved two missionaries who had been imprisoned for violating a Georgia statute requiring whites to get state approval before living on Indian lands. The statute was part of Georgia's attempt to remove Native Americans from lands that a federal treaty had given to the Cherokee Nation in 1791. Gold was discovered on these lands in 1828, and the state wanted to clear the lands of their Native American occupants so that the gold could be recovered. There were several conflicts between the Supreme Court and the state of Georgia over the matter; the state even refused to send lawyers to the Supreme Court to argue on its behalf in the *Worcester* case. In the *Worcester* decision, the Court overturned the convictions of the missionaries and ordered their immediate release from state prison. In doing so, the Court declared the specific Georgia statute at issue, as well as all the other Georgia statutes dealing with the Cherokee, to be unconstitutional (see also Remini 1988, 69). Emboldened by instructions from the state legislature that the governor was to ignore the Court's decision, Georgia officials refused to abide by the Court's order. President Jackson refused to enforce the order, and the journalist Horace Greeley reported that President Jackson allegedly had said, "John Marshall has made his decision, *now let him enforce it!*" (see Remini 1988, 70). Although most scholars now believe that this quote attributed to Andrew Jackson is apocryphal (see, e.g., Murphy 1962, 26; and Ellis 1987, 31), it nonetheless reflects the president's general distain for the powers of the federal judiciary.

President Andrew Jackson and his supporters in Congress refused to implement the decisions of the Supreme Court in part because they viewed the Court as an elitist body that could not be reconciled with their notion of majoritarian democracy (see, e.g., Remini 1988, 24–31). Jackson supporters in Congress introduced legislation to strip the U.S. Supreme Court of the ability to hear appeals from state supreme courts, and they strongly supported efforts to have federal judges run in partisan elections (see Geyh 2006, 55). As Frederick Robinson, a Jacksonian

Democrat in Congress, argued, "Judges should be made responsible to the people by periodical elections. The boast of an independent judiciary is always made to deceive you. We want no part of our government independent of the people" (qtd. in Volcansek and Lafon 1988, 90). It is important to note that although President Jackson had a clear aversion to judicial supremacy, he never attacked the courts as an institution (see Geyh 2006, 56). Jacksonians made a lot of noise about the evils of judicial supremacy, but they never took the actions necessary to reign in what they perceived to be courts out of control. Jackson would attack specific court decisions, but he would not destroy the overall independence of the judiciary. He needed the courts to help him implement some of his political agenda.

Jackson thus did not oppose the concept of judicial independence, although he was skeptical of the notion of judicial supremacy. But the customary independence of the federal courts had evolved to such a point by this time that direct attacks on judicial independence could be dangerous. In this era, "respect for the judiciary as a separate and independent branch of government counseled Congress against radical reform, in favor of incremental adjustments that adhered to legislative precedent and preserved the stability of the courts" (Geyh 2006, 64–65). Or as Robert McCloskey argued, by this time in American history, "the nation in general thought of the Court as the principal authority and conceded its right to supervise the states in most matters" (1994, 51). Walter Murphy reports that by the end of Chief Justice Marshall's time on the Supreme Court, "almost all of the basic measures to curb the Court had been seriously suggested or actually tried. . . . But despite all the threats, no anti-Court legislation passed Congress between the Judiciary Act of 1802 and the Civil War" (1962, 63). Thus American society came to see the federal courts as legitimate participants in the inter-institutional dialogue about the nation's constitutional future, bringing with them their legal reasoning and legal analysis.

Instead of attacking the Supreme Court directly, President Jackson moved to control the Court by appointing Jacksonian loyalists to the bench, including his nomination of Roger Brook Taney as chief justice after the death of John Marshall in 1835 (see, e.g., Schlesinger 1953, 322–23). Americans have always seemed to have accepted the notion that presidents have the right to shape the course of the nation by putting on the Supreme Court men or women who agree with their vision of the future. As Chief Justice Rehnquist proclaimed, "There is no reason in the world why a President should not 'pack' the Court," that is, "appoint people to the Court who are sympathetic to his political and philosophical principles" (qtd. in O'Brien 2005, 33). By the end of his two terms in office, Jackson had appointed six justices to the U.S. Supreme Court, more than any of his predecessors except George Washington and more than any of his successors except Franklin D. Roosevelt (see Stephenson 1999, 77). The Supreme Court thus became a Jacksonian Court. Although Jackson did not take actions to attack the Court as an institution, he took control of the Court by appointing justices who shared his values and his vision. He changed the contributions that federal courts could bring to the constitutional conversation without preventing them from being heard in the first place.

Dred Scott and the Civil War

Political uproar over a Supreme Court decision erupted again when the Court handed down its decision in *Dred Scott v. Sandford* in 1857. The case concerned whether a slave taken to free territory remained enslaved. While the decision was a landmark ruling that violated the rights of persons of color, the details of the case are nevertheless interesting.

Dred Scott was born into slavery about 1800 in Virginia. Scott's original owner took him from Virginia to Alabama and then, in 1830, to St. Louis, Missouri. In 1832, following the death of his original owner, Scott was sold to an army surgeon, Dr. John Emerson. Emerson took Scott to the free state of Illinois for more than two and a half years. In the spring of 1836 Emerson moved to a fort in the Wisconsin Territory (present-day Minnesota), taking Scott along. Slavery was also prohibited in the Wisconsin Territory. While staying in Wisconsin, Scott met and married Harriet Robinson, a slave owned by a local justice of the peace. (Marriages between slaves were illegal in slave states, but persons of color were free to marry in free states and territories.) The Scotts were legally married in Wisconsin. After the marriage, Emerson treated both Scott and his wife as his property. The army then transferred Emerson to St. Louis, then to Louisiana, and then back to St. Louis. The Scotts remained in the free Wisconsin Territory during this time. Eventually Emerson, recently married, ordered the Scotts to join him in Missouri. Instead of staying in the free territory of Wisconsin, going back to the free state of Illinois, or suing for their freedom, the Scotts traveled more than a thousand miles, apparently unaccompanied, down the Mississippi River to meet their owner. Soon a daughter, Eliza, was born to the slave couple. After Emerson's death in 1843, his widow hired Scott out to an army captain. At this point Dred Scott tried to buy his freedom for three hundred dollars, but Mrs. Emerson refused. He then sued for his and his wife's freedom in court in Missouri in 1847. Mrs. Emerson then handed control of the case over to her brother, John Sandford. Dred Scott's first suit failed because he could not prove that he was a slave. Eventually the case was reheard, and in 1850 a lower court in Missouri ruled that Mr. Scott was no longer a slave. The Missouri Supreme Court overruled this decision, and Scott appealed the ruling all the way to the U.S. Supreme Court.

In its ruling, written by Chief Justice Roger Taney, the Supreme Court ruled that Congress had no power to prevent the spread of slavery, that the Missouri Compromise of 1820, preventing the spread of slavery to the free territories, was unconstitutional, and that blacks had no rights that the United States would ever recognize. In fact, the Court's ruling stated that blacks were not considered persons under the U.S. Constitution and that they were not entitled to any of its protections. This sweeping decision outraged the abolitionists and contributed to the rise of the new Republican Party, headed by Abraham Lincoln. In many ways the Supreme Court's *Dred Scott* decision, often known as the Court's "greatest self-inflicted wound" (see Hughes 1928, 50), propelled the country into the Civil War (see, e.g., O'Brien 2005, 16).

The abolitionists were livid about the *Dred Scott* decision. The antislavery movement had some of its intellectual roots in Jacksonian notions of democracy. Thus antislavery politicians adopted the Jacksonian view against what they saw as "aggression by the judiciary" and "judicial usurpation" (see Schlesinger 1953, 485). They roundly condemned the *Dred Scott* decision, and it became a focal point in many congressional campaigns. Radical abolitionists introduced many bills in Congress to restrict the power of the federal courts, including the U.S. Supreme Court (see, e.g., Murphy 1962, 31). The antislavery movement took up the mantra that the Supreme Court had no moral or legal authority over the slavery question.

The Supreme Court's decision in *Dred Scott* became a dominant issue in the 1858 Senate election between Democrat Stephen Douglas and Republican Abraham Lincoln. These two candidates would also oppose each other in the presidential election of 1860. The famous Lincoln-Douglas debates occurred during the senatorial campaign. As Stephenson notes, "*Dred Scott* and slavery consumed so much of the candidates' attention that one wonders what the two men would have discussed without them" (1999, 99). During the debates, Lincoln often repeated the Jeffersonian and Jacksonian views that the Supreme Court was not the only institution that could interpret the Constitution (see, e.g., Whittington 2007, 34–35). Thus as a political candidate Lincoln called for a dialogue among the institutions of government about the meaning of the Constitution, especially on the issue of slavery.

Abraham Lincoln was generally a moderate when it came to notions of judicial power. As a political candidate, he did not attack the Supreme Court as an institution as did many of the more radical members of his party. Lincoln certainly opposed the *Dred Scott* decision, but during the debates he stated that he would abide by the part of the decision that affected the specific parties to the case. But then he went on to quote Jefferson, who had argued that judges should not be considered the ultimate authority on constitutional questions, because doing so would "reduce us to the despotism of an oligarchy" (qtd. in Fisher and Adler 2007, 28–29). Lincoln is also quoted as saying, "Our judges are as honest as other men and not more so. . . . Their power is the more dangerous as they are in office for life, and not responsible, as the other functionaries are, to elective control" (qtd. in Simon 1973, 10).

It is unclear whether Lincoln was opposed to judicial supremacy in general or just to the decision in the *Dred Scott* case. In another debate, Lincoln demanded that the Supreme Court fix its ruling in *Dred Scott:* "We know the court that made it, has often over-ruled its own decisions, and we shall do what we can to have it to over-rule this" (qtd. in Stephenson 1999, 99). Thus Lincoln implied that he would take whatever action was necessary to change the Court's decision, including changing its personnel. As president, Lincoln generally ignored the *Dred Scott* ruling (see Whittington 2007, 34–35), but he did take a variety of steps to avoid judicial involvement in his Civil War policies.

Clearly, the *Dred Scott* decision was an important issue in the presidential election of 1860. The Democratic Party split over the ruling, and Democrats were unable to nominate only one candidate for the presidency that year (see Stephenson 1999, 101–2). Thus both Stephen Douglas and John Breckinridge ran as Democrats for the presidency in 1860. John Bell ran under the banner of the Constitutional Union Party. The Republicans united behind Abraham Lincoln, and although Lincoln eventually won the presidency, he clearly received only a minority of the popular votes cast in the election. Many have argued that Chief Justice Taney's decision in the *Dred Scott* case was directly responsible for Abraham Lincoln's election to the presidency (see, e.g., Warren 1926, 357; and

Fehrenbacher 1978, 485). The *Dred Scott* ruling was directly overturned by the passage of the Thirteenth, Fourteenth, and Fifteenth amendments to the Constitution, ratified just after the end of the Civil War.

Once in office, Lincoln did not attack the courts as expected; he just ignored them (see, e.g., McGinty 2008). Although he called for respect for the judiciary, Lincoln in his first inaugural address stated, "If the policy of the government, upon vital questions, affecting the whole people, is to be irrevocably fixed by the decisions of the Supreme Court, . . . the people have ceased to be their own rulers" (qtd. in Murphy et al. 2006, 359). Instead of directly attacking the federal courts, Lincoln and the Republicans turned to the time-honored tradition of packing the Supreme Court with sympathetic justices. Within two months of his first inauguration, Lincoln was able to fill three vacancies on the Court following the death of one justice and the retirements of two others. In 1863 Congress expanded the size of the Court to ten, in part because of the creation of a new western circuit court of appeals and in part to allow Lincoln to make additional appointments to the Court. In 1864, following the death of Chief Justice Taney, Lincoln named his secretary of the treasury, Salmon P. Chase, chief justice. In all, Lincoln was able to name five justices to the U.S. Supreme Court during his presidency (see Rehnquist 2001, 212–13).

During the early years of the Civil War members of the Republican Party in Congress introduced many bills to restrict the general power of the federal courts, but the war caused Congress to worry about other issues (see Murphy 1962, 31–32). Nevertheless, the 1860s are generally seen as the low point in the Supreme Court's influence (see, e.g., Stephenson 1999, 103). Not surprisingly, during the Civil War the Supreme Court upheld Lincoln's actions in such cases as *The Prize Cases* (1863), *Roosevelt v. Meyer* (1863), and *Ex Parte Vallandigham* (1864). As Rehnquist (1998) and Mark Graber (2006), among others, have noted, throughout U.S. history the Supreme Court has almost always upheld even extraordinary governmental powers during wartime. As McCloskey has written, "War is never a favorable environment for judicial power" (1994, 64). Thus the Supreme Court became subservient to the wishes of the Lincoln administration during the Civil War and was thus excluded from the constitutional conversation about the future of the nation.

Lincoln's greatest wartime confrontation with the Supreme Court came in the case of *Ex Parte Merryman* (1861). John Merryman, of Maryland, was a Southern sympathizer who was arrested by Union soldiers after a riot in Baltimore. He was imprisoned at Fort McHenry, in Baltimore. Just after the riot and the Southern attacks on Fort Sumter, President Lincoln suspended the writ of habeas corpus. Nevertheless, Merryman filed for a writ of habeas corpus with the U.S. Court of Appeals in Maryland, demanding to be released from his military confinement. Chief Justice Taney, the author of the much hated *Dred Scott* decision, was riding circuit and sitting on the U.S. Court of Appeals for the Maryland District at the time. Taney ruled that only Congress could suspend the writ of habeas corpus and that President Lincoln's actions were unconstitutional. Lincoln simply ignored the Taney opinion, and Congress eventually ratified the president's actions in 1863.

As president of a nation disintegrating around him, Lincoln approached the inter-institutional constitutional conversation about the future of the Union by ignoring the other institutions. Lincoln saw holding the Union together as his sole duty, regardless of what other political actors thought at the time. The views of Congress, the state legislatures still in the Union, and the Supreme Court were irrelevant. Lincoln saw it as his burden, and his burden alone, to preserve the United States. "Perhaps the most important constitutional interpretation in American history," writes Michael Comiskey, "was authored by a president, Abraham Lincoln, who decided in the absence of any constitutional language on the question that a state may not leave the Union, and enforced that decision on the battlefields of the Civil War" (2008, 206).

Reconstruction and the Courts

After the Civil War ended, and President Lincoln having been assassinated, the Radical Republicans, who were then in control of Congress, could never forgive the Supreme Court for its *Dred Scott* decision, and anti-court sentiment ran deep in the legislative branch. As Barry Friedman notes, "During Reconstruction, quite unlike any other period in American history, the Supreme Court's independence was in almost constant jeopardy" (2002, 3). The Radical Republicans proposed a number of steps designed to limit the power of the U.S. Supreme Court and the rest of the judiciary, including impeachment threats against justices who rendered decisions with which the Radical Republicans disagreed, but most of these attacks against the courts were never actually enacted into law (see, e.g., Murphy 1962, 36–37). Many viewed the threats against the Supreme Court as an attempt to silence its voice in the inter-institutional constitutional conversation. Of course, through their impeachment of President Johnson in 1868 the Radical Republicans in Congress also attempted to silence any dissent from the executive branch as well. The

Radical Republicans wanted legislative supremacy to be the new constitutional paradigm for the recently reunited nation.

In Congress, the Radical Republicans proposed a number of court-curbing initiatives during and after the Civil War. Some of the Radicals wanted to abolish the federal judicial system then in place and start over. Some even talked of "annihilating" the Supreme Court (see, e.g., B. Friedman 2002, 6). The House of Representatives passed legislation to require a two-thirds vote of the Supreme Court before a federal statute could be declared unconstitutional (see Fisher and Adler 2007, 1044), but the bill died in the Senate. Although most of the anti-court proposals failed to be enacted, the Radical Republicans took some very important actions against the courts. During Reconstruction the Radical Republicans enacted one of the first court-stripping bills in American history (discussed in more detail below), and they decreased and increased the size of the Supreme Court as their political needs dictated. As mentioned above, Congress had expanded the number of justices on the Court to ten in 1863, in part to give President Lincoln an additional appointment to the Court. After the Civil War, however, in 1866, the Radical Republicans reduced the size of the Court to seven in order to prevent President Andrew Johnson from naming any justices to the High Court (see B. Friedman 2002, 39). The reduction in the size of the Court would occur through attrition.

After the Civil War ended, the Supreme Court began to reassert itself and attempted to reclaim what the justices felt was the Court's rightful place in the constitutional dialogue. After President Lincoln's death, the Court declared a variety of President Lincoln's actions to be unconstitutional. For example, in *Ex Parte Milligan* (1866) the Court declared that the use of military tribunals in the North, where the regular federal courts were fully functioning, was unconstitutional. In this case, the Court also questioned the constitutionality of Lincoln's suspension of the writ of habeas corpus for U.S. citizens in the North who were not part of the military. Lambdin Purdy Milligan was a Confederate sympathizer who lived in Indiana. Milligan and several others were arrested for plotting to steal weapons from the Union army with the goal of liberating Union prisoner-of-war camps holding Confederate soldiers. Milligan and his compatriots apparently thought that the liberated Confederate soldiers would help to overthrow the government of the state of Indiana and that Indiana would then join the Confederacy. Milligan was arrested by the Union army and sentenced to death by a military tribunal. The Supreme Court did not address the use of military tribunals in the South after the

Civil War, but it did declare that military tribunals could not be used to try civilians in the North.

Although the *Milligan* ruling did not impede Reconstruction efforts in the South, the Radical Republicans in Congress were nonetheless furious over the Court's actions. Some compared the *Milligan* decision to *Dred Scott,* with Senator Thaddeus Stevens declaring that the *Milligan* decision was "far more dangerous" than the *Dred Scott* ruling because of "its operation upon the lives and the liberties of the loyal men, black and white, in the South" (qtd. in B. Friedman 2002, 14).

The Supreme Court then issued a string of decisions that further outraged the Radical Republicans in Congress. In *Cummings v. Missouri* (1866) and *Ex Parte Garland* (1866) the Court declared unconstitutional certain of the loyalty oaths required of Southerners in the state and federal Reconstruction Acts. In *Hepburn v. Griswold* (1870) the Court by a vote of 4-3 declared unconstitutional an 1862 federal statute requiring that creditors of the United States accept paper money not backed by gold or other precious metals in payment for debts owed by the United States. The Lincoln administration had considered this act necessary to maintain the Civil War effort. The Radical Republicans were furious about the *Hepburn* decision, and they moved quickly to increase the size of the Court to nine justices, giving President Grant two very quick appointments to the High Court. The *Hepburn* decision was quickly overturned by *Knox v. Lee* (1871), by a vote of 5-4, after President Grant appointed the two new justices to the Court. Thus the Supreme Court had become directly involved in the political battles of the day. It reasserted its right to participate in the constitutional dialogue of the time, directly challenging the Radical Republican preference for legislative supremacy in the new constitutional order.

After the Court's *Milligan* ruling and the loyalty-oath decisions discussed above, the Radical Republicans feared that the Supreme Court would use the *Ex Parte McCardle* (1869) case to declare the Reconstruction Acts unconstitutional. *McCardle* was a military-tribunal case involving William H. McCardle, a Mississippi journalist. William McCardle was a former Confederate soldier. He had been arrested and jailed by a military commander under the Military Reconstruction Act of 1867 for publishing a series of editorials in his Mississippi newspaper that were sharply critical of Reconstruction. McCardle sought a writ of habeas corpus from the regular federal courts on the grounds that the Reconstruction Acts under which he was arrested were unconstitutional. Note that unlike the Milligan case, this case involved the use of military tribunals in the Reconstruction South. To prevent the possibility that the Supreme Court would use the McCardle case to challenge their Reconstruction efforts, the Radical Republicans in Congress enacted over President Johnson's veto legislation to strip the Supreme Court of jurisdiction to hear any habeas corpus cases, including the McCardle case (see Murphy 1962, 38–40). In its decision in *Ex Parte McCardle* (1869) the Supreme Court accepted the limits Congress had placed on its jurisdiction. The Supreme Court thus backed down from a fight with the Radical Republicans, who had already initiated impeachment proceedings against President Johnson. However, in its later decisions in *Ex Parte Yerger* (1869) and *United States v. Klein* (1872) the Supreme Court implied that its decision in *Ex Parte McCardle* may not have settled the long-term question of the constitutionality of court-stripping legislation (discussed in more detail in chapter 5).

Most scholars see the Supreme Court as clearly acquiescing to the demands of the Radical Republicans during this era. Barry Friedman (2002) writes that the Supreme Court was under extreme duress from a determined and angry Congress and had little choice but eventually to back down from the fight with the Radical Republicans. The Radical Republicans did not attack the lower federal courts, however, because they needed them to carry out their Reconstruction agenda (see Geyh 2006, 70). Although the Radical Republicans' threats against the Supreme Court were certainly real and the Court did back down in the *McCardle* decision, its later rulings in *Yerger* and *Klein* indicate that the justices were unwilling to silence themselves completely in the constitutional conversation of that critical time in American history. The Supreme Court clearly retreated in *McCardle,* but the Radical Republican notion of legislative supremacy failed to prevail in the long-term struggle between these institutions of government.

The Lochner Era of Economic Conservative Activism on the Court

Another period of strong conflict between Congress and the federal courts began during the 1890s. At this time the federal courts and especially the U.S. Supreme Court were gaining power and playing a more important role in policymaking (see, e.g., Gillman 2002, 512). Anger over the Supreme Court's protection of corporate interests and its conservative activism led to many rhetorical attacks against the federal courts by the liberals of the time. The Populists and the Democrats eventually united in their opposition to what they termed "judicial tyranny." The Republicans embraced the Supreme Court as the protector of America's sacred values. As Stephenson writes, "The Court became identified institutionally as an agent of the forces of law and order, respectability, and economic wealth" (1999, 107). Howard Gillman argues that the Republican Party intentionally increased the power of the courts in this era as part of its effort "to restructure national institutions better to facilitate national economic development" (2002, 512). Thus the Republicans increased the power of the federal courts in order to achieve some of their long-term political and ideological goals.

Large corporations were key to the Republican economic plans at this time, but the Republican electoral coalition was fragile. The Republicans thus strengthened the federal courts in order to help protect their ideological interests and became the protectors of judicial independence against Democratic and Populist attacks. Baum argues that during this period large corporations benefited the most from the Supreme Court's policies. These large business concerns hired the best legal talent in the country to argue their positions before the Supreme Court, which paid off in a long series of Court decisions striking down a variety of governmental regulations of business practices. "Corporate interests came to the judiciary because of their defeats elsewhere in government. . . . In scrutinizing these regulations closely, the Court served as a court of last resort for corporations in a political sense as well as the legal sense" (Baum 2004, 178).

Three key Supreme Court decisions in 1895 infuriated the liberals of the time, the Populists and their allies in the Democratic Party. The Court declared the income tax to be unconstitutional in *Pollock v. Farmers Loan and Trust Co.,* emasculated the Sherman Antitrust Act in *United States v. E. C. Knight,* and refused to recognize workers' rights by allowing management to continue using court-ordered injunctions as strikebreaking measures in *In re Debs.* The Populist leader Sylvester Pennoyer, formerly governor of Oregon, asserted, "Our government has been supplanted by a judicial oligarchy," and he called on Congress "to impeach the nullifying judges." Governor John Peter Altgeld, of Illinois, declared that the Supreme Court "has come to the rescue of the Standard Oil kings, the Wall Street people, as well as the rich mugwumps" (both qtd. in Stephenson 1999, 125).

This period of economic conservative activism on the part of the U.S. Supreme Court later became known as the Lochner era, named for the Court's landmark decision in *Lochner v. New York* (1905). In the *Lochner* case, the Supreme Court struck down a New York state law setting maximum working hours for bakers. In its decision, the Court read into the Fourteenth Amendment's due-process clause a substantive right to liberty of contract with which governments could not interfere. Thus the Court struck down as unconstitutional almost all governmental economic regulations. In his famous dissent in *Lochner,* Justice Oliver Wendell Holmes criticized the Court for deciding the case based "upon an economic theory which a large part of the country does not entertain" (198 U.S. 45, 75–76). This period of economic judicial conservatism is also often referred to as the era of substantive due process.

Despite the Supreme Court's pronouncements, governments at many levels continued to enact various economic regulations. The liberals of the time did not accept the notion of judicial supremacy on these issues, and the political branches continued to voice their concerns in the inter-institutional constitutional conversation. Eventually, the Sixteenth Amendment, which went into effect in 1913, overturned the *Pollock* decision, thus constitutionalizing the federal income tax. In 1914 Congress enacted the Clayton Act and created the Federal Trade Commission in part because of a fear of judicial hostility to progressive reforms.

The Lochner era of conservative economic judicial activism did not end, however, until the Court's decision in *West Coast Hotel Co. v. Parrish* (1937), in which the Supreme Court took a much broader view of the government's power to regulate economic activities. Thus the economic conservatism of the Supreme Court continued until the mid-1930s, when the Supreme Court eventually reversed itself in the famous "switch in time that saved nine" (discussed in more detail below) and ruled that the New Deal was a constitutional governmental response to the Great Depression.

During the early part of this long period of conservative judicial activism, the courts in general and the Supreme Court in particular became key targets in political campaigns. For example, the presidential campaign of 1896 became in part a grand debate about the proper role of the Supreme Court in American society. Alan Westin has called this election the second of the two "great anti-Supreme Court campaigns of American party politics" (1953, 38), with the 1860 election following the Supreme Court's *Dred Scott* decision having been the first. Both the Democratic Party and the Populist Party supported William Jennings Bryan for president in 1896, while the Republicans nominated William McKinley. The Bryan campaign was able to get three anti-court planks included in the Democratic Party platform in 1896 (see Murphy 1962, 45). The Populist Party then endorsed Bryan and added similar anti-court planks to their party platform. The Populists pushed the concept that the courts should reflect majoritarian views.

The Republicans countered that the Democrats and the Populists, because of their anti-court positions, were extremists who were enemies of law and order intent on undermining constitutional government (see Stephenson 1999, 125). The Republicans also argued that if the Democrats won in the 1896 presidential election, they would pack the Supreme Court with like-minded extremists. Thus the Republicans became the protectors of the courts, because their judicial economic conservatism was clearly in line with the political goals of the Republican Party. As former president Harrison told the Republican faithful, "I cannot exaggerate the gravity and the importance and the danger of this assault upon our constitutional form of government; [upon] the high-minded, independent judiciary that will hold the line on questions between wealth and labor, between the rich and poor" (qtd. in Stephenson 1999, 127). The Republican victory in the 1896 election prevented Congress from enacting any anti-court measures at that time. But the era of liberal unhappiness with the courts would extend for quite a few years beyond this period. As William Ross noted, "Between 1890 and 1937, populists, progressives, and labor leaders subjected both state and federal courts to vigorous and persistent criticism and proposed numerous plans to abridge judicial power" (1994, 1).

The Progressive Era

The Progressives in the 1920s also opposed the right-wing court decisions discussed above. They thus inherited the anti-court sentiments of their Populist predecessors. The Progressives argued that the courts should reflect majoritarian values instead of always siding with the rich and powerful minority in society. They became more and more skeptical of judicial power in general, in addition to opposing specific Supreme Court decisions. In the early decades of the twentieth century the Progressives advocated a variety of means to prevent the courts from exercising too much power (see Ross 1994), including legislation to require the popular election of federal judges, to allow Congress to overturn Supreme Court rulings by a two-thirds vote (see Murphy 1962, 50), and to require the vote of seven justices before a law could be struck down as unconstitutional (see G. Rosenberg 1992, 384). Some Progressives also wanted to institute recall provisions for the justices of the Supreme Court, which would have ended life terms for federal judges and thus allowed the voters to decide whether justices could remain on the Supreme Court (see Culp 1929, 391). Theodore Roosevelt even proposed having the voters vote on constitutional questions not yet decided by the U.S. Supreme Court in what has been called a "program of recall of judicial decisions" (see Ross 1994, 134–35).

The Progressives were quite critical of the way the courts protected big businesses in the United States during this period. Robert La Follette, running for president under the Progressive Party label in 1924, called judges "petty tyrants and arrogant despots" (qtd. in Murphy 1962, 50). There were hints that impeachment procedures should be used against conservative judicial activist judges. Teddy Roosevelt, another important figure in Progressive politics, once stated, "I may not know much law, but I do know that one can put the fear of God in judges" (qtd. in Stephenson 1999, 130). Roosevelt advocated popular referendums on constitutional decisions, but he never supported more direct institutional attacks on the judiciary. Others called for the initiation of provisions for recalling federal judges just like those available for recalling many political officeholders in some states. Some scholars have argued that the Populist and Progressive attacks on the courts were, as John Schmidhauser and Larry Berg put it, "all manifestations of lack of confidence in the integrity and impartiality of the judiciary" (1972, 36). Other scholars question whether these complaints against the judiciary rose to this level, noting that almost none of the institutional attacks on the courts were ever enacted. This was owing in part to LaFollette's loss in the 1924 presidential election, but other factors also led to the failure of the anti-court proposals.

Ross (1994) provides a variety of explanations for the Progressives' and other court critics' inability to curb the power of the courts. One reason why the courts maintained their power despite these pointed attacks has to do with the deep and solid respect for the courts among the American people. A second reason, according to Ross, was the Progressives' belief that judicial decision making should be based on expert scientific examination, not formal legal doctrines or the needs of partisan politicians. Third, at times during this era the courts did provide some victories for progressive causes, including judicial intervention to preserve some civil liberties, such as the right of private and public schools to teach foreign languages in their classrooms. Ross argues that instead of the courts being single-minded protectors of business interests, the precedents from the Supreme Court and other federal courts at this time were more nuanced than previous studies indicated. According to Ross, some other factors played a role in protecting the courts, including the political savvy of some of the judges, the elite bar's defense of the courts, and the implementation of modest reforms that derailed the most sweeping calls for change. Thus, Ross argues, the critics of the federal courts in this era, despite their anti-court rhetoric, did not truly question the courts' right to make decisions. They opposed specific court decisions but never the inherent need for the courts to be part of the inter-institutional constitutional dialogue in the first place. Ross concluded that the most vehement anti-court proposals "arose out of an angry reaction to adverse decisions or an attempt to rally support, rather than out of reasoned reflection about the proper place of the courts in American government" (1994, 320). The defenders of the courts took advantage of the disjointed nature of the anti-court forces by characterizing these various judicial reform efforts as unprincipled and shortsighted.

FDR and His Court-Packing Plan

One period of great conflict between the Supreme Court and the political branches that has received a lot of scholarly attention is that of the fight between the Court and President Franklin D. Roosevelt over the constitutionality of the president's New Deal programs. The courts remained conservative judicial activists despite FDR's landslide victory in the 1932 presidential elections, an election that also produced large Democratic majorities in both houses of Congress. C. Herman Pritchett (1948), Murphy (1962), Stephenson (1999), Thomas Keck (2004), David O'Brien (2005), and Louis Fisher and David Adler (2007) all discuss this gargantuan political battle between the Supreme Court and the political branches at length. Remember that liberals had been angry with the conservative activism of the federal courts since the 1890s. As Ross notes, "The conflict between Franklin D. Roosevelt and the Supreme Court that reached its denouement in 1937 was merely the culmination of a struggle that had raged with varying degrees of intensity for a half century" (1994, 2).

The generalities of the struggle between FDR and the Supreme Court are easy to outline. In the mid-1930s the majority of the Supreme Court continued to be conservative activists who believed that Roosevelt's New Deal programs were an unconstitutional assault on their notion of a limited federal government that could not constitutionally regulate the national economy. In more than a dozen rulings in that period the Court struck down various New Deal programs as unconstitutional. "For the first time since the Jacksonian era," notes Stephenson, "the Court squarely opposed the defining policies of the administration in power" (1999, 136).

Roosevelt was furious, but during the 1936 presidential campaign he rarely mentioned the Supreme Court. FDR's supporters in Congress, however, introduced more court-curbing bills in the 1935–37 period than in any other time in American history (see Nelson 1988). Their anger against the federal courts ran very deep. As Ross points out, "Antagonists of the courts between 1890 and 1937 alleged that a 'judicial oligarchy' had usurped the powers of Congress and thwarted the will of the people by interfering with the activities of labor unions and nullifying legislation that was designed to ameliorate the more baneful effects of the Industrial Revolution" (1994, 1). On the other hand, the 1936 Republican Party platform declared that the GOP was the defender of the Supreme Court and of the nation's constitutional democracy (see Stephenson 1999, 151).

Following his landslide reelection of 1936, FDR broke his silence about the courts and proposed a radical plan to change the makeup of the Supreme Court. In his so-called Court Packing Plan, Roosevelt wanted to almost double the size of the Supreme Court so that he could appoint a new majority of the justices. FDR stated that he wanted to appoint another justice to "assist" each of those justices over the age of seventy, thus allowing him to appoint six new justices to the Court immediately. FDR couched his plan in terms of judicial efficiency instead of attacking the Court directly for striking down his New Deal legislation (see Stephenson 1999, 156). While most scholars see FDR's Court-Packing Plan as motivated by the desire to protect the New Deal while at the same time ending the era of conservative economic judicial activism, Kevin McMahon argues that FDR's plan was motivated in part by the president's desire "to revolutionize the judiciary as an institution. . . . He hoped to transform the judiciary into an agent of the modern presidency, deferring to the expertise of the newly enhanced administrative state" (2004, 61–62). While pressuring Congress to enact his Court-Packing Plan, Roosevelt at the same time urged judges to follow a philosophy of judicial restraint and judicial deference, demanding that the Supreme Court especially follow the institutional will of the elected branches (see, e.g., Keck 2004, 19). One of FDR's eventual appointments to the Supreme Court, Justice Felix Frankfurter, came to epitomize FDR's ideal liberal restraintist judge.

Although the Court had struck down New Deal programs in a consistent series of 5-4 votes, starting in the spring of 1937 it switched its position and began to uphold the constitutionality of the New Deal in a set of 5-4 votes in favor of Roosevelt's legislation. Justice Owen Roberts had switched his vote, which became known as "the switch in time that saved nine." Although FDR's Court-Packing Plan is widely credited with forcing the Supreme Court to change its position on the constitutionality of the New Deal, it should be noted that Justice Roberts changed his vote at conference in December 1936, two months before FDR unveiled his Court-Packing Plan, in February 1937 (see, e.g., O'Brien 2005, 57). Nevertheless, it does appear that Justice Roberts may have read the handwriting on the wall stemming from the election results of the 1936 Democratic landslide. He may have feared that the threats against the judiciary advocated by the congressional Democrats before the election would become reality after their landslide victory. On the other hand, Barry Cushman (1998) argues that the change in the Court's jurisprudence resulted more from internal legal forces within the Court than from external factors such as the 1936 election results. Peter Irons (1982) and Ronen Shamir (1995), among others, have argued that certain key legal considerations, such as the fact that the early New Deal statutes were poorly drafted, were as important as external political concerns in the dramatic shift in the Supreme Court's approach to the constitutionality of the New Deal. Probably the Court's shift was caused by a combination of legal, political, and strategic factors. Whatever the cause, the shift occurred too late to prevent President Roosevelt from promoting his Court-Packing Plan.

Congress never approved FDR's Court-Packing Plan, mainly because public opinion was strongly against the proposal (see Stephenson 1999, 156–57). Ross reports that a 1935 Gallup poll showed that 53 percent of those polled opposed limits on the Supreme Court's power. Ross concludes that "the poll demonstrates the resilience of public support for judicial power, even when the Court was under widespread attack for striking down popular legislation" (1994, 297). However, Congress did pass legislation that would allow justices who had served on the Court for at least ten years to retire at age seventy at full salary instead of the half-salary previously given to retired justices. Thus Congress provided huge financial incentives for the conservative justices on the Supreme Court to retire quickly (see O'Brien 2005, 348). In part because of this generous early-retirement program, Roosevelt was able to appoint eight justices to the Court over the next six years, thus giving his supporters a huge majority on the Court. Although the Court-Packing Plan failed, FDR nevertheless was able to alter dramatically the future course of the judiciary.

One clear result of the defeat of FDR's Court-Packing Plan was that popular opinion in the United States continued to be against institutional attacks on the Supreme Court. "In the late 1930's, after nearly a half century of sustained efforts to curtail the powers and responsibilities of state and federal courts, the American judiciary found itself barely bruised and more powerful than ever," concludes Gillman (1996, 736). Many scholars have pointed out that the general public, in Lauren Bell's words, "holds the judicial branch in higher esteem than it holds either the legislative or the executive branches of government" (2008, 39). As discussed in the introduction, the conventional academic wisdom became that the courts were protected by a general sense of reverence toward them. Murphy argues that beginning in the 1890s and early years of the twentieth century, "judges were revered as high priests . . . who made neither law nor policy, but . . . [were] dispensing divinely ordained justice" (1962, 47). Ross notes "the public's profound respect for the Supreme Court" (1994, 282). Ross also argues that FDR's Court-Packing Plan failed largely because "it contravened the respect for the judiciary so deeply ingrained in the American character" (1994, 302). Pritchett wrote that the Supreme Court at least was protected from attack by "the most potent myth in American political life—the myth that the Court is a non-political body, a sacred institution on which politics must not lay its profane hands" (1948, 14). Since the courts were held in such reverence, those who attacked them did so only at their peril. Thus in the early 1960s Murphy and Pritchett argued that "courts are protected by their magic; only rarely can a hand be laid on a judge without a public outcry of sacrilege" (1961, 554–55). Of course the courts depend on the goodwill of the American people, since they generally cannot enforce their own decisions. As former member of Congress, federal judge, and White House counsel Abner Mikva argued, "The Supreme Court's mandates are usually obeyed not because of soldiers in the street but because of public perceptions of the Court's legitimacy" (1992, 555).

Another paradoxical result of the Court-Packing Plan's defeat was that many Americans came to realize that the Court often made political as well as legal decisions. While the Court was revered by the public at large, many came to consider it a political institution. As McCloskey notes, "The critical assault on judicial review that culminated in the Battle of 1937 did not destroy the Court, but it did impair many of the ancient myths which had long served as justifications for the Court's activities" (1994, 207). If the Supreme Court is merely a political institution making purely politically based decisions, then the elected branches have every right to challenge judicial rulings and to attempt to pack the Court with justices whose ideologies agree with their own. Among others, Gillman argued that as part of the constitutional dialogue, "judges take on those powers, responsibilities, and agendas that are assigned to them by other power-holders in the political system" (2002, 513; see also Peretti 1999). McMahon, for example, argues that President Roosevelt eventually packed the Supreme Court with rights-centered liberals whose beliefs naturally culminated in the Court's famous *Brown v. Board of Education* (1954) decision. McMahon stresses the importance of the president in shaping judicial policymaking and the political choices that the justices make. He concludes: "Through its judicial policy, the Roosevelt administration aided in constructing the federal judiciary's institutional norms and commitments, especially with regard to the High Court. These norms and commitments conditioned behavior on that tribunal for the middle third of the twentieth century" (2004, 7). Thus increasingly the Supreme Court came to be seen as another political voice in the inter-institutional constitutional conversation.

The Warren Court Era

Although almost all of the previous attacks against the courts had come from liberals complaining about conservative judicial activism, the climate changed dramatically after the liberal activist Warren Court handed down a whole series of decisions that infuriated conservatives. Many scholars point to the famous fourth footnote in *United States v. Carolene Products Co.* (1938) as the point when things began to change dramatically. In that famous footnote, the Supreme Court stated that it was turning away from economic cases to deal more with cases involving civil rights and civil liberties. The footnote implied that the Court would turn its attention to the protection of fundamental rights such as the First Amendment and to the protection of "discreet and insular minorities." The liberal Warren Court issued a series of decisions on a number of topics that created an enormous amount of friction with conservatives in Congress. Instead of liberals attacking a Supreme Court that they felt was too protective of the status quo, as had occurred throughout much of American history, now conservatives attacked the Court for trying to make drastic changes in American society too fast. For example, in response to the Supreme Court's landmark decision in *Brown v. Board of Education* (1954), Senator Richard Russell (D-GA) stated, "Ways must be found to check the tendency of the court to disregard the Constitution and the precedents of able and unbiased judges to decide cases solely on the basis of the personal predilections of some of its members as to political, economic, and social questions" (qtd. in McMahon 2004, 4).

The conflict between Congress and the Warren Court has received a great deal of scholarly attention. Sheldon Elliott (1958), Pritchett (1961), Murphy (1962), Schmidhauser and Berg (1972), Lucas Powe (2000), and Michael Klarman (2004) have all written extensively on the controversy in this era. Cornell Clayton (1992) and McMahon (2004), among others, have argued that the liberal judicial activism of the Warren Court was promoted either directly or indirectly by the executive branch under Presidents Roosevelt, Truman, Eisenhower, Kennedy, and Johnson. Clayton concludes that "the executive branch originally supported—even drove—the Supreme Court in its new political role . . . welcom[ing] judicial activism of the Warren Court variety" (1992, 126).

Conservatives were furious about a wide variety of the Warren Court pronouncements. Generally the conservatives in Congress, however, reacted most vigorously to Warren Court decisions regarding race discrimination, congressional investigations of Communism, other national-security issues, freedom of speech and expression, the rights of accused criminals, and the redrawing of legislative districts to ensure the "one person, one vote" principle. Senator James Eastland (D-MS) set the tone for the attacks when he asked Senator Joseph McCarthy this question on the floor of the Senate in 1957: "Is there any more certain road to the destruction of the American system of government than an irresponsible Supreme Court usurping the power of Congress?" Senator McCarthy replied, "You are right." Echoing the notion that the Court had become an extremely political body, Senator Eastland concluded, "We have politicians instead of lawyers on the Court" (qtd. in Murphy 1962, 88).

Conservative reactions to the Warren Court's decisions regarding race discrimination, starting with *Brown v. Board of Education* (1954), were pointed. "Impeach Earl Warren" bumper stickers and billboards were quite common in the South after the 1954 decision (see, e.g., Geyh 2006, 109). Congressional opponents of the Court's desegregation decisions even drafted the infamous Southern Manifesto, which stated that the *Brown* decision was a "clear abuse of judicial power" that encroached on the proper role of the legislature and the legislative function. Because the Supreme Court had abandoned its duty to enforce the Constitution, other public officials had to work to reclaim constitutional principles in an effort to overturn the *Brown* decision (see Powe 2000, 61). In other words, the Southern Manifesto called for "massive resistance" to the Supreme Court's unanimous ruling. The signers of the Southern Manifesto included every U.S. representative and senator from the Deep South. One of the clear ramifications of the Court's decision in *Brown* was that the issue of race became critically important in politics throughout the South (see Klarman 2004, 365).

The Supreme Court's confrontations with Congress over the Communist witch hunts of the McCarthy era also produced an outcry from various members of Congress (see Powe 2000, 96–98). In *Watkins v. United States* (1957) the Supreme Court ruled that Congress had violated the rights of witnesses testifying before the House Un-American Activities Committee, in part because the questions posed were too vague. In response, furious member of Congress introduced a wide variety of bills to curb the Court. As Powe describes the situation, "The summer of 1958 witnessed a battle over judicial power not quite comparable to Roosevelt's Court-packing plan twenty-one years earlier, but close enough for Court supporters" (Powe 2000, 127). Members of Congress were extremely angry over the Supreme Court's attempt to limit congressional investigative powers. Responding to this determined opposition from Congress to its ruling, just two years later the Court significantly softened its position in *Barenblatt v. United States* (1959), upholding basically the same practices that it had ruled unconstitutional in *Watkins.* Fisher and Adler term the *Barenblatt* decision a clear "retreat" by the Court in the face of "a groundswell of opposition from legislators" (2007, 225). Clearly, the Supreme Court backed down from a direct confrontation with Congress on this issue.

In addition to its decisions regarding congressional investigations of potential Communists, the Supreme Court handed down a variety of decisions that made it almost impossible to arrest someone for mere membership in the Communist Party. *Yates v. United States* (1957) was one of the cases in this line of rulings. One of the swiftest congressional reactions came after the Supreme Court's decision in *Jencks v. United States* (1957), in which the Court ruled that a person under investigation by the Federal Bureau of Investigation for being active in the Communist Party was entitled to see all the FBI reports regarding his or her case. Because the *Jencks* decision was involved statutory interpretation, Congress quickly acted to overturn the decision by a vote of 74-2 in the Senate and 315-0 in the House (see Fisher and Adler 2007, 1034). Congress also considered, but did not enact, numerous bills designed to curb the Court and severely restrict its jurisdiction over a wide variety of issues. At the 1957 meeting of the American Bar Association, in London, ABA members expressed their strong reservations about many of the recent Supreme Court rulings. After that meeting, Chief Justice Warren resigned from that organization (see Stephenson 1999, 174; and Powe 2000, 100). The next year, the Conference of State Chief Justices adopted six resolutions opposing various U.S. Supreme Court decisions.

Of course, social conservatives also were extremely upset by the Supreme Court's decisions having to do with school prayer, abortion, and the rights of criminal defendants in the 1960s and 1970s. During this time, Governor George Wallace, of Alabama, referred to the Supreme Court as "that sorry, lousy, no account outfit" (qtd. in Simon 1973, 8). Senator Strom Thurmond, of South Carolina, was reported to have told Richard Nixon during his 1968 presidential campaign that there was no stronger issue in the South than the future direction of the Supreme Court (Simon 1973, 8). Conservative members of Congress frequently introduced legislation to curb the Court and to restrict the jurisdiction of both the lower federal courts and the Supreme Court. However, very little of this legislation was ever enacted into law. Geyh argues that the Court was protected from attack in part because legislators needed its voice in the constitutional conversation on a variety of issues: "These efforts to curb the Warren Court failed miserably," revealing "a high degree of congressional respect for and reliance on the federal courts, respect and reliance that a few unpopular decisions simply could not erode" (2006, 109–10).

Goldwater, Nixon, and Reagan Attack the Courts

During and after the Warren Court era, conservatives continued to attack the courts. In 1964 Senator Barry Goldwater (R-AZ), the Republican presidential candidate, made the judiciary a significant campaign issue (see McCloskey 1972, 359). Goldwater was especially upset with the Warren Court's decisions regarding civil rights and the protection of the rights of accused criminals. Thus he adopted the anti-court rhetoric of the social conservatives of the 1950s during his campaign, and this rhetoric became standard for social and economic conservatives in future elections. As Clayton and J. Mitchell Pickerill note, "In the view of many New Right Republicans, the Warren Court had formed an activist partnership with liberal Democrats to liberalize broad swaths of American social policy" (2006, 1385–86). Probably the most famous statement from Goldwater came in his acceptance speech at the 1964 Republican Convention, in which he proclaimed, "Extremism in the defense of liberty is no vice. Moderation in the pursuit of justice is no virtue" (see, e.g., Whittington 2007, 162).

Goldwater thus helped make anti-court rhetoric part of the conservative mantra, tying liberal judges to the rest of the liberal social engineering Goldwater and other conservatives so despised. As Keck notes, "Goldwater's frequent criticisms of the Supreme Court were part of a more general denunciation of the New Deal/Great Society Democratic order" (2004, 94). Most importantly, Goldwater started to make the Republican Party the home for social conservatives and supporters of what we would now call the Religious Right. Kenneth Wald argues that "Goldwater's candidacy appeared to galvanize many evangelicals who had previously stayed outside the political arena" (1997, 221).

During the 1968 presidential campaign, Richard Nixon made "law and order" and political attacks on liberal activist judges two of his main campaign issues (see, e.g., Phillips 1970; Rae 1989; Edsall and Edsall 1991; and O'Brien 2001). The law-and-order rhetoric, as well as his so-called Southern Strategy, were designed in large part to bring more social conservatives into the Republican coalition. From Nixon's perspective, the only groups in society who supported the Warren Court agenda were northern liberals, blacks, and the poor (see Simon 1973, 21), and these were not groups of voters that Nixon would win anyway. Nixon believed that the great Silent Majority wanted a complete overhaul of the U.S. Supreme Court. After he won his party's nomination, Nixon reportedly said about the federal courts, "I think some of our judges have gone too far in assuming unto themselves a mandate which is not there, and that is to put their social and economic ideas into their decisions" (qtd. in Simon 1973, 8). Nixon then promised to appoint only strict constructionists to the federal courts, meaning judges "who saw their duty as interpreting law and not making law. They would see themselves as caretakers of the Constitution and servants of the people, not super-legislators with a free hand to impose their social forces and political viewpoints on the American people" (qtd. in Stephenson 1999, 181). He wanted judges who would uphold the decisions of Congress and the president, in other words a judiciary that would defer to the decisions of the elected branches. According to Simon, "Nixon wanted a [Supreme] Court majority that thought more like lawyers than statesmen" (1973, 8).

Nixon's strongest attacks against the courts had to do with the rights of accused criminals (see, e.g., Clayton and Pickerill 2006, 1387). For example, during his campaign Nixon declared that court decisions "have inhibited law-enforcement officials and encouraged criminals" (qtd. in Stephenson 1999, 181). Nixon divided the world into criminal forces and law-and-order forces, and the Supreme Court was clearly on the wrong side of that divide (see Simon 1973, 21). Complaining about many Supreme Court decisions concerning the rights of the accused, Nixon said the result was that "the tragic lesson of guilty men walking free from hundreds of courtrooms across the country has not been lost on the criminal community" (qtd. in Keck 2004, 111). Thus both Nixon and George Wallace in 1968 were able to blame the Supreme Court for rising crime rates and for fostering social unrest, as evidenced by the growing antiwar and civil rights movements (see Keck 2004, 110). Although the rhetoric concerned law and order or race issues, the intent was really to reach out to a broader coalition of social conservatives in the nation. Social conservatives hated the Warren Court, and Nixon wanted to tap that mistrust of the courts in order to bring more social conservatives into his camp. According to Stephenson, the 1968 presidential campaign was "a watershed event for the Supreme Court both institutionally and jurisprudentially. It inaugurated an era of conspicuous politicization of the judiciary" (1999, 183).

The 1968 presidential campaign thus was another signal that the Republican Party would strive to become the party of social conservatives, just as it had been the party of economic conservatives since the late nineteenth century. Nixon's positions on law and order, race issues, and other such public policy questions were designed in part to make social conservatives more comfortable in the Republican Party. John Blum has observed that the conservatives were able successfully to "link the issue of law and order to the disruptions caused by other questions agitating and dividing the American people, particularly race, poverty, and war" (1991, 214). Following Nixon's election in 1968, Congress passed the Crime Control Act of 1968, which included many anti-court measures, including one that attempted to overturn the Supreme Court's *Miranda v. Arizona* (1966) decision (see chapter 2). Even though the 1968 legislative provision had never really been enforced, the Supreme Court nonetheless eventually struck down the statute as unconstitutional in *Dickerson v. United States* (2000). Nixon also made his attacks on a liberal activist judiciary an important part of his reelection campaign in 1972, vowing that if reelected, he would appoint even more conservatives to the bench (see Simon 1973, 291). Ever since Nixon, Republican presidential candidates have made the perceived liberal activism of federal judges a central campaign issue (see O'Brien 2001, 71).

Following Nixon's lead, Ronald Reagan made the federal courts and their perceived liberal activism a major campaign issue during his 1980 and 1984 presidential campaigns. Reagan attempted to unite a coalition of social conservatives and economic conservatives under the Republican Party umbrella. He tapped into the rise of the Moral Majority and other Religious Right groups (see chapter 3). During the 1980 campaign, Reagan announced that in contrast to his Democratic opponents, he would appoint judges with "integrity" who believed in "judicial restraint" (qtd. in Stephenson 1999, 204). Reagan often attacked liberal judicial activism in his 1980 presidential campaign. After Reagan won the 1980 election and brought a Republican majority to the Senate and an increased GOP minority to the House, numerous of court-curbing bills were introduced in Congress, although none were enacted. President Reagan then made it clear that he would appoint only conservatives to the federal bench. Vetting of judicial nominees, in what O'Brien calls the "most rigorous and decidedly ideological screening process ever" (2001, 72), was centralized in the Justice Department under Attorney General Edwin Meese. As Meese made clear, social conservatives saw judicial appointments as the best way to further their agenda in the long term. The Reagan administration clearly intended to pack the courts with conservatives in order, as Meese stated, "to institutionalize the Reagan Revolution so it can't be set aside no matter what happens in future presidential elections" (qtd. in O'Brien 1988, 63). Gillman defines this approach to packing the judiciary as "political entrenchment" (2006a, 139).

Thus after Goldwater, Nixon, and Reagan, the Republican Party became the anti-court party, while the Democrats became the party that worked to protect the courts from institutional attack. As one liberal Democratic Senate staffer told me, "The conservative agenda is to attack judges, and this has been their plan since the days of Nixon's anti-court activism." Agreeing with this view, a liberal lobbyist said, "The current resentment of the judiciary from the Right dates back to their reactions to the *Brown* decision and Nixon's exploitation of that resentment." Thus social conservatives will attack the courts as institutions when it suits their political needs. As another Democratic Senate staffer told me, "The Right's lesson from the Warren Court era is that the courts are political. They now see the courts as a means to a political end because law and politics have merged." Even in the aftermath of *Bush v. Gore* (2000), it still appears that social conservatives in the Republican Party will attack the federal courts, while the more liberal Democrats will generally work to protect judicial independence in part because even the conservative-dominated federal courts of today seem to be fairly aligned with the needs of liberal Democrats and the interest groups that support them (see, e.g., Silverstein 1994, 62; and Bell 2008, 39).

This chapter demonstrates that tensions between Congress and the federal courts have occurred throughout American history. As William Ross reminds us, "During every period of the Republic's history, critics of the courts have assailed the judiciary with invective and have proposed measures to curtail the institutional prerogatives of the courts" (1994, 1).

Until about the 1950s, the most vigorous attacks upon the power of the federal courts came from the more progressive elements in American politics, who felt that the conservative-dominated federal courts were impeding social progress. Thus liberals often called for the courts to be more majoritarian in their decisions, and progressive elements supported a variety of ways to make the courts more accountable to them. Beginning in the 1950s, however, the federal courts took on a more liberal activist bent, and conservatives complained that the federal courts no longer reflected majoritarian values. Social conservatives in particular have been quite critical of federal judges and their decisions since the days of the Warren Court. The anti-court conservatives found a home in the Republican Party beginning in part with the presidential campaign of Barry Goldwater. Since then, in order to appease social conservatives, Republican presidential candidates and Republican presidents have made the courts a clear political issue in their campaigns and programs. Even though most federal judges today are Republican appointees, certain social conservatives in the Republican Party continue to attack the federal courts in an attempt to change the voice of the courts in the constitutional dialogue. Chapter 3 explores how the Religious Right has begun to put its anti-court views into practice in recent years as social conservatives have come to dominate the Republican Party, at least in the U.S. House of Representatives.

TWO

Regular Interactions between Congress and the Courts

Although some of the interactions between Congress and the federal courts bring about inevitable intense conflict, many of the day-to-day contacts between the two branches involve more regularized and often even routine matters. A variety of scholarship (e.g., Graber 1993; Rogers 2001; Gillman 2002; Lovell 2003; and Pickerill 2004) reminds us that the relationship between Congress and the courts can be quite cooperative at times, as the legislative branch may purposely increase the power of the courts or defer decisions to the courts for a variety of reasons. Of course, even these regularized interactions may lead to conflicts because of the institutions' differing perspectives and wills, but mostly these routine interactions occur without much fanfare (see e.g. Resnik 2000b; and Resnik, Boggs, and Berman 2004).

While the huge fights between Congress and the courts get the most attention in the media and among academics, the regularized interactions deserve examination as well. As J. Mitchell Pickerill describes the situation, "Those who expect a constitutional revolution, a constitutional moment, or other form of severe confrontation between the Court and Congress simply do not appreciate the more routine and typical type of interaction between Court and Congress in the political process" (2004, 130). This chapter focuses on the regularized interactions between Congress and the federal courts, which may or may not lead to highly publicized conflicts between them.

One source of potential conflict between the two branches is the inevitable communication problems between two institutions with such differing perspectives and wills. As Roger Davidson and Walter Oleszek observe, "Communications between Congress and the federal courts are less than perfect. Neither branch understands the workings of the other very well" (2004, 350). One lobbyist told me, "The courts and Congress don't talk to each other enough." Katzmann (1988, 1995, 1997), whose works often captured the more regularized interactions between Congress and the federal courts, frequently called for better communication between the two branches. A Senate staffer remarked that when the Senate Judiciary Committee invited Justice Anthony Kennedy to testify before the committee in February 2007, it was the first time a Supreme Court justice had ever testified before that committee. This staffer noted, "Both Chairman Leahy and ranking Republican Senator Specter want more exchange and dialogue with the courts. They are both respectful of the dignity of the judicial institution." The difference in perspectives of these two institutions is illustrative. Judges see the courts as an independent and coequal branch of government, but Congress sometimes views them as just one more federal agency begging for money and other resources.

There are few regularized communication channels between Congress and the federal courts, and this often leads to problems. Katzmann has often called for formalizing methods for increasing routine communication between Congress and the courts. He sees an overall lack of communication and understanding as causing undue friction in the relationship between the judicial and legislative branches. "Congress," he writes, "is largely oblivious of the well-being of the judiciary as an institution, and the judiciary often seems unaware of the critical nuances of the legislative process. But for occasional exceptions, each branch stands aloof from the other" (1988, 7).

In order to improve interbranch communication and to help diffuse some of the anti-judge rhetoric and actions in Congress, Representatives Adam Schiff (D-CA) and Judy Biggert (R-IL) created the Congressional Caucus on the Judicial Branch. This organization has invited Supreme Court justices and other judges to meet with members of Congress in informal settings in order to encourage members of the two branches to find ways to better understand each other. In 2006 Schiff and Biggert introduced legislation to improve judicial salaries. From the judicial side, in his *2007 Year-End Report* Chief Justice John Roberts called for finding additional methods to improve communication and cooperation among the branches of government, especially between the federal courts and Congress. As he stated in his report, "The separate Branches may not always agree on matters of mutual interest, but each should strive, through respectful exchange of insights and ideas, to know and appreciate where the others stand" (2008, 5).

Confirmation of Judicial Nominees

One area of regularized interactions between Congress and the federal courts involves the judicial confirmation process. Presidents have long used their appointment powers to put judges on the federal courts who supported their agendas. Of course, these presidential appointments must be confirmed by the U.S. Senate, so there is a regularized appointment and confirmation process. Presidents may find that their judicial appointees are easily confirmed, or the confirmation process itself may become the focus of interbranch conflict. Michael Gerhardt (2000) notes that this regularized process has the potential to create conflict between the president and the Senate, but it can also highlight conflicts between the federal courts and Congress. All participants in the inter-institutional constitutional dialogue thus understand the importance of lifetime judicial tenure. As one lobbyist told me, "Both left and right groups attack federal judges during the confirmation fights."

Clearly, presidents often see their judicial appointments as a way to perpetuate their ideological and constitutional visions. Thus presidents want to appoint like-minded judges to the federal bench, especially to the U.S. Supreme Court. As James Simon reminds us, "Throughout American history, Presidents have encouraged the politicalization of the Supreme Court." "In his own way," says Simon, "every U.S. president has tried to mold the Supreme Court in his own political image" (1973, 9, 288). In fact, the Federalists started the practice when they attempted to pack the federal courts with Federalist judges in the Judiciary Act of 1801, which was repealed by the new Democratic-Republican Congress in the Judiciary Act of 1802. As David O'Brien has argued, "The presidential impulse to pack the Court with politically compatible justices is irresistible" (2005, 56).

Presidents certainly understand that although their term in office is relatively short, federal judges are appointed for life. Thus the federal judges appointed today will continue to be part of the inter-institutional constitutional conversation long into the future. As President Nixon stated, "There is probably no more important legacy that a President of the United States can leave . . . than his appointments to the Supreme Court" (qtd. in Valis 1981, 54). To illustrate this point, during the 1984 presidential campaign a famous editorial cartoon showed nine justices who looked exactly like Ronald Reagan chanting, "Forty more years" (see Pacelle 2002, 93). By making careful judicial appointments, presidents can ensure that they have an enduring legacy. Kevin McMahon argues that presidents devote a lot of time and political capital to changing the makeup of the federal courts. "In comparison to legislative achievement—which is often difficult to carry out, and which subsequent presidents and Congress can wipe away—constitutional change is more permanent," concludes McMahon. "Simply stated, constitutional revolutions are both rare and enduring" (2004, 18).

What sometimes receives less attention, however, is the fact that senators often use their role in the confirmation process to attempt to shape constitutional interpretation (see, e.g., Gerhardt 2005). According to Gerhardt, "Senators, and presidents, employ their authority over appointments to impress their constitutional views upon other institutions (and the public)" (2000, xxvi). For example, during the Warren Court era, Congress would make nominees to the Court "jump through some additional hoops" in order to send a message to sitting justices that some members of Congress were unhappy with the direction of a variety of Warren Court decisions (see Pacelle 2002, 94). Lauren Bell argues that immediately after the Supreme Court declares an act of Congress to be unconstitutional, that judicial decision becomes a key part of the senators' questions in the confirmation process for even federal district court nominees. As Bell notes, following activist rulings from the Supreme Court, "senators who supported the original legislation sought nominees' views on the appropriateness of striking down acts of Congress" (2008, 39). Certainly Senator Arlen Specter (R-PA), the former chair of the Senate Judiciary Committee, among others, asked such questions of Chief Justice Roberts and Justice Samuel Alito during their confirmation hearings.

Even though federal judges at all three levels are appointed by the president and confirmed by the Senate for life terms, presidents have used different approaches to the judicial nomination process, especially for nominees to the lower federal courts. For example, Presidents Lyndon Johnson and Bill Clinton seemed to use a patronage approach for lower court nominees, basically allowing home-state Democratic senators to name the nominee. Presidents Reagan and George W. Bush, on the other hand, made judicial conservatism a litmus test for nomination to the federal bench (see, e.g., Baum 2001, 103). Senator John McCain hinted that if he became president, he would follow that practice (see Toobin 2008). Because vacancies on the U.S. Supreme Court are so rare, every president will have his staff prepare a short list of potential nominees in case an unexpected vacancy suddenly occurs.

Judicial nominations and confirmations have received a great deal of scholarly attention, with works by Mark Silverstein (1994), John Anthony Maltese (1995), David Yalof (1999), Michael Comiskey (2004), Lee Epstein and Jeffrey Segal (2005), Benjamin Wittes (2006), and Christine Nemacheck (2007) serving as good examples of this kind of research. Not surprisingly, most of this research deals with presidential appointments to the Supreme Court, with works by Sheldon Goldman (1997), Gerhardt (2000), Nancy Scherer (2005), and Bell (2002a, 2002b, 2008) serving as the clear exceptions. In general, the president is able to get most of his federal judicial appointments through the Senate with little problem. Even nominations to the U.S. Supreme Court may be treated by Congress as routine events. The confirmation processes for Justices Kennedy, O'Connor, Souter, Ginsburg, Breyer, and even Scalia are illustrative. These nominations received very little opposition in the Senate, and the justices were confirmed with overwhelming Senate approval despite some interest-group opposition to each of the nominees. In fact, Yalof (1999) notes that in the twentieth century the Senate confirmed 89 percent of the president's Supreme Court nominees. The president's winning record for the appointment of lower federal judges is even higher. Thus most of the time the judicial confirmation process proceeds with little fanfare and little attention from the media or the public. However, some judicial nominations create extraordinary tensions between Congress and the federal courts.

One of the most important modern confirmation fights was over President Johnson's 1968 nomination of Associate Justice Abe Fortas to the chief justice's chair following the announced retirement of Chief Justice Earl Warren. During the committee hearings on the nomination, conservatives attempted to blame Fortas for all the evils they saw in the activism of the Warren Court era (see Silverstein 1994, 22–28). This was ironic, of course, because Fortas had served on the Court for a very short period before his nomination to be chief justice; most of the more controversial decisions of the Warren Court predated his service on the High Court bench. Seeing President Nixon's election as imminent, Republicans and conservative southern Democrats filibustered the Fortas nomination on the floor of the Senate, using alleged financial improprieties on the part of Justice Fortas as the publicly stated excuse for the filibusters (see Maltese 1995, 71; and Epstein and Segal 2005, 98). Because Senate rules allow an individual senator to debate any issue without time limits, senators may attempt to "talk a bill" to death or delay a nomination indefinitely through a filibuster. Today, it takes sixty votes in the Senate to invoke cloture and end a filibuster. Filibusters have been rare when it comes to judicial nominations, but following the disputed 2000 presidential election Democrats used the filibuster to block several of President George W. Bush's nominations to lower federal courts (see Epstein and Segal 2005, 98–99).

After the filibuster of his nomination for the post of chief justice, Justice Fortas eventually withdrew his name from consideration and resigned from the Supreme Court. The decision on whom to name as the next chief justice then passed to President Nixon. Chief Justice Warren carried out his promise to retire, and President Nixon nominated Warren Burger to replace him as chief justice. There was little conflict over this nomination. At Chief Justice Burger's swearing-in ceremony, held at the Supreme Court, Chief Justice Warren administered the oath of office, while Nixon beamed. Simon (1973) paints a very clear picture of the importance President Nixon placed on this event signaling the end of the Warren Court era and his perception of the changes that Chief Justice Burger would bring to the country in the future. At Burger's swearing-in ceremony, President Nixon delivered a speech to the Court, the first time in American history that a sitting president had addressed the Supreme Court directly in its own courtroom. President Nixon appropriately thanked Chief Justice Warren for his dedication to his country and for all of his hard work, but he was really celebrating the fact that Warren was no longer the formal or symbolic voice of the Supreme Court in the inter-institutional constitutional dialogue. Richard Nixon, the former Republican U.S. senator from California, despised his former political rival Earl Warren, the former Republican governor of California, and the values of his so-called Warren Court. The two men had never really trusted each other. Despite their differences, Nixon, Warren, and Burger smiled for the cameras at the ceremony. "There was a surrealistic uneasiness to the scene," wrote Simon. "It was not what it appeared to be and no formal statement of unity, however forceful, could brush over that fact. The whole affair had the air of a celebration, produced, directed, and celebrated by a single man: Richard Nixon" (1973, 2). The Warren Court era had come to a close, and President Nixon wanted to immortalize that event for all eternity.

Several of Nixon's other nominations to the Supreme Court created much more political controversy, however. Coming right after the filibuster of the Fortas nomination, these fights in the Senate over Nixon's

Supreme Court nominations have greatly affected the current state of interactions between the federal courts and the other branches. Following Fortas's resignation, President Nixon had a great deal of trouble in filling the seat of the associate justice. The Senate rejected two of Nixon's nominees for the Supreme Court, Clement F. Haynsworth and G. Harold Carswell, in part because they were viewed as unqualified to sit on the nation's highest court (see Maltese 1995). Nixon was furious about these defeats, primarily because he believed that the president had the constitutional responsibility to appoint federal judges without undue interference from the Senate (see, e.g., Simon 1973, 98–99). He felt that the Senate should rubber-stamp his judicial nominations, but the majority of the Senate felt otherwise. In retaliation for the failure of the Senate to confirm the two Nixon appointees, conservatives in the House persuaded House Minority Leader Gerald Ford in 1970 to consider impeachment efforts against Justice William O. Douglas, an outspoken liberal on the Court (see Canellos 2006a). Those efforts failed after the successful nomination of Harry Blackmun as an associate justice (see O'Brien 2003, 100–104).

Later, other Supreme Court confirmation fights became highly contentious. Liberal interest groups persuaded the Senate to vote down President Reagan's nomination of Judge Robert H. Bork to the Supreme Court, in part because of his unwavering judicial conservatism. Silverstein (1994) and Bell (2002b, 2008), among others, argue that changes in the norms and traditions of the Senate have made it much easier for interest groups to influence the judicial confirmation process. Interest groups that tend to win in the federal courts become key allies for the courts when they are under attack. "Increased access to the courts has combined with new tools of judicial power to make the judiciary an attractive ally for a host of powerful constituent groups," writes Silverstein (1994, 62). Of course, these groups care deeply that the judicial confirmation process produces federal judges who will continue to rule in their favor. Among many others, Bell (2002b, 2008) has highlighted the role of interest groups in the confirmation process. Comiskey summarized the vast new literature on the role of interest groups in judicial confirmations when he wrote that "the tactics of these groups in confirmation battles are similar to those in any legislative struggle" (2004, 51).

Coming soon after the failed nomination of Judge Bork to the Supreme Court, the 1991 nomination of Clarence Thomas to replace Justice Thurgood Marshall also proved difficult, although he was eventually confirmed. Even though they had filibustered the nomination of

Abe Fortas to be chief justice, conservatives took great offense at the nomination fights over these Republican nominees. As one journalist has described the situation, "In the 1980's and 90's, liberal attacks on conservative Supreme Court nominees like Robert Bork and Clarence Thomas spawned a new era of political hostility" (D. Rosenberg 2005, 24). Conservatives then made the courts a larger focus of their overall political efforts. They would not allow liberals to control the voice of the Supreme Court through the appointment process. One should not underestimate the lessons conservatives took away from these failed judicial nominations, and these inter-institutional fights have clearly affected the political memories of conservatives today. The political mantra from the Right became that liberal activist judges had to be prevented from joining the bench, and the conservatives decided to fight liberal nominations in the Senate Judiciary Committee and on the floor of the full Senate. Former attorney general Edwin Meese stated the conservative view quite bluntly: "The Senate should use its confirmation authority to block the appointment of activist federal judges" (Meese and DeHart 1997, 181).

The battles over Supreme Court nominations provide the context for understanding the fights over lower federal court nominations during the presidency of George W. Bush. On average, about 80 percent of presidential nominations to the lower federal courts have been confirmed by the Senate (Epstein and Segal 2005, 99–100). Recently, however, the lower federal courts have become increasingly important political prizes for liberals and conservatives alike. These courts are now seen as key political players in the inter-institutional constitutional conversation, gaining attention that previously was given only to the Supreme Court. During the Clinton presidency, the Republicans in the Senate slowed down as many Clinton nominations for the lower federal bench as they could because their conservative base still was quite angry over what they perceived as continued liberal judicial activism on the federal courts. For example, during the Clinton presidency Republicans in the Senate put "holds" on more than a hundred of Clinton's nominations to the lower federal courts. These "holds" prevented the nominations from even being considered by the Senate Judiciary Committee. This "extra-parliamentary" practice has often been referred to as a "silent filibuster" (see Tolley 2006, 81).

Because President Bill Clinton was having difficulty getting some of his judicial nominees confirmed, he used his recess-appointment power to appoint some federal judges for a limited period of time. Recess appointments allow an individual to fill an executive or judicial position temporarily until the election of a new Congress. The use of recess appointments for federal judges broke several long-standing norms in the judicial selection process, including the norm that presidents would not make recess appointments to the federal appellate courts (see Tolley 2006, 82–83). President George W. Bush also made recess appointments for federal judges, but his appointees were individuals who had been defeated previously in the U.S. Senate (see Tolley 2006, 83–84). The use of recess appointments for federal judges has thus exacerbated partisan tensions over the judicial confirmation process.

When George W. Bush won the disputed 2000 presidential election, the Democrats decided to do what they could to prevent the most conservative Bush appointees from gaining federal judgeships. Several nominations were filibustered on the Senate floor, and the Republicans could not gather the necessary sixty votes to invoke cloture and end the filibusters. Members of the Religious Right were especially angered by these filibusters, because they felt that the targets of the filibusters were properly minded social conservatives who would bring Religious Right values to the federal bench. In an event entitled "Justice Sunday" they brought together thousands of people both in person and through television to protest the filibusters "against people of faith" (see Wilcox and Larson 2006, 3). The Religious Right urged Republicans in the Senate to use whatever means were necessary to end the filibusters and confirm the social conservatives to the bench.

The Republicans in the Senate, who held the majority of seats in that body, responded to the Democratic filibusters by attempting to eliminate the filibuster option for all judicial appointments, which became known as the "nuclear option." If the majority of Republicans had eliminated the filibuster as an option for the minority party, the Democrats likely would have used every parliamentary weapon available to them to prevent the Senate from conducting any business (see Stolberg 2006; and Bell 2008). A compromise was finally reached in 2005, crafted by the so-called Gang of 14, made up of moderate senators from both political parties, and the showdown over the so-called nuclear option was averted. Thus the Gang of 14 not only prevented further filibusters against Bush appointees but also prevented conservatives from eliminating the filibuster entirely for judicial nominations (see Nather 2005). Senator John McCain, the Republican candidate for president in 2008, was part of that Gang of 14 in 2005. The Religious Right has never quite forgiven him for his role in protecting the right of potential filibusters for judicial nominees (see, e.g., Hulse 2008; Meckler 2008; and Reston 2008). In fact, James C. Dobson, of Focus on the Family, a Religious Right group, has said that he could never support Senator McCain in his bid for the presidency because of his role in the compromise on filibusters for judicial nominees (see, e.g., Bumiller 2008). Since many in the Religious Right mistrust Senator McCain and his role in the Gang of 14, he took pains in a major speech in May 2008 outlining what types of persons he would nominate to the federal bench if elected president (see, e.g., Eilperin 2008; and Quaid 2008). Regarding the Gang of 14 proposal, McCain said in his speech, "[The compromise offered by the Gang of 14] showed that serious differences can be handled in a serious way, without allowing Senate business to unravel in a chaos of partisan anger" (qtd. in Bumiller 2008).

When President George W. Bush finally was able to fill two vacancies on the Supreme Court, he acted to nominate strong social conservatives who were acceptable to the Religious Right. Because the Religious Right was so consumed with changing the nature of judicial decisions in the country, Bush felt obligated to honor its wishes (see chapter 3). Senator John McCain indicated that if elected president, he would have followed George W. Bush's example in the appointment of federal judges. One commentator concluded, "McCain plans to continue, and perhaps even accelerate, George W. Bush's conservative counter-revolution at the Supreme Court" (Toobin 2008). On the other hand, Barack Obama said that if he were elected president, he would not appoint federal judges who tilt to the side of "the powerful against the powerless" and who favor corporations and the government against the individual (qtd. in Savage 2008).

George W. Bush, in his desire to transform American society, has long seen the federal courts as his long-term legacy. Robert McKeever states that as early as the beginning of his presidency President Bush "wanted to complete the Reagan revolution by nominating more radical conservatives to the Court" (2006, 165). In 2005 Bush found himself with two vacancies to fill on the Supreme Court because of the retirement of Justice Sandra Day O'Connor and the death of Chief Justice William Rehnquist. To fill the chief justice's chair, President Bush nominated John Roberts Jr. He then nominated his White House Counsel, Harriett Miers, to fill the seat being vacated by Sandra Day O'Connor. In response to the nomination of Harriett Miers, the ultraconservative Pat Buchanan blasted the president for "running from a fight and wasting 'a once-in-a-generation opportunity to return the Supreme Court to constitutionalism' and overthrow 'the judicial dictatorship imposed on the United States since the Warren Court'" (qtd. in Greenburg 2007, 271). Because social conservatives complained bitterly about the Miers nomination (see, e.g., Toobin 2007, 284–94), Bush withdrew her name and nominated Samuel A. Alito, who was much more acceptable to the Religious Right (see, e.g., McKeever 2006, 173–74).

The confirmation processes in 2005 and 2006 for Roberts and Alito nicely illustrate the tensions between the institutional cultures and perspectives of Congress and the federal courts. Liberals took the opportunity of the Roberts nomination to criticize the Supreme Court's conservative activist decisions in the area of federalism, where the Court had restricted congressional power in favor of the states by declaring various federal statutes to be unconstitutional. In a letter to then Judge Roberts, Senate Judiciary Committee Chairman Arlen Specter (R-PA) "blasted the 'judicial activism' of the Supreme Court under Chief Justice William H. Rehnquist." "My immediate reaction," stated Specter, "is to wonder how the Court can possibly assert its superiority in its 'method of reasoning' over the reasoning of Congress" (qtd. in Perine 2005). Reacting to Senator Specter's letter, Nan Aron, president of the Alliance for Justice, a liberal interest group, stated, "It's nice to see a Republican senator drawing attention to what every constitutional law scholar in the country has recognized as the real story about the Supreme Court: the aggressive, activist efforts of the court's conservatives [to overturn legislation] that protects ordinary Americans" (qtd. in Stolberg 2005b). Objecting to statements in various Supreme Court opinions that he felt denigrated the role of Congress, Senator Specter declared during Judge Roberts's confirmation hearings: "There isn't a method of reasoning which changes when you move across the green from the Senate columns to the Supreme Court columns. And we do our homework, evidenced by what has gone on in this hearing. And we don't like being treated as schoolchildren [by the Supreme Court]" (qtd. in Greenhouse 2005a).

Even though Senator Specter eventually voted to confirm now Chief Justice Roberts, this episode makes it clear that both liberals and conservatives in Congress are unhappy with the Supreme Court's judicial activism. At one point, it appeared that the Roberts nomination might become highly ideological and partisan (see, e.g., Stern 2005). In the end, however, the vote to confirm him was 78-22, with many liberals eventually voting for him both in committee and on the floor. Two notable liberals who voted against the Roberts nomination were Senators Hillary

Clinton and Barack Obama, both of whom were considering running for president at the time. As two journalists covering the confirmation process reported, "Roberts' swearing-in capped a relatively trouble-free nomination highlighted by three days of polished testimony before the Judiciary Committee that left Democrats grasping for a rationale to oppose his nomination" (Stern and Perine 2005, 2651).

The Senate vote on Justice Samuel Alito, by contrast, did become a highly ideological and highly partisan political event. In fact, the confirmation vote for now Justice Alito was the most partisan in history. Since President Bush nominated Judge Alito only after conservatives had successfully killed his previous nomination of White House Counsel Harriett Miers to fill Justice O'Connor's seat on the Supreme Court, Alito was seen as the darling of the right wing of the Republican Party. Liberals voted against Judge Alito on purely ideological grounds, and some even tried to filibuster his nomination. The filibuster failed because all the Republicans and about half of the Democrats voted in favor of cloture to end the filibuster. On 31 January 2006 Alito was confirmed by a vote of 58-42, with only four Democrats voting in favor of his nomination and one liberal Republican senator voting against it (Stern and Perine 2006). Immediately after his confirmation, Justice Alito attended President Bush's State of the Union address along with three other justices, raising the eyebrows of some political commentators, given the degree of partisanship in his confirmation vote. The only Supreme Court justice who received more negative votes than Justice Alito was Justice Clarence Thomas (see Reynolds 2006).

Clearly, the confirmation process for judicial nominees has become highly contentious, partisan, and extremely ideological. Both liberals and conservatives use the confirmation process for political gains, and both complain about judicial activist judges. Both sides use the confirmation process for federal judges to raise enormous amounts of money for interest groups and candidates alike (see, e.g., Bumiller 2005; and Bell 2008). As one reporter explained, "Nothing rallies the bases of both parties like the issue of judges. For conservatives, who have fought for decades to curb what they regard as the liberal activism of the judiciary, the Alito nomination is a sweet reward. For liberals, it is terrifying" (Stolberg 2006). Some do believe that the current conformation process has become too political. As one liberal member of Congress told me, "The courts have become too politicized today. Ideological litmus tests for federal judges are just plain wrong."

Appropriations for the Courts and Judicial Salaries

Another regularized interaction between Congress and the federal courts involves the annual budget process for the federal judiciary. Congress has the power of the purse, and each year Congress must appropriate funds for the operation of the federal court system. Each year, one or two justices travel across the street to testify before the Appropriations Committee of either the House or the Senate to explain the proposed budget for the federal judiciary. In a rare occurrence, in February 2007 Justice Kennedy even testified before the Senate Judiciary Committee concerning the judicial branch's request for higher salaries for federal judges (see Biskupic 2007; and Mauro 2007). Thus overall appropriations for the judicial branch have long been a source of concern and conflict between Congress and the federal courts (see, e.g., Walker and Barrow 1985; Perry 1999; and Rishikof and Perry 1995). In her study of congressional appropriations for the federal judiciary, Eugenia Toma found that from 1946 to 1977, Congress rewarded the Supreme Court with budget increases when it handed down conservative decisions and attempted to punish the Court for its liberal decisions by withholding budget increases. Toma concluded that Congress "signals its overall approval or disapproval of the Court's direction through budgetary allocations" (1991, 146). However, even Toma agrees that this control mechanism works only "at the margin" (145).

Members of Congress do often threaten to use their power of the purse against the federal courts, even if those threats usually do not materialize. Thus when Majority Leader Tom DeLay bellowed, "We set up the courts. We can unset the courts. We have the power of the purse!" (qtd. in Klein 2005), or when Congressman Steve King (R-IA) expressed his frustration with the courts by declaring, "When their budget starts to dry up, we'll get their attention" (qtd. in Marcus 2005), these threats seemed to ring hollow. The fact that Congress rarely cuts the federal judiciary's budget, however, does not reduce the seriousness of these threats. It is certainly possible in the future that if Congress becomes angry enough with the Supreme Court or with the other federal courts, the judicial branch's annual budget will suffer.

In addition to judicial salaries, the federal courts depend upon Congress for funds for new judgeships, for courthouses, for staff, for technology, and for a variety of other purposes. Chief Justice Warren was upset with Congress because it would not even provide the necessary funds for a library messenger for the Court (see Peretti 1999, 143). As I have written previously, "The annual appropriations process provides a clear avenue to see the different institutional perspectives of the Supreme Court and of Congress. The courts rightly see themselves as an independent third branch, and many judges seem to resent Congress's interference with their budget requests" (Miller 2004, 64). Congress, however, often views the federal courts as just one more federal agency begging for funds (see, e.g., Resnik 2000b, 1011). Judicial salary increases are not at the top of the agenda for many politicians. As one staffer to a liberal Democrat told me, "Federal judges already make more money than most of our constituents. It's hard to be sympathetic to their salary concerns." Another staffer for a liberal Democrat told me, "There's no way we are raising judicial salaries until we get a decent increase in the minimum wage first." Echoing the point that the courts are just one more federal agency begging for money, a Democratic staffer in the Senate told me, "Judges are public servants, and the courts aren't special. There are other benefits to being a judge other than the salaries." Thus judicial salaries are not high-priority items on the congressional agenda each year, although federal judges have long complained that they were severely underpaid.

While Congress is constitutionally barred from reducing the salaries of federal judges, an angry Congress can refuse to grant them salary increases. In 1964, for example, Congress increased the salaries for lower federal judges by $7,500 per year but increased those for Supreme Court justices by only $4,500 per year, a clear indication that Congress was unhappy with several Court decisions (see Schmidhauser and Berg 1972, 9). During the fight between FDR and the Supreme Court over the constitutionality of the New Deal, Congress did the reverse by enacting financial incentives for early retirement for the justices, hoping to encourage some retirements from the Court so that Roosevelt could appoint justices more favorable to his views (see Murphy et al. 2006, 337).

Today judicial salaries remain a key point of contention between Congress and the federal courts. Seth Stern noted that "salaries [for federal judges] are far lower than what fresh-faced law school grads can make at big corporate firms" (2002). Chief Justice Roberts said in his *2006 Year-End Report* that keeping judicial salaries well below those of many *law professors* today is a "constitutional crisis" and a potential threat to judicial independence (2007, 1). In his appearance before the Senate Judiciary Committee in February 2007, Justice Kennedy echoed this theme: "The Committee knows that judges throughout the United States are increasingly concerned about the persisting low salary levels

Congress authorizes for judicial service. Members of the federal judiciary consider the problem so acute that it has become a threat to judicial independence" (U.S. Senate 2007). In his *2007 Year-End Report* Chief Justice Roberts again raised the concern of inadequate judicial salaries, noting that many federal judges received lower salaries than some *first-year lawyers* at the largest firms in major U.S. cities, where many of the federal judges serve. The chief justice also praised congressional efforts to increase judicial salaries, including action by the House Judiciary Committee in late 2007 to give federal judges cost-of-living adjustments that had been denied to them since 1989. The Senate Judiciary Committee passed similar legislation in February 2008. In his *2007 Year-End Report* Roberts declared, "I am resolved to continue Chief Justice Rehnquist's twenty-year pursuit of equitable salaries for federal judges" (2008, 6).

The main problem for federal judges is that since 1989, annual cost-of-living increases for federal judges have been linked to congressional salary increases. When Congress votes to raise its own pay, it often hides behind the fact that federal judges will also enjoy the salary increase. When members of Congress refused to vote themselves annual cost-of-living increases (usually during election years), these increases were automatically denied to federal judges. Members of Congress also are hesitant to allow other federal employees, including federal judges, to earn higher salaries than they do. In December 2007 *The Third Branch,* a newsletter published by the Administrative Office of the Federal Courts, carried an interview with Congressman Howard Berman (D-CA), the then chair of the House Judiciary Committee's Subcommittee on Courts, the Internet, and Intellectual Property, the subcommittee in which legislation to decouple judicial salaries from congressional salaries originated. When asked about the opposition of some members of Congress to the legislation, Congressman Berman responded, "Some of my colleagues believe that linking the salaries of federal judges to our own salaries will somehow make it politically more palatable for Members of Congress to approve cost-of-living adjustments for themselves. The evidence simply does not bear this out" (Berman 2007, 1).

Others also agree that federal judicial salaries are currently too low. One Democratic member of the Judiciary Committee told me, "Salaries for judges are woefully inadequate. Since Congress keeps increasing the caseloads of federal judges, it is our duty to pay them what they deserve." Echoing this theme, another member of Congress told me, "Public sector salaries are all too low, but we need experienced judges and their legal wisdom on the bench. First year associates at large law firms earn more than federal judges. It's outrageous."

In early 2008 Congressman Berman and the other Democrats on the House Judiciary Committee supported legislative efforts to increase judicial salaries substantially and end a twenty-year policy "that holds judicial salaries hostage to the politics of congressional pay raises" (Berman 2007, 1). Federal judges did receive a normal cost-of-living increase in their salaries in 2007, but it remains to be seen whether the full House and the full Senate will eventually approve this legislation, which would substantially increase the salaries of federal judges.

Concerns over the annual appropriations process led Chief Justice Roberts to also argue that the independence of the courts was under attack. He wrote in his 2005 annual report that "in recent years, the budget for the federal judiciary and the ever-lengthening appropriations process have taken a toll on the operation of the courts." He went on to complain about the overly high rents that the judicial branch pays to the federal General Services Administration for courthouses and other office space. He continued, "Escalating rents combined with across-the-board cuts imposed during fiscal years 2004 and 2005 resulted in a reduction of approximately 1,500 judicial branch employees as of mid-December 2005 when compared to October 2003" (2006). Congress may also be able to use its taxing power against federal judges, although that seems unlikely (see, e.g., Entin and Jensen 2006).

The legislature can use its power of the purse in other ways to make life more difficult for federal judges, such as refusing to give them adequate courthouses, technology, or staff. Some members of Congress have used the appropriations process to attempt to force the Supreme Court and other federal courts to allow cameras in their courtrooms (see, e.g., Biskupic 2007; and Mauro 2007). One federal judge told me that Congress may require federal district court judges to share courtrooms, which he interpreted as an attack on the professionalism of the judiciary. Judge Harry T. Edwards, of the U.S. Court of Appeals for the District of Columbia Circuit, agrees: "In the process of deciding to allocate funds, Congress and the President can sometimes turn courthouse funding into a political football" (2006, 233).

When it comes to the annual appropriations process, it seems that Congress often does not consider significant the fact that the courts are a coequal third branch. As a former chair of the House Appropriations subcommittee with jurisdiction over the budget for the judicial branch explained, "The courts do not have many advocates in Congress. They do not have a constituency. Congress continues to pass more and more laws that require the courts to assume jurisdiction of more cases and add to their workload. Congress is eager to authorize more judges, but when it comes to paying for them, the members of Congress do not think that is a very high priority" (N. Smith 1996, 177).

In fact, the courts are often at a disadvantage when it comes to funding because there is little that they or federal judges can do for the reelection-minded legislators. Certainly, as John Walker and Deborah Barrow note, "judges cannot exchange their decisions for favorable congressional treatment without destroying the very foundations of the judiciary's independence and authority" (1985, 44). Or as Chief Justice Warren noted, it is difficult for the courts to lobby Congress, because "we can't trade anything with the Committees" (qtd. in Walker and Barrow 1985, 44). None of the liberal congresspersons or liberal congressional staff whom I interviewed would admit that they or their bosses would support cutting the budgets of the courts in retaliation for conservative judicial decisions. As one Democratic staffer told me, "Liberals don't want to hurt judges because we are fighting for increased access to the federal judiciary. Increased access to the federal courts always serves the interests of justice." With the courts lacking a clear constituency, it becomes far too easy for Congress to treat the courts as just one more federal entity begging for money from the legislative purse.

Changing the Boundaries of the Circuit Courts of Appeals

Another area of regularized interactions between Congress and the federal courts involves the process of drawing boundaries for the U.S. circuit courts of appeals. Congress has long used its power to create new judgeships and determine the boundaries of the federal circuit courts to express its displeasure with decisions of the U.S. Supreme Court and other federal courts. As John Schmidhauser and Larry Berg have written, "During a good many decades, Congress' manipulation of the size and geographic location of the circuits served as a barometer of its approval or disapproval of the Supreme Court's decisions" (1972, 29).

The U.S. Courts of Appeals, often referred to as the U.S. circuit courts, were first established in the Judiciary Act of 1789. At that time, Supreme Court justices "rode circuit" and thus also served on one of the federal courts of appeals. Early in the nation's history, the number of circuits and their boundaries changed fairly often to meet the demands of population growth. After the Civil War, Congress increased the jurisdiction of the lower federal courts, giving rise to an eventual backlog in cases before these courts. In 1891 Congress greatly modified the old circuit courts of appeals, creating the current system of permanent U.S. Courts of Appeals (see Stephenson 1999, 114; and Martinek 2008).

Drawing the boundaries of the federal circuits has always been a highly political undertaking. For example, during the administration of Jimmy Carter the old Fifth Circuit was eventually split in half, largely because of the circuit's increasing caseload. The old Fifth Circuit U.S. Court of Appeals covered many of the states of the old Confederacy (Florida, Georgia, Alabama, Mississippi, Louisiana, and Texas). The request to divide the circuit had come from the circuit judges themselves, who unanimously requested that Congress redraw the boundaries of the circuit, thus splitting the circuit into two. President Carter stated that the large number of judges serving on the circuit court and the size of its caseload had produced "an unwieldy bench, one that was beset with management problems and that found it difficult to preserve consistency and predictability in the law" (qtd. in Barrow and Walker 1988, 1). Even though the division of the Fifth Circuit was based primarily on management issues, politics clearly entered into the lengthy discussions about if and how to divide up the circuit. The division of the Fifth Circuit was first proposed more than eighteen years before Congress finally acted to create the new Eleventh Circuit in 1980.

The newly created Eleventh Circuit included Florida, Georgia, and Alabama, while the new Fifth Circuit included Mississippi, Louisiana, and Texas. There were very real concerns about how the new circuits would approach civil rights cases because in the late 1970s the judges in the western states of the old Fifth Circuit seemed to favor civil rights plaintiffs, while judges in the eastern states favored civil rights defendants. Thus liberals in Congress and interest groups like the NAACP generally opposed dividing the circuit (see Wasby 1993, 56) until President Carter had appointed enough liberal and African American judges to the circuit to allay their fears (see Goldman 1997, 251).

Today, members of Congress who are upset with the liberal bent of the Ninth Circuit have called for that court to be divided into several circuits in order to curb its perceived liberal judicial activism, although they often use the size of the circuit as another reason to divide it (see, e.g., Kasindorf 2003). The Ninth Circuit covers an enormous area of the western region of the country, including the states of California, Alaska, Arizona, Idaho, Hawaii, Montana, Nevada, Oregon, and Washington and the Pacific territories of Guam, American Samoa, and the Mariana Islands. Because the Ninth Circuit has long been regarded as the most liberal circuit in the country, conservatives have often supported efforts to divide it. The ideological opposition to the Ninth Circuit and the resulting desire to divide the circuit are evident in two different arguments. One argument is that dividing the circuit would reduce the general liberalism of the circuit; the other is that the more conservative states in the circuit, such as Montana and Idaho, should not be forced to follow the liberal precedents of judges who reflect California's societal views (see *New York Times* 2006a). Proponents of dividing up the huge Ninth Circuit also argued that this action would create new judgeships, allowing President George W. Bush to make more judicial appointments in that region (see Fagan 2005). Some proponents of splitting the circuit have noted that the Supreme Court reverses the decisions of the Ninth Circuit more than it does those of any other appellate court (see Fagan 2005; and Fitzpatrick 2007).

Recently, there have been several legislative attempts to divide the Ninth Circuit. In the fall of 2004 the House passed regular legislation introduced by Congressman Sensenbrenner (R-WI), the then chair of the House Judiciary Committee, that would have split up the Ninth Circuit, but the bill died in the Senate that year (see Tobias 2005). In November 2005 conservatives were able to add a rider to a budget reconciliation bill that would have divided the Ninth Circuit by creating a new Twelfth Circuit comprising all the states of the current Ninth Circuit except California, Hawaii, and the Pacific Ocean territories of Guam and the Northern Mariana Islands. The rider was eventually deleted from the conference report on the bill. In 2005 Senator Dianne Feinstein (D-CA) called the death of the circuit-splitting bill a "victory for judicial independence, for the legislative process, and for California and the other Western states that comprise the Ninth Circuit" (qtd. in Tobias 2005). Then Minority Leader Nancy Pelosi (D-CA) called the rider "the latest in a series of Republican attacks on an independent judiciary. . . . It is simply a partisan exercise to appease the radical right" (qtd. in Fagan 2005). The judges on the Ninth Circuit have historically opposed such efforts to split up the circuit (see Wasby 1993, 56), and they were virtually unanimous in their opposition to the 2005 proposal (see Tobias 2005).

In 2006 both the Senate Judiciary Committee and the House Judiciary Committee considered legislation to split up the Ninth. Liberals continued to object, and in September 2006 the *New York Times* ran an editorial opposing continuing efforts to divide the Ninth Circuit (*New York Times* 2006a). The House passed new legislation to split the Ninth in 2006, but the bill again died in the Senate in large part because of the opposition of the Democratic senators from California (see Fitzpatrick 2007). Again, the judges on the Ninth Circuit overwhelmingly opposed the move, as did many law professors and politicians from the region (see Weinstein 2006b). The Ninth Circuit remains the largest and busiest circuit court in the federal system today.

Deciding the Number of Judges per Court

The creation of new judgeships is another area of regularized interactions between Congress and the federal courts. Congress, and not the Constitution, sets the number of justices who serve on the U.S. Supreme Court. Likewise, Congress can determine how many judgeships there should be on the lower federal courts. When Congress is upset with the federal courts, it can refuse to authorize additional judgeships to an overworked district court or court of appeals, or it can delay filling vacancies on those courts.

Early in the nation's history, the size of the U.S. Supreme Court fluctuated. The Judiciary Act of 1789 created a six-person Court, but the justices also "rode circuit" and thus served on a U.S. Circuit Court at the same time. A seventh justice was added in 1807, when a new circuit court of appeals was added to the system. In 1837 the size of the Supreme Court was increased to nine, reflecting the addition of new circuit courts because of the westward expansion of the country. In 1863 Congress increased the number on the Court to ten to provide for the addition of a new circuit court and to give President Lincoln an additional appointment (see Fisher and Adler 2007, 123). In 1869 the Court return to nine justices, and it has remained at that number ever since.

Reducing or increasing the number of justices on the Supreme Court has often been used by Congress to express its displeasure with court decisions or to influence the future direction of the Court. In the Judiciary Act of 1801 the Federalist Congress reduced the number of justices on the Court from six to five (to take effect with the next vacancy) partly in an attempt to prevent the new Democratic Republican president, Thomas Jefferson, from appointing someone from his party to the Court. At the beginning of the Civil War, Congress added three justices to the existing seven in order to give President Abraham Lincoln a working majority on the Court (see Pacelle 2002, 95). After the Civil War, the Radical Republicans gradually reduced the number of justices on the Court in order to prevent President Andrew Johnson from filling any vacancies. The size of the Court went from ten to eventually seven. Following the 1868 election of the Republican Ulysses S. Grant as president, Congress returned the number to nine in 1869, and it has stayed at that number ever since (see Pacelle 2002, 96). Of course, Franklin D. Roosevelt attempted unsuccessfully to increase the size of the Court in his Court-Packing Plan, discussed in chapter 1. Since then, many have argue that, as Terri Peretti writes, "altering the size of the Court remains a potential, but unlikely, tool of political control of Congress" (1999, 139).

There are other ways to create more judicial vacancies, such as enacting age limits or term limits for federal judges. Term limits for federal judges and the election of federal judges were the favorite proposals of some liberals during the era of conservative activism of the Supreme Court, from the 1890s until the mid-1930 (see Ross 1994). Because of the importance of the Supreme Court, some academics today have returned to these calls for term limits for Court justices. To date, very few politicians have picked up this proposal for limiting the power of individual justices (see Greenhouse 2007a). One liberal member of Congress opposed to such proposals told me, "There are no age limits or term limits for Congress. Why should we enact such limits for judges? We need to insulate judges from political pressures on their decision-making, not further politicize them."

Congress also has control over the number of judges who sit on the lower federal courts. At times in American history the legislature has greatly increased the number of federal judges, especially when the same political party controlled both Congress and the presidency. Thus Congress would increase the number of federal judgeships in part to allow a president of the same party the ability to make many judicial appointments (see, e.g., C. Smith 1993, 235; McCubbins, Noll, and Weingast 1995; and Songer, Sheehan, and Haire 2000, 24). As discussed in chapter 1, the Federalists in Congress attempted to increase the number of federal judges through the Judiciary Act of 1801, which was quickly repealed by the Judiciary Act of 1802. The Radical Republicans during Reconstruction also greatly increased the size of the federal judiciary because, "notwithstanding its occasional bullying of the Supreme Court, the Reconstruction-era Congress had a vested interest in preserving and promoting a strong, stable, and expanded federal judiciary that would enforce the statutes that Congress enacted in the teeth of regional resistance" (Geyh 2006, 70). As another example, in 1891 the Republican-controlled Congress created new U.S. courts of appeals and greatly expanded the number of judges on the existing circuits. The bill was passed the day before the new Democratic-controlled House of Representatives took office, although the presidency and the Senate stayed in Republican hands.

Thus the lame-duck House created many new federal judgeships for the Republican president to fill, allowing the Republican Senate to confirm many new federal judges, over the protests of the new Democratic House of Representatives (see DeFigueiredo and Tiller 1996, 437).

The Democrats too have used the creation of new federal judgeships to enhance their party's control of the federal judiciary. For example, the number of judges on the lower federal bench was greatly increased during FDR's administration, allowing Roosevelt to appoint a large number of federal judges (see Songer, Sheehan, and Haire 2000, 44). Following the Democratic takeover of both Congress and the presidency in 1960, for example, Congress acted three times to increase the size of the federal judiciary substantially, enlarging it by almost 33 percent from 1960 to 1968. Howard Gillman notes that this push to increase the number of lower federal judges was probably in part highly partisan in nature, allowing Democratic presidents to appoint a large number of federal judges to the bench (2006a, 145–46). At the beginning of the Kennedy administration, in 1961, federal judges were about evenly split between Democrats and Republicans, but by the end of the Johnson administration, in 1968, more than 70 percent of the federal judges then on the bench had been appointed by Democratic presidents (see Gillman 2006a, 152). One of the largest expansions of the federal judiciary occurred with the passage of the Omnibus Judgeship Act of 1978, which gave President Carter many new judicial appointments. This increase in the number of federal judges was in part motivated by the increased workload in the federal courts because of the increase in the number and scope of new federal crimes, but it was also motivated in part by partisan purposes, to allow the Democrats in the Senate to confirm more Democratic judges (see Goldman 1997, 241). More judgeships were also created by the Democrats in 1984 and in 1991, for example (see Wasby 1993, 55).

Some of the changes in the numbers of federal judges have occurred because of the western expansion of the country, increased workloads and backlogs in the federal courts, and requests from the federal judiciary itself for more judges. When the Eleventh Circuit was created in 1980 with the division of the old Fifth Circuit, it was the first circuit created since the Tenth Circuit, in the mid-1920s (see Wasby 1993, 56). However, John DeFigueiredo and Emerson Tiller's (1996) research indicates that expansion in the size of the federal judiciary is more likely to occur when the same political party controls the U.S. House of Representatives, the U.S. Senate, and the presidency. The work of Deborah Barrow, Gary Zuk, and Gerald Gryski (1996) also supports this conclusion. These scholars also found that vacancies on the federal bench are more likely to occur when the party of the retiring judge and the party of the current president are the same. Thus federal judges seem hesitant to retire if a president of the opposite party would be able to appoint their replacement. Some scholars argue that Congress often turns a deaf ear to complaints from federal judges about their workloads and usually does not increase the number of judgeships merely because of such concerns (see, e.g., Barrow and Walker 1988, 253). Often Congress increases the size of the federal judiciary for purely partisan reasons.

Congressional Reactions to Court Decisions Involving Statutory Interpretation

Congress and the federal courts also have routine interactions regarding federal court decisions involving statutory interpretation. Federal courts routinely interpret the statutes enacted by Congress. As Lawrence Baum and Lori Hausegger remind us, "The largest share of the Court's work is interpretation of statutes enacted by Congress" (2004, 107).

Of course, when the majority in Congress is unhappy with a judicial decision involving statutory interpretation, they can simply pass a new statute to overturn the court's decision (see, e.g., Henschen 1983). For example, in 1978 Congress enacted the Pregnancy Discrimination Act after the Supreme Court held that pregnancy was not a protected disability under the Civil Rights Act of 1964 (see Pacelle 2002, 94). The Civil Rights Restoration Act of 1991 overturned at least a dozen Supreme Court statutory-interpretation decisions regarding the ability of victims to sue for alleged race and sex discrimination. In fact, it is not uncommon for Congress to move to overturn judicial decisions involving statutory interpretation (see, e.g., Eskridge 1991a; and Baum and Hausegger 2004). R. Shep Melnick (1995, 101) believes that Congress overturns many more judicial-policy statements than Eskridge has found, in large part because many members of Congress may not even realize that they are taking action to overturn a court decision in any given piece of legislation. Mark Graber (1993) and George Lovell (2003), among others, argue that at times Congress intentionally passes statutes with ambiguous language, thus further empowering the courts by almost requiring them to interpret the ambiguous statutes. In other words, Congress punts the most controversial decisions to the courts in order to preserve a fragile coalition in the legislative branch.

After the courts issue rulings involving statutory interpretation, Congress may decide to review its original ambiguous compromise.

Davidson (1993) reports that Congress now pays increasing attention to the statutory-interpretation decisions of the courts. According to Davidson, "An increasingly frequent source of the lawmaking agenda is found in judicial interpretations of existing statutory language" (1993, 103). Jeb Barnes (2004b) has found that Congress pays a great deal of attention to the statutory-interpretation decisions of the federal courts. As Barnes has summarized the changing nature of the such rulings by the courts, "Put simply, today's federal judges not only serve their traditional role of resolving politically important constitutional disputes, but also pay a significant role in administering conflicts among competing agencies over the meaning of statutes and considering public challenges to regulatory procedures and decisions" (J. Barnes 2004a, 36).

It needs to be stated, however, that Congress generally does not routinely overturn most judicial decisions involving statutory interpretation. One study found that only 5.6 percent of the Supreme Court's statutory-interpretation cases were overturned by Congress in the 1978–89 period (see Hausegger and Baum 1998, 228). In some cases, the courts actually invite Congress to correct the statutory-interpretation decisions, as Hausegger and Baum (1999) discovered in their research. The dominant view among scholars is that the Supreme Court and other federal courts clearly take the views of Congress into account when interpreting statutes (see Baum 1997, 119), although some scholars have challenged that conventional wisdom (see, e.g., Baum and Hausegger 2004). Thus congressional consideration of decisions involving statutory interpretation has become part of the regularized interactions between Congress and the federal courts.

Congressional Reactions to Constitutional Decisions from the Courts

In theory, when the Supreme Court or another federal court issues a constitutionally based decision, the only way for Congress to overturn that decision is through a constitutional amendment. In fact, a variety of amendments to the Constitution have been enacted mainly to overturn Supreme Court decisions, including the Eleventh Amendment, the Civil War amendments (the Thirteenth, Fourteenth, and Fifteenth), the Sixteenth Amendment, and the Twenty-Sixth Amendment. In addition, a variety of constitutional amendments designed to overturn specific Supreme Court decisions have been proposed but never ratified. For example, there have been efforts to pass constitutional amendments prohibiting abortion, prohibiting flag burning, allowing prayer in schools, and prohibiting gay marriage. To date, none of these proposed amendments have received the two-thirds vote in both houses of Congress necessary to send them to the states for ratification. Even when Congress enacts a constitutional amendment, however, the inter-institutional conversation does not end. As Comiskey has noted, "Because the courts can rule on disputes over the meaning of an amendment's terms, amendments do not always end the constitutional dialogue on the subjects they address" (2008, 207).

Some of the most persistent proposals for constitutional amendment proposals have been aimed at prohibiting burning of the American flag as a form of political protest. Votes on proposed constitutional amendments to prohibit flag burning have been taken nearly every year since the Supreme Court's decisions in *Texas v. Johnson* (1989) and *United States v. Eichman* (1990) allowing it. Almost every year since these cases were handed down, one house of Congress has gotten the necessary two-thirds vote to pass the proposed amendment, but the other house has failed to reach that threshold. Thus the proposed amendment has never been sent to the states for ratification because it has never gotten the necessary vote in both houses of Congress at the same time.

In reality, Congress can also take statutory steps to reverse the policy announced by the Court, if not the constitutional decision itself. Davidson notes that the same partisan and ideological fights that Congress engages in over a wide variety of policy issues clearly spill over into issues of constitutional interpretation. "Partisan and ideological allegiances are as divisive as ever," he writes, "and are especially salient in congressional responses to pressing constitutional questions" (1993, 118). But one Democratic member of Congress warned that Congress should not rush to overturn constitutionally based decisions of the Supreme Court. This member said to me, "The President has said that he has an equal role in interpreting the Constitution with Congress and the Supreme Court, but that is not true. Congress and the President must follow the Supreme Court in constitutionally based cases because the job of the courts is to interpret the Constitution. We can't just ignore court rulings on the Constitution like the President has tried to do."

Of the twenty-three Supreme Court decisions studied by Robert Dahl (1957), in effect seventeen were reversed by Congress. Likewise, Joseph Ignagni and James Meernik (1994) found that in the years 1954–90 Congress had in effect reversed the policy direction in thirteen of the sixty-five decisions they studied. For example, in 1978 the Supreme Court ruled that the Fourth Amendment did not protect the offices of a newspaper from police searches if the police had a search warrant. Congress responded by passing legislation granting additional protections to newspapers (see Peretti 1999, 142). Using a different methodology, Pickerill (2004, 41) found that in almost half of the cases he studied, Congress acted to save statutes found to be unconstitutional by the courts. Pickerill argues that although at times Congress will directly confront the Court's constitutionally based decisions, "it is much more common for Congress to amend legislation in a manner that makes clear concessions to the Court's decision" (2004, 49).

Nevertheless, at times Congress will attempt to use statutory means to reverse a constitutionally based ruling by the Supreme Court. But the Court has usually declared most of the congressional statutory efforts to reverse its decisions to be unconstitutional. For example, when the Supreme Court declared that burning of the American flag was protected political speech in *Texas v. Johnson* (1989), Congress responded by enacting a federal statute making flag burning illegal. The Court quickly declared that statute to be unconstitutional in *United States v. Eichman* (1990). In 1968 Congress passed the Omnibus Crime Control and Safe Streets Act, which was designed in part to overturn a number of Supreme Court decisions regarding criminal procedure (see Gillman 2006a, 156). One of the legislative provisions in this act was intended to overturn the Supreme Court's decision in *Miranda v. Arizona* (1966) decision. That statutory effort was declared unconstitutional by the Supreme Court in *Dickerson v. United States* (2000). In *Dickerson,* the Supreme Court made its position on congressional interference with judicial constitutional interpretations quite clear. Said the majority in *Dickerson,* "Congress retains the ultimate authority to modify or set aside any judicially created rules of evidence and procedure that are not required by the Constitution. But Congress may not legislatively supersede our decisions interpreting and applying the Constitution" (530 U.S. 428, 437).

Fights between Congress and the Supreme Court over the interpretation of the Free Exercise Clause of the First Amendment have also occurred recently. After Congress overwhelmingly enacted the Religious Freedom Restoration Act in an attempt to overturn the Supreme Court's decision limiting the free exercise of religion in *Employment Division v. Smith* (1990), the Supreme Court promptly struck down that statute in *City of Boerne v. Archbishop Flores* (1997) (see, e.g., Bragaw and Miller 2004). Congress responded by enacting the Religious Land Use and Institutionalized Persons Act of 2000, which reestablished some of the rights protected by the Religious Freedom Restoration Act (see Baum

2004, 212). In striking down the Religious Freedom Restoration Act, the Supreme Court said in the *Boerne* case, "Our national experience teaches that the Constitution is preserved best when each part of the government respects both the Constitution and the proper action and determinations of the other branches. When the Court has interpreted the Constitution, it has acted within the province of the Judicial Branch, which embraces the duty to say what the law is. When the political branches of the Government act against the background of a judicial interpretation of the Constitution already issued, . . . it is this Court's precedent . . . which must control" (521 U.S. 507, 535–36). Thus the *Boerne* decision will long be remembered for "its stunning assertion of the Court's supremacy in settling all governmental disputes" (Bragaw and Perry 2002, 21). Therefore, the U.S. Supreme Court claims to be the last word on issues of constitutional interpretation. However, many scholars doubt that Congress will refrain in the future from attempting to modify or to overrule Supreme Court decisions through statutory means (see Murphy et al. 2006, 339).

Of course, when the Supreme Court issues a constitutionally based decision, there is no guarantee that Congress will actually follow the ruling. At times, Congress just ignores constitutional decisions from the courts. For example, in *Immigration and Naturalization Service v. Chadha* (1983) the Supreme Court ruled that Congress could not constitutionally use a one-house veto to overrule decisions by federal agencies. The response from Congress has been to continue to enact such legislative vetoes, and a variety of presidents have signed them into law. Thus Congress has effectively ignored the Court's decision in *Chadha* (see Fisher and Adler 2007, 222–24). It is difficult for the Supreme Court to be an active participant in the inter-institutional constitutional dialogue when the other branches simply ignore the Court's pronouncements.

Pickerill has found that Congress pays a great deal of attention to constitutionally based judicial decisions, at least those from the Supreme Court. Congress may not devote much time to constitutional issues in its initial debates on legislation (Pickerill 2004, 67), but it does respond when the courts declare congressional actions to be unconstitutional. As Pickerill notes, "Congress is highly responsive to Supreme Court decisions striking federal statutes; that is, Congress usually responds formally to the Supreme Court by repassing the statute in modified form, amending the Constitution, or taking other official action" (2004, 7). "When it comes to constitutional issues," he concludes, "Congress is often a reactive body" (2004, 145). Congress is certainly aware of the voice of the courts in the inter-institutional constitutional debate, although the legislative branch may not always yield to the dictates of the judicial branch.

The more routine interactions between Congress and the federal courts illustrate that the two institutions have very different perspectives and wills. At times, these regular interactions inevitably produce friction and tension between the two institutions. At times, Congress has attempted to use its institutional powers in the judicial confirmation process and in the budgetary process, among others, to help shape the direction of judicial decisions. At other times, Congress has been more direct in its attempts to guide or alter the scope of judicial decisions. Since constitutional interpretation is a continuous dialogue among the political actors in American society, these interactions between Congress and the courts will probably continue well into the future. Congress will always attempt to influence the decision making of federal judges, including the justices who sit on the U.S. Supreme Court. While this continuous conversation among the branches of government is certainly healthy, there are limits as to how far Congress should go in its attempts to influence judicial decisions. When Congress goes too far, the majority in Congress may get what they want in the short term, but at the expense of the fundamental principle of judicial independence. Independent federal courts must remain key participants in the ongoing inter-institutional constitutional conversation.

THREE

The Courts as Pawns in the Culture Wars

Today the interactions between Congress and the federal courts seem to have entered a new phase. As indicated in the introduction, many believe that the relationship between the courts and Congress is at its lowest point since the 1950s or even since Reconstruction. The courts are under increasing attack in Congress, in part because they have become the pawns in the brutal culture wars taking place in American society.

There has always been a tension between certain fundamentalist religious elements in American society and the more rationalist federal judiciary. As Richard Ellis reports, even in colonial times evangelical religious leaders were highly suspicious of the courts and of the legal system in general: "The law, they believed, was too rational, too complex, and too much under the control of designing intellectuals" (1971, 255). For much of the nation's history, social conservatives have paid very little attention to the courts, because the courts were more concerned with economic issues than with civil rights and civil liberties cases. That all changed with the long line of liberal activist Warren Court decisions, which some would argue signaled the beginning of the contemporary culture wars.

Accentuated by the Warren Court's deciding quite a few cases dealing with the role of religion in American society, religious conservatives have rarely found federal judges to be their allies in the culture wars. Social conservatives certainly criticized the Warren Court decisions on religion, but they could never muster a majority in Congress to reverse the judicial decisions that they so detested or to prevent the courts from hearing such cases in the first place. During the Warren Court era, the Religious

Right was not a well-organized political force in society, preferring to remain apart from politics for many decades, even many generations (see, e.g., Reed 1996, 5). However, beginning in the 1970s and accelerating in the 1980s and 1990s, the Religious Right eventually became a key component of the Republican Party coalition.

The Religious Right is certainly an important political and social movement in America today. However, the term *Religious Right* and the narrower term *Christian Right* can be somewhat difficult to define. In general, the academic literature and political commentators tend to use the two terms interchangeably. Scholars and others have provided various definitions for the movement. Clyde Wilcox and Carin Larson define this political movement as follows: "The Christian Right is a social movement that attempts to mobilize evangelical Protestants and other orthodox Christians into conservative political action" (2006, 6). Ralph Reed, a founder of the Christian Coalition, a powerful Religious Right lobbying group, defined the Christian Right as "an emerging coalition of evangelicals, Greek Orthodox, and traditionalist Roman Catholics. Their goal: to limit government, reinvigorate the family, and restore the culture's Judeo-Christian principles" (1996, 8). Others stress the evangelical or fundamentalist Protestant roots of the Religious Right. Sara Diamond, for example, states that the Religious Right "is a political movement rooted in a rich evangelical subculture, one that offers participants both the means and the motivation to try to take dominion over secular society" (Diamond 1998, 1).

Part of the difficulty in defining the Religious Right is that it is in fact a coalition of a wide variety of socially conservative subgroups, each with its own powerful leaders and its own specific agenda. Drawing on this multidimensional element of the movement, Steven Brown defines the Christian Right in this way: "The New Christian Right cannot rightly claim the status of political monolith so often imputed to it by both critics and supporters. The movement can be more accurately characterized as a vast mosaic of interests dominated by a handful of influential leaders and a growing number of special interest organizations that seek to convert the socially conservative views of their followers into political activism" (2002, 3). Most commentators agree that one of the main goals of the Religious Right is to transform American society through the use of the political process. According to Judith Garber, "Ultimately, the goal of the Christian Right is a seamless integration of religious, political, and legal institutions achieved through elected officials, appointed officials, and actors in civil society who share a religiously conservative worldview" (2006, 24–25).

The Religious Right controls a large number of religious broadcast radio and TV stations and publishing houses, in addition to counting many local churches among its followers (see Diamond 1998, 1). Despite its attempts to reach out to other, like-minded social conservatives, the movement remains generally concentrated among primarily white evangelical Protestant Christians (see, e.g., Green 1995; Brown 2002; and Wilcox and Larson 2006). When their political needs demand it, the Religious Right can also include Orthodox Jews, conservative Catholics, and conservative Mormons, although some evangelical Protestants remain extremely wary of those groups mostly for theological reasons (see, e.g., Luo 2007; Salmon 2007; and Feldman 2008). Certainly that is one of the lessons former Massachusetts Governor Mitt Romney, a devout Mormon, learned in his failed run for the presidency in 2008, since he failed to gain enough votes from evangelical and fundamentalist Protestants in that race despite reaching out specifically to those groups (see Luo 2008). Because the most powerful elements of the Christian Right are evangelical Protestants, at least in the interest groups that usually lead the movement, in this book I use the terms *Religious Right* and *Christian Right* interchangeably, although *Religious Right* can certainly imply a somewhat broader political coalition than does *Christian Right.*

I use these terms to refer to the social movement that has become a powerful political element in American society. Not all religious conservatives, and certainly not all religious evangelicals or fundamentalists, agree with the political objectives or tactics of this movement, nor are all social conservatives driven by its perspective. Nonetheless, when I use the term *Religious Right,* I am referring to the political force led by Jerry Falwell, Pat Robertson, Ralph Reed, Phyllis Schlafly, James Dobson, Tony Perkins, and others. Some of the key interest groups in this movement include the Moral Majority, the Christian Coalition, the Eagle Forum, the Family Research Council, Focus on the Family, the Concerned Women of America, and other, like-minded pressure groups. While in the past many Christian Right followers traditionally avoided politics, today these groups are a strong political force. As James Guth, Lyman Kellstedt, John Green, and Corwin Smidt describe the current political mobilization efforts of the Religious Right, "In recent years . . . the Christian right has promoted what we call the 'civic gospel' to justify a new religious insurgency, urging conservative Christians to link their faith to political choices, fight attacks on the rights of religious people, and mobilize churches to advance these objectives" (2002, 171). The Religious Right has become a key element in the current Republican Party coalition, bringing its anti-court views with it.

There is little doubt that the Religious Right is an important player in current Republican Party politics. As one journalist noted upon the death of Jerry Falwell, one of the founders of the contemporary Religious Right, "[Falwell's] positions on a number of core issues have become canonical for the mainstream of the modern Republican Party" (Holley 2007, A6). Many commentators credit the Religious Right with helping Ronald Reagan win the presidential election of 1980 and bringing a Republican Senate majority with him, the first time that had occurred in decades. The Religious Right may have also been important in Reagan's 1984 reelection campaign (see, e.g., Durham 2006). Certainly the Republican takeover of the House of Representatives and the U.S. Senate following the 1994 elections was due in part to Religious Right support for the GOP candidates (see, e.g., Wilcox, 1995; and Wald 1997, 217–18). Most commentators also note that the Religious Right was an important part of George W. Bush's victories in the presidential elections of 2000 and 2004 (see, e.g., Guth et al. 2002; Rozell 2002; and Durham 2006). In addition, John Green and Nathan Bigelow (2005, 196–97) claim that the Religious Right was an important player in more than one hundred House races in 2000, and the movement was also quite active in the 2002 elections. In the 2008 presidential race there was much speculation about whether Religious Right voters would eventually support Republican Senator John McCain (R-AZ), whom many social conservatives perceive as too moderate for their taste (see, e.g., Hallow and Dinan 2008; and Hulse 2008).

Estimates of the size of the Religious Right component of the Republican coalition vary. Since Jerry Falwell's founding of the Moral Majority in 1979, most public opinion polls have indicated that about 10–15 percent of white voters have supported the Religious Right's political agenda in various elections (see, e.g., Wilcox 1992; and Wilcox, DeBell, and Sigelman 1999). Although this percentage has remained fairly constant in recent decades, the Religious Right has become much better organized recently, making it an important player in contemporary Republican Party politics (see Wilcox and Larson 2006, 5). Religious Right leaders and voters rarely support Democrats these days, and most of the harshest criticism of the Religious Right comes from liberal Democratic activists.

While the Religious Right is an important part of current electoral politics, the movement has been far less successful in actually changing American society and culture, and remains angry about the direction in which American society is moving. Wilcox and Larson write, "The Christian Right has paradoxically been the most successful social movement in influencing elections and party politics over the past century, and the least successful in influencing policy and culture" (2006, 182). Mark Tushnet argues that even though the Religious Right has been a potent force in Republican electoral politics, it could not win in the federal courts because they were dominated by the more moderate wing of the Republican Party (2006a, 9). Downplaying the strength of the Religious Right in helping to determine electoral results, Tushnet writes, "The reason the Court's economic conservatives won and its cultural conservatives lost is simple. In the arena of politics, economic conservatives were winning and cultural conservatives were losing. . . . The patterns discernible in the Rehnquist Court's decisions reproduced the patterns occurring in American politics generally" (2006a, 10). Thus much of the Religious Right's frustration concerning its inability to reform American society has been directed toward courts and the judges who sit on them.

The Religious Right and the Courts

Because it has been so upset by what it perceives as the extreme liberal activism of the federal courts, the Religious Right has adopted a three-pronged approach to changing the direction of federal judicial decisions. The irony, of course, is that the federal courts in general and the U.S. Supreme Court in particular are currently dominated by Republican appointees. Nevertheless, the Religious Right wants to bring major changes to the policies pronounced by the federal courts. First, it has become very active in the judicial selection process. For example, President George W. Bush has furthered the Religious Right agenda by attempting to put only social conservatives on the federal bench. Second, the movement has supported many efforts to restrict the power of federal judges and to weaken the federal courts institutionally (see chapter 5). Finally, it has increased its litigation efforts in an attempt to overturn those federal precedents it finds so objectionable. As one journalist writes, "Judges are a key issue for conservatives, who have concluded that they can't advance their agenda unless they have backing from the courts" (Meckler 2008).

Despite this three-pronged approach to changing the direction of federal judicial decisions, most of the political rhetoric of the Religious

Right is extremely anti-court and anti-judge. A quick survey of the titles of many recent anti-court books written by Religious Right leaders illustrates their heightened rhetoric against the courts: *The Supremacists: The Tyranny of Judges and How to Stop It,* by Phyllis Schlafly (2006); *Men in Black: How the Supreme Court Is Destroying America,* by Mark Levin (2005); *Courting Disaster: How the Supreme Court Is Usurping the Power of Congress and the People,* by Pat Robertson (2004); *Disrobed: The New Battle Plan to Break the Left's Stranglehold on the Courts,* by Mark W. Smith (2006); and, going a bit further, *Outrage: How Gay Activists and Liberal Judges Are Trashing Democracy to Redefine Marriage,* by Peter Sprigg (2004).

Members of the Religious Right often see themselves as the victims of social, political, and legal discrimination. As Ralph Reed, a founder of the Christian Coalition, wrote in 1994, "In a country founded on the principle of basic freedoms guaranteed to all its citizens, people of faith find themselves marginalized and ridiculed" (41). Reed said that the Religious Right often feels as if the United States "treats faith as a form of pathology" (49). Followers of the Christian Right believe that the apparatus of government is trying to destroy their way of life and force them into accepting ideas and beliefs that they find abhorrent. The courts are often at the center of this concern, especially when judges hand down socially liberal decisions on the relationship between government and religion. As Cynthia Burack explains, "Christian Right leaders routinely instruct their followers that it is they—born-again, Bible-believing Christians—who are denied tolerance by a society whose descent into cultural evil is increasingly apparent and aggressive" (2003, 337).

The Religious Right has long been mistrustful of the Supreme Court as an institution, and this mistrust often spills over into distrust of all courts. The Religious Right is in many ways a grass-roots, populist movement that believes in a faith-based approach to politics, which is the exact opposite of the rationalist, law-based approach of most judges. In the 1960s and 1970s, while Religious Right leaders viewed big government in general as taking away the duties and responsibilities traditionally performed by the family, they saw the Supreme Court as an elitist institution dominated by wealthy, well-educated advocates of the big-government myth. One of the founders of the Christian Right, Pat Robertson, writes that "America is the only society in which the ruling elites turned against their own culture" (2004, xxi). Along these lines, Andrea Lafferty, of the Traditional Values Coalition, stated that "many judges view themselves as the real rulers of our nation" (qtd. in Brandenburg and Kay 2007, 16).

As early as 1977, a Gallup poll found that Religious Right supporters had less confidence in the Supreme Court than did other U.S. citizens (Moen 1989, 13). Along these same lines, Amy Steigerwalt (2007) found that religious conservatives have continued to have a much lower level of diffuse support for the courts than the general population, and thus they see the courts much more negatively than do other Americans.

The Religious Right has always objected to nine unelected judges telling them how to run their affairs, especially when it comes to questions of the interchange between government and religion. According to religious conservatives, the elitist Supreme Court wanted to take prayer out of the schools; allow innocent babies to be killed by abortionists; promote the agendas of feminists, pornographers, and gays; and remove all vestiges of religious faith from public spaces and the public schools. Ralph Reed calls this situation "the cultural hegemony of the institutions controlled by elites in the United States" (1994, 130). The rhetoric of the Religious Right often becomes anti-court and anti-judge.

The organized Religious Right groups, starting with Jerry Falwell's founding of the Moral Majority in 1979, clearly tapped into these already existing anti-court feelings among Christian Right supporters. What is more important, their leaders gave this alienated segment of American society a strong and organized political voice.

The following quotations are illustrative of the views of Religious Right leaders toward the courts in general and toward the U.S. Supreme Court in particular. According to one Religious Right activist, "The biggest myth about judges is that they're somehow imbued with greater insight, wisdom, and vision than the rest of us; that for some reason God Almighty has endowed them with superior judgment about justice and fairness" (Levin 2005, 1). Religious conservatives see liberal activist judges as arrogant in forcing their views upon the rest of American society. They strongly object to the notion that the Constitution is a living, changing document that judges can update and reinterpret to fit modern circumstances. While liberals see progress, flexibility, and tolerance resulting from judicial reinterpretations of the living Constitution, social conservatives view them as an attack on their preferred way of life. For example, James Dobson, a leader of the Religious Right movement, has complained that "each time the Supremes meet, it's as though they are holding a 'Constitutional Convention', because the foundational document becomes whatever any five of these justices say it is" (2004, 40).

For members of the Religious Right, tolerance in American society is a secular humanist concept that offends their clear sense of biblically determined right and wrong. They are especially suspicious of court-imposed tolerance, which they regard as intolerance toward religious people. As Cynthia Burack explains the views of the Christian Right, "For many, tolerance—and especially tolerance mandated by U.S. law or the Constitution—is itself an abuse of political authority and an invitation to Christian resistance" (2003, 336). This notion of Christian resistance to liberal activist court decisions has led Ralph Reed to call for "a new theology of political activism for religious conservatives" (1996, 255). This new political activism is the method by which the Religious Right feels it can begin to correct the evils imposed on U.S. society by liberal activist judges. According to Phyllis Schlafly, a leader of the Christian Right, "The United States Constitution did not create judicial supremacy or consign us to be ruled by a judicial oligarchy. . . . But Congress, the legal establishment, and the American people have all failed in their duty to keep the judiciary in its proper place" (2006, 3).

Followers of the Religious Right often believe that liberal activist judges are destroying the very fabric of American society. "Were our forefathers to view the American federal government of the twenty-first century, I believe they'd be appalled. Activist judges have taken over," writes Mark Levin (2005, 11). A 2005 e-mail message from the group Focus on the Family to its supporters is illustrative:

> What kind of judges do the liberals want? Those like the one who allowed Terri Schiavo to be starved and dehydrated to death. Those like the ones who don't believe it should be illegal for abortionists to suck the brains out of nearly-delivered children. Those who believe pornography showing women being raped, mutilated and defecated upon is protected by the First Amendment—but the Ten Commandments are not. (qtd. in Wilcox and Larson 2006, 1)

James Dobson, chairman of Focus on the Family, said at Justice Sunday, an event staged in order to draw support for President George W. Bush's social conservative nominees to the federal bench, "There is a majority on the Supreme Court that is . . . unelected, unaccountable, arrogant, imperious, and determined to redesign the culture according to their own biases and values, and they are out of control. I think they need to be reined in" (qtd. in Wilcox and Larson 2006, 3). Leaders and supporters of the Religious Right feel that it is their destiny to restore American society to what it was before liberal activist judges destroyed Americans' shared social and moral values. For example, Tony Perkins, president of the Family Research Council, said at the same Justice Sunday event, "As American citizens we should not have to choose between believing and living by what is in the [Bible] and serving the public" (qtd. in Wilcox and Larson 2006, 3). Dobson said earlier that liberal activist judges "were threatening to destroy the family and bring down the nation" (qtd. in Kaplan 2004, 260–61). And the Reverend Louis Sheldon, president of the Traditional Values Coalition, called federal judges "robed tyrants" (qtd. in Van den Brook 2002).

Many of these arguments sound similar to the anti-court rhetoric of earlier periods in American history. Certainly Presidents Jefferson, Jackson, Lincoln, and the two Roosevelts complained about what they saw as the arrogance of judicial decisions with which they disagreed. And social conservatives in the 1950s and 1960s certainly attacked the liberal activist decisions of the Warren Court. What seems different today, however, is that the Religious Right is not only attacking specific judicial decisions with which they disagree; it is disputing the fundamental right of federal judges to make any policy decisions that deviate from a certain Religious Right orthodoxy. Many Religious Right leaders seem to be attacking the pivotal right of the judiciary to settle public policy issues in America. They are attacking the courts as institutions and attacking judges who do not take a very strict, religiously focused view of the Constitution or of the rule of law in general. The Religious Right appears to object to any form of judicial decision making based on legal reasoning and legal analysis that deviates from its narrow political agenda. Not only do religious conservatives want to change the course of judicial decisions but they also demand that judges follow a purely political and results-oriented approach to judicial decision making. If they cannot force federal judges to follow their preferred political agenda, then they want to weaken the courts to the point that judges and justices can no longer participate in the inter-institutional constitutional conversation.

The fact that Religious Right leaders and followers view the use of law differently than do most judicial scholars is illustrated by the movement's distrust of the Rehnquist Court. Although the rest of the country considered the Rehnquist Court to be a fairly conservative judicial body (see, e.g., Schwartz 2004), Religious Right advocates saw it as being captured by liberal judicial activists. The Religious Right leaders focused on liberal decisions from the federal courts, but they tended to ignore the many conservative activist decisions of the Rehnquist Court because those decisions had to do with issues such as federalism, which are not that important to Religious Right constituencies. The Christian Right sees the courts as dominated by liberal activism, while there is broad scholarly agreement that the federal courts have been steadily moving to the right for the last several decades (see, e.g., Balkin and Levinson 2001; Chemerinsky 2003; Tushnet 2003; Keck 2004; and Clayton and Pickerill 2006). Pat Robertson has even argued that although Justices Scalia, Thomas, and Rehnquist were good judges in his view, "the members of today's Supreme Court are hell-bent on ruling from the bench without the slightest concern for what history or tradition or jurisprudence should say" (2004, 16).

Thus the Religious Right sees a liberal activist federal judiciary where others see a more conservative federal bench. The quotations below are illustrative of the movement's general views toward the courts. These criticisms are quite striking, especially when one remembers that the federal courts are basically conservative Republican bodies today. For example, Phyllis Schlafly argues that "judges have convinced themselves that they are infallible and should have the final say over our nation's controversial political and social issues. Judges use their assumed powers to enforce their liberal agenda on us, and they preempt criticism by repeatedly proclaiming the false court-invented notions that their rulings are the law of the land and that the Constitution is whatever the Supreme Court says it is" (2006, 187–88). And Pat Robertson proclaimed that "we have come to a time and place where nothing short of national revival, accompanied by a radical overhaul of our justice system, can save us" (2004, 18–19). Robertson even announced Operation Supreme Court Freedom, "in which he and others would pray for God to create vacancies on the Court that Bush could fill" (Wilcox and Larson 2006, 115).

The Religious Right sees itself as a defensive movement against the evils of the Left. It considers the nation's basic social and religious values to be constantly under attack, especially by the courts. "In one decision after another," writes James Dobson, "the judiciary has torn into the fabric of the home" (2004, 39). Ralph Reed highlighted this defensive posture of the Religious Right when he described the agenda of the Christian Coalition in these terms: "We are not revolutionaries but counterrevolutionaries, seeking to resist the left's agenda and to keep them from imposing their values on our homes, churches, and families" (1996, 195). That religious conservatives think they are merely defending the American way of life becomes evident when they discuss the so-called liberal activist approach of the federal judiciary. The Religious Right also believes that its views reflect the thinking of the majority of American voters. According to Mark Smith, "These days conservatives rail against the courts, and with good reason. Liberals win victory after victory after victory in the judiciary—advancing a radical agenda that could never win approval in the democratic process" (2006, 5). The fact that conservative forces are currently winning many battles in the federal courts goes unnoticed.

Scholarly accounts of the views of the Religious Right toward the courts capture this same idea: the Religious Right leaders believe that the courts are corrupting American society. As Steven Brown concludes in his analysis of the Religious Right, "Increasingly alarmed by what they perceived as rampant judicial activism, particularly in such areas as obscenity and privacy, many conservative Christians came to view the Court as the promoter of moral decadence that permitted almost any form of expression except for the religious" (2002, 21). Of course, there is a long list of judicial decisions that social conservatives find the most objectionable. Religious Right leaders cite these judicial decisions on a regular basis in order to energize their base. Andrew Taylor summarizes the situation as follows: "Religious and social conservatives, then, are using highly publicized judicial decisions on affirmative action, abortion, criminal defendants, homosexuality, and the relationship between church and state as devices to mobilize millions of supporters for political action. They especially have the federal courts in their cross hairs" (2005, 94).

Religious Right leaders often define the good judge as one who upholds the original intent of the framers of the Constitution. As part of the second prong of their overall strategy, by forcing judges to follow the views of the framers, they are reducing judicial discretion, and they hope they are also reducing the ability of judges to force liberal social policies on an unwilling nation. It is also important to note that Religious Right leaders also claim, through the use of revisionist-history techniques, that the framers created a Christian American ideal to which America as a society should return. Many liberal commentators find this notion that the Founding Fathers created an ideal Christian nation fictional or even delusional (see, e.g., Dershowitz 2007). But Christian Right leaders insist that strict constructionist judges would restore the religious principles on which they feel this nation was built. For example, Levin argues that "the plain language of the Constitution should govern judges when rendering constitutional decisions. Judicial decisions should not be based on the personal beliefs and policy preferences of a particular judge" (2005, 12). Along these same lines, Phyllis Schlafly writes, "Judicial supremacists have grabbed unconstitutional powers for the courts, and Congress has failed to restrain their power grab" (2006, 4).

One very clear argument from the Religious Right is that the United States was founded as a Christian nation, and the liberal activist federal courts are ignoring the plan provided by the Founders. The Religious Right has advocated a revisionist history for America, one that clearly precludes judicial decisions that deviate from that vision. This vision is often expressed in some form of the statement that the United States was founded and remains a Christian nation. D. James Kennedy, in his book *What If America Were a Christian Nation Again?* writes, "What made us great in the first place is our rich Christian heritage. It's time to reclaim it" (2003, 4). In other words, Christian Right leaders claim that historical democratic figures would have supported the current political and social agenda of the Religious Right. They make these claims in order to "reconstruct the political terrain" and thus bolster their own claims to the American democratic tradition (see Burack 2003, 342). For example, Peter Sprigg has written that "Christianity supplied the moral foundations of the founding fathers" (2004, 112). Along these lines, Pat Robertson has argued that Jefferson's metaphor of the "wall of separation of church and state" was merely a clever literary turn of phrase and was "never meant to convey any great message about either theology or social policy" (2004, 10); it was merely "an arbitrary phrase" that reflected little of Jefferson's true thinking on the issue (see also Reed 1994, 74–80). Most Jeffersonian scholars would disagree with this analysis. Critics of the Religious Right also note this attempt to create a revisionist history for the United States. Alan Dershowitz proclaims, "The Religious Right is engaged in a crusade to convert the United States into a Christian theocracy based on the Bible and, more specifically, on the divine authority of Jesus Christ" (2007, 1).

Various Religious Right advocates in the United States clearly feel that the federal courts are trampling on the will of the people. They believe that the Religious Right views are those of the majority in the United States and that the liberal activist courts are thus thwarting the will of the people and destroying majoritarian democracy. The quotations below are illustrative. Pat Robertson, for example, has written that "through systematic reinterpretation and misreading of the Constitution, by disregarding the will of the people in dozens of politically charged cases, and by attempting to enshrine their own liberal notions of 'social justice' through tortured readings of the law, justices have substantially changed the form and substance of our American democracy—and have repeatedly distorted the true meaning of the Constitution" (2004, 4). Along these same lines, Mark Smith writes, "The American judiciary issues a never-ceasing line of rulings that are totally out of sync with ordinary Americans and the values they hold dear" (2006, 19). Expressing his views on the importance of the courts for the Religious Right agenda, Tony Perkins argues that "conservatives want judges who will not legislate from the bench, because when we allow judges to legislate from the bench we get abortion on demand, we get same-sex marriage, we get everything that's bad for society" (qtd. in Reston 2008).

Even some judges who are supported by the Religious Right complain about the need to stop liberal judicial activism among their colleagues. For example, Judge Tom Parker, an associate justice on the elected Alabama Supreme Court, strongly criticized the U.S. Supreme Court's decision in *Roper v. Simmons* (2005), which declared it unconstitutional to execute defendants who were juveniles at the time when a crime was committed. Judge Parker wrote: "I am not surprised that the liberal activists on the U.S. Supreme Court go to such lengths to usurp more political power. I am also not surprised they use such ridiculous reasoning to try and force foreign legal fads on America" (Parker 2005). Judge Parker's extraordinary solution to the situation was to urge his colleagues on the Alabama Supreme Court to ignore the U.S. Supreme Court precedent.

As stated above, the first prong of the Religious Right's strategy for restoring the federal courts to what it considers its rightful place in society is to pack the courts with social conservative jurists. Of course, presidents have always tried to put on the bench those who would support their political agenda. The Religious Right seems to want only true believers in its cause to be seated as federal judges. For example, former Congressman Tom Feeney (R-FL), a strong supporter of the Religious Right, called for Congress to carefully examine the religious faith of any nominee to the U.S. Supreme Court (House Committee on the Judiciary 2005b, 6). This could create a new religious litmus test for federal judges, something that most academic commentators would consider unconstitutional given the Constitution's Article VI prohibition on a religious test for public office.

Given how important the Religious Right was to the presidential campaigns of George W. Bush in 2000 and 2004, it is no surprise that President Bush attempted to appease the movement leaders by appointing many social conservatives to the federal bench. As Robert McKeever argues, "Because so many of the issues that matter most to evangelicals are determined in whole or in part by the federal judiciary, the only means of achieving their agenda is through the appointment of judges whose constitutional views coincide with the policy goals of that agenda" (2006, 166). A Democratic staffer on the Senate Judiciary Committee agreed: "President Bush caters to the Religious Right when it comes to the courts, and he selects his nominations to appease the right wing base of his party. He wants a fight over these ultra-conservative nominees." Thus fights over judicial appointments became both symbolic political events and occasions to rally the social conservative troops to push harder for the creation of a morally just society. And as Charles Tiefer writes, "Beyond practicality, social conservatives saw judicial appointments in symbolic terms. Judicial pronouncements established the socially approved meaning of liberty and morality" (2004, 68).

The leaders of the Religious Right have been uncompromising in their opposition to the appointment of moderates to the federal bench, as evidenced by their strong opposition to the appointment of Sandra Day O'Connor to the Supreme Court (see, e.g., Moen 1989, 153). They have also complained bitterly about the moderate rulings of Republican judicial nominees, such as Justices David Souter and Anthony Kennedy (see, e.g., Reston 2008). Even President George W. Bush's nomination of Harriett Miers to the U.S. Supreme Court was opposed by most Religious Right activists because she was perceived as being too soft in her support of the Christian Right agenda (see Toobin 2007, 284–94). Some in the Religious Right have even called for the impeachment of moderates such as Justice Kennedy, who is a Reagan appointee to the High Court. The Religious Right fears that other conservative nominees will become moderates after they receive life appointments to the federal judiciary, as happened with Justices John Paul Stevens and Harry Blackmun, both Republican appointees (see, e.g., Baum 2004, 132; and Comiskey 2004, 2). According to Pat Robertson, "For a time, some people believed that if Republican presidents could simply appoint enough conservative justices to the bench, there might be a chance of restoring balance in the Court. It is apparent now that was a mistake" (2004, 15).

When the Democrats in Congress in 2005 attempted to filibuster many of these conservative Bush nominees to the lower federal courts (see chapter 2), religious conservatives were furious. The leaders of the Religious Right then organized Justice Sunday, a televised event to protest the state of the federal judiciary and to urge the Republicans in the Senate to use any means necessary, including the so-called nuclear option of eliminating the filibuster altogether for judicial nominations, in order to get judges acceptable to the Religious Right confirmed to the federal bench. Held in a megachurch in Louisville, Kentucky, the event was simulcast to several hundred churches around the country via satellite, broadcast over the Internet, and carried by a variety of Christian radio and television stations. Even Senate Majority Leader Bill Frist (R-TN), a moderate Republican who was then contemplating a run for president, spoke via satellite. The anti-court rhetoric at the event ran extremely high. Religious Right leaders accused the Senate Democrats of filibustering the Bush nominees merely because of their religious views, while even President Bush admitted that the filibuster had more to do with the nominees' judicial philosophy than it did with their religious faith (see, e.g., Wilcox and Larson 2006, 3–4). Pleased with the success of their first Justice Sunday, Christian Right leaders then organized a two-day conference called "the Judicial War on Faith," at which, among other things, many Religious Right leaders called for the impeachment of Justice Kennedy because he did not always vote according to their preferences (see, e.g., Durham 2006, 215–16).

Not only did the Religious Right care about the social conservative bona fides of new nominees to the bench but as part of the second prong of their overall plan they wanted to impeach those judges who they thought were forcing a liberal social agenda on the nation. Various conservative activists at a conference entitled "Remedies to Judicial Tyranny," organized by a group called the Judeo-Christian Council for Constitutional Restoration, argued that judges whose opinions did not support the views of the Religious Right should be impeached. Michael P. Farris, chair of the Home School Legal Defense Association, stated at the conference, "If about 40 [federal judges] get impeached, suddenly a lot of these guys would be retiring" (qtd. in Milbank 2005).

Following the Terri Schiavo controversy, discussed below, many Religious Right conservatives called for the impeachment of judges who refused to follow their preferred ideological views. For example, former House majority leader Tom DeLay has been quoted as saying, "Judicial independence does not equal judicial supremacy." He did not rule out impeaching judges, because the current situation depended on "a judiciary run amok." "The failure is to a great degree Congress's," he said. "The response of the legislative branch has mostly been to complain. There is another way, . . . and that is to reassert our constitutional authority over the courts. . . . This era of constitutional cowardice must end" (qtd. in Hulse and Kirkpatrick 2005). Michael Schwartz, then chief of staff to Senator Tom Coburn (R-OK), agreed. "I'm in favor of impeachment," he said; he even suggested that "mass impeachment" of federal judges might be in order (qtd. in Hulse and Kirkpatrick 2005).

Tony Perkins proposed that "there's more than one way to skin a cat, and there's more than one way to take a black robe off the bench" (qtd. in Garber 2006, 23).

The anti-court message of the Religious Right has been picked up by a variety of politicians who need votes from the Religious Right to get elected. Senator John McCain, who was often viewed with skepticism from those in the Religious Right, in part because he once called Jerry Falwell and other Religious Rights leaders "the political agents of intolerance" (see, e.g., Holley 2007, A6), has since spoken out against liberal judicial activism in a naked nod to the Religious Right. In the May 2007 Republican presidential debates, for example, McCain said, "One of our greatest problems in America today is justices that legislate from the bench, activist judges." Religious Right leaders were generally suspicious of Senator McCain when it came to judicial appointments because he was a part of the Gang of 14 group of moderate senators from both parties who reached a compromise to retain filibusters against judicial appointments in extreme circumstances but also prevented George W. Bush's nominees from being filibustered (see, e.g., Tobias 2008). Senator McCain also has aroused the ire of the Religious Right because of his strong support for Justice Souter in his confirmation process (see, e.g., Bumiller 2008; and Hallow and Dinan 2008), as well as his support for campaign-finance reform (see, e.g., Reston 2008). Justice Souter was thought to be a conservative jurist when he was appointed to the Supreme Court by the first President Bush, but after he arrived at the Court, he quickly joined the liberal wing of the High Court (see, e.g., Comiskey 2004, 2). Describing McCain's stances on judicial confirmations, one journalist said that since Reagan's presidency "Mr. McCain . . . has been a loyal soldier but not a major player in the effort to put more conservatives on the federal courts" (Bumiller 2008). McCain's apparent indifference to packing the courts with social conservatives has led to a great deal of mistrust toward him among some in the Religious Right movement. In order to attempt to counter this concern, in May 2008 Senator McCain gave a major speech at Wake Forest University in which he praised Chief Justice John Roberts and Justices Antonin Scalia and Samuel Alito, promising to nominate judges with a similar judicial philosophy (see, e.g., Eilperin 2008; Meckler 2008; and Reston 2008). "Mr. McCain's speech was a clear embrace of the judicial philosophy of President Bush and other recent Republican presidents," reported Elisabeth Bumiller (2008).

Other GOP presidential hopefuls also blasted liberal activist federal judges, mainly to garner the votes of Religious Right supporters. For example, former Arkansas governor Mike Huckabee, who is also a Southern Baptist minister, said on his presidential campaign Web site:

> One of the greatest ongoing threats to our constitutional republic is the ever-increasing politicization of the federal judiciary. Instead of interpreting the law according to its plain or original meaning, many judges are using the Constitution and statutes passed by Congress as a mere pretense for imposing their policy preferences on the American people. As president, I will appoint justices and judges who not only share my judicial philosophy (e.g., Chief Justice John Roberts, Justice Antonin Scalia, Justice Clarence Thomas, and Justice Samuel Alito), but who also have established themselves within the *conservative legal community* as faithful adherents of originalism and textualism. The stakes are simply too high to do otherwise. (Huckabee 2008, emphasis added)

Huckabee was the darling of the Religious Right, even using this slogan and giving his campaign Web site the title "Faith, Family, Freedom."

Another presidential hopeful and strong supporter of Religious Right causes, Senator Sam Brownback (R-KS), stated on the floor of the Senate that it was necessary for Congress to "reign in an increasingly reckless judiciary" by "stripping courts of authority they have usurped from the people and their legislative representatives" and "through impeachment, when necessary at both the Federal and State level" (2004). Also reaching out to the Religious Right, the GOP presidential hopeful and former governor of Massachusetts Mitt Romney said in reference to the state supreme court's ruling legalizing same-sex marriage that "activist judges struck a blow to the foundation of civilization, the family" (qtd. in D. Jackson 2006). Attempting to appeal to Religious Right voters, former Senate majority leader Bill Frist (R-TN), when he was considering a run for the presidency, denounced Supreme Court justices as "unelected and unaccountable, arrogant and imperious, determined to redesign the culture to their own biases and values" (qtd. in Taylor 2005, 89). Also in a nod to the Religious Right, the GOP presidential candidate Rudy Giuliani called liberal federal judges "imperial" and said that they thought "they were put here by God" (qtd. in A. Lewis 1999, 285).

The Religious Right has clearly taken its anti-judge crusade to the halls of Congress, and various allies in Congress are strongly advocating that agenda (see chapter 4). For example, with support from the Christian Coalition in 2005 Congressman Ron Lewis (R-KY) introduced the Congressional Accountability for Judicial Activism Act. This bill would have allowed Congress to overturn any constitutionally based U.S. Supreme Court decision with a two-thirds vote. In the press release to announce the introduction of this legislation, Congressman Lewis said that in his view *Marbury v. Madison* (1803) had been wrongly decided, because it gave too much power to the courts. He concluded, "The exercise of such broad judicial authority, expanded over time and by political tradition, has a growing adverse affect [*sic*] on co-equal branches of government" (R. Lewis 2005). Some of the Republican members of the House Judiciary Committee seem to agree with this Religious Right agenda. A staff member for a conservative Republican member of the Judiciary Committee told me, "The judiciary is not totally independent because Congress has the authority for oversight in order to narrow the focus of decisions where the judges have overreached."

Increased Rates of Conservative Litigation before the Courts

Ironically, given the Religious Right's strong anti-court and anti-judge rhetoric, the third prong in its approach to changing the direction of judicial decisions in America is their quiet increase in litigation designed to reverse what they perceive to be liberal activist court precedents. Although many leaders of the Religious Right continue to denounce the federal courts and federal judges in their public statements, they nonetheless have quietly started to work behind the scenes to advance a more conservative judicial agenda. This litigation strategy is almost never highlighted in their fundraising appeals or in their public speeches, but pursing litigation is clearly another strategy of contemporary Christian Right leaders. For example, one of the first subgroups created just after the founding of the Moral Majority was its Legal Defense Fund. After Ronald Reagan started to increase his appointments of social conservatives to the federal bench, the Christian Right began to actively pursuing a new conservative litigation strategy (see Moen 1989, 171–72). Lee Epstein (1985) was among the first scholars to study the role of litigation initiated by conservative interest groups. Building on this effort, Brown (2002) and Hans Hacker (2005a) both have looked at the litigation strategies of the Religious Right in particular. Works by Kevin Den Dulk, Dennis Hoover, and J. Mitchell Pickerill (Den Dulk and Hoover 2003; Den Dulk and Pickerill 2003; Den Dulk 2006) also examine these Christian Right litigation strategies. These groups take on both critically important cases pending before the U.S. Supreme Court and less well known cases in the lower courts, such as a ruling by the California Supreme Court that prohibited an apartment owner from renting to a couple because they were unmarried (see Diamond 1998, 84–85). As Hacker describes, "A new generation of litigators are now using sophisticated litigation strategies pioneered decades earlier by liberal interest groups to achieve extraordinary results. Among the most active and best funded public interest law firms in the nation, they have developed highly responsive organizations capable of shifting emphases in response to political changes" (2005b, 365). These law firms and interest groups are using litigation in order to bring about, in Ralph Reed's words, quoted above, the "new theology of political activism for religious conservatives" (1996, 255). As Brown concludes, these new litigation groups have come into existence "with the intention of using the courts as the next battleground of conservative Christian activism" (2002, 5).

One key Religious Right group today that quietly uses litigation as a key part of its social conservative strategy is the American Center for Law and Justice, founded by Pat Robertson in 1990. Robertson promotes the organization as the "Christian counterpart to the American Civil Liberties Union" (Wilcox and Larson 2006, 116). The chief counsel for the group is Jay Alan Sekulow, who has argued numerous cases before the Supreme Court of the United States. A Jewish convert to Christianity, Sekulow is "the Christian Right's attorney of first resort" (Diamond 1998, 86). In a recent book, *Witnessing Their Faith: Religious Influence on Supreme Court Justices and Their Opinions* (2006), Sekulow argues that Supreme Court justices have long used their Christian faith as a lens for understanding the Constitution. Notably missing from the book are liberals like Justice Harry Blackmun, who was a devout United Methodist all of his life. Nor does Sekulow discuss any of the Jewish justices who have had seats on the Court over the years.

The number of Religious Right litigation firms is growing. In addition to the Alliance Defense Fund and the Center for Law and Religious Freedom, these include, among others, the Rutherford Institute, the American Center for Law and Justice, and the Liberty Counsel (see Brown 2002, 11). Much like their public-interest counterparts on the left, these Religious Right law firms combine both interest-group activities and traditional legal practices (see Hacker 2005b, 369). These groups often portray the liberal-leaning American Civil Liberties Union (ACLU) and other liberal litigation groups as their enemy, even though they sometimes cooperate on certain specific cases. In a book promoting the Religious Right's litigation strategy, Alan Sears and Craig Osten write that the Alliance Defense Fund and its litigation allies "have quickly grown to become a formidable opponent and have been successful with a growing legal army of allies through strategy, training, funding, and litigation to defeat the ACLU and its allies several times in courtrooms and in the battle for minds across the nation" (2005, 5–6). Note the war metaphor, with the army of Religious Right lawyers fighting the great battle against the secular humanists in the courts and in the hearts and minds of the American people. Because the Religious Right sees the courts as so important, Pat Robertson founded the Regents University Law School to help train Christian Right lawyers. Graduates from this ultraconservative law school controlled key positions in the U.S. Department of Justice under Attorney General Alberto Gonzales (see, e.g., Lithwick 2007; and Vegh 2007). Thus Religious Right litigation groups have grown in number and in activity in recent years.

The Lessons from the Terri Schiavo and Kelo Cases

The Religious Right often uses the pejorative "judicial activism" when they feel that judges have made improper decisions. For example, Tom McClusky, of the Family Research Council, argued, "Judges are not above the law. Recent legislation seeking to rein in judicial activism is an effort to restrain judicial power within the limits of Constitutional design, not an attack on 'judicial independence'" (2006).

However, the Terri Schiavo episode and the conservative reaction to the Supreme Court's decision in *Kelo v. City of New London* (2005) illustrate that the Religious Right really wants extremely activist judges to uphold their vision and their ideological agenda. Thus social conservatives actually object not to the philosophy of judicial activism but to the ideological outcome of liberal activism. The Christian Right would be quite happy with conservative activist judicial decisions, as the following discussion of the Terri Schiavo episode and the Supreme Court's *Kelo* decision illustrates. In both instances conservatives wanted activist judges to step in and settle these issues according to the conservatives' preferred outcomes. When the judges acted more like judges than like political and ideological operatives, the movement conservatives were outraged. So while Religious Right leaders use the rhetoric of judicial restraint, they really advocate a narrow form of conservative judicial activism in order to bring about the legal and political results they desire.

The Terri Schiavo episode is a clear indication that conservatives were upset that the judges involved used legal reasoning and legal analysis instead of arriving at the policy outcome that the Religious Right wanted. The key political events occurred in the spring of 2005. Terri Schiavo had been in a severe car accident and as a result had spent the past fifteen years in a persistent vegetative state. She was being kept alive by artificial means. Her husband wanted to remove the life support, while her parents wanted to keep her alive through all medical means possible. The technical legal question in the case was whether under Florida law the husband or the parents ultimately had the right to decide whether to remove her artificial life support apparatus. The husband and the parents could not reach agreement on this life-and-death decision. When eventually the husband sued to have the life support machines removed, the Florida state judges hearing his case all ruled in his favor. The Religious Right, furious with these decisions, persuaded members of Congress and President Bush to try to reverse the rulings. Congress, which was out of town for the Easter recess, returned for an emergency session and enacted legislation supported by President Bush to give federal judges jurisdiction to hear the case. This action granted extraordinary power to the federal courts, and Congress and the president were clearly trying to force a specific legal outcome on the judges hearing the appeals. When the federal judges in this case all upheld the decision of the Florida state courts, the Religious Right was outraged. They wanted the judges to rule to keep Terri Schiavo alive by any possible means, but the judges used legal analysis in their rulings instead of deciding as a conservative politician might have done in the case (see, e.g., Durham 2006, 214–15; and Toobin 2007, 246–49).

When the judges did not rule as the Religious Right had tried to dictate, leaders of the movement greatly increased their anti-court rhetoric. There were many calls for impeachment of federal judges and Supreme Court justices, as discussed above. It was also clear that the Republican leadership in Congress and the White House hoped to use the anger of the Religious Right in this case to help get more social conservatives confirmed to the federal bench (see, e.g., McKeever 2006, 168–69). As Wilcox and Larson conclude, "The furor over the Schiavo case in 2005 made clear both the symbolic power of the Christian Right with Congress and its substantive weakness" (2006, 113). Eventually Congress and the president realized that they could not force federal judges to adopt a specific legal outcome in this case.

In *Kelo v. City of New London* (2005) the U.S. Supreme Court ruled that local governments had the right to define the phrase "public use" in the Takings Clause of the Fifth Amendment. The City of New London,

Connecticut, wanted to take an individual's house by eminent domain in order to redevelop the area as a privately owned commercial office park. The constitutional question in this case was whether this commercial development was a public use under the language of the Fifth Amendment. The Fifth Amendment states that governments can take private property for public use as long as fair compensation is given to the property owner. Following a long line of judicial restraintist precedents in this area of the law, the majority of the Court ruled that in fact the local governments could define "public use" even if that meant that the taken property would eventually be developed by private developers. If the Court had said that the Supreme Court should define "public use" in these cases, that would clearly have been an activist decision by the Court. Again, the religious conservatives were outraged at the decision because it did not protect private property from governmental intrusion, but this time they were allied with economic conservatives.

Congress reacted quickly to this decision. The Subcommittee on the Constitution of the House Judiciary Committee held hearings in September 2005 regarding the Supreme Court's *Kelo* decision and possible congressional responses to it. Then-Congressman Tom Feeney (R-FL) found the Court's *Kelo* decision to be "just indicative of the larger trend in the Court to substitute their own prejudices and biases for the constitutional language itself" (House Committee on the Judiciary 2005b, 6). Representative Trent Franks (R-AZ), a strong supporter of the Religious Right, after attacking the Supreme Court for its decisions on abortion, religion, and other issues, said about the *Kelo* decision, "We've seen the courts diminish our liberty to a great extent and now, with the *Kelo* decision, we've seen the courts make a frontal assault on the right to property" (House Committee on the Judiciary 2005b, 7).

Congressman Steve Chabot (R-OH), chair of the subcommittee, made some very interesting comments at the hearing regarding the *Kelo* ruling. In addition to claiming that the Supreme Court's decision would increase the likelihood that local governments would use their powers of eminent domain more frequently, he argued that religious people had a great deal to fear from the decision. Using language directly from Christian Right political propaganda, he predicted that local governments would take church property in eminent-domain proceedings in order to increase their local tax base. Congressman Chabot described the threat to religion from this property-rights decision in this way: "Houses of worship and other religious institutions are also, by their very nature, non-profit and almost universally tax exempt. These fundamental characteristics of religious institutions render their property particularly vulnerable to being taken under the rationale approved by the Supreme Court in favor of for-profit, tax generating businesses" (House Committee on the Judiciary 2005b, 2).

In both of these cases, the Religious Right wanted the judges to approach the case as a politician might instead of using legal analysis to come to a decision supported by the law. In other words, the Religious Right was furious that the judges would not follow their preferred activist approach in deciding these two cases. In the Schiavo case, social conservatives wanted activist judges to overrule the Florida law that gave Terri Schiavo's husband the right to decide if and when to remove life support from her. In the *Kelo* case, the Supreme Court ruled in a restraintist manner, saying that the Court should not decide what is the "public good" in an eminent-domain case and leaving that decision to local elected officials instead. Conservatives in both episodes wanted activist judges to step in and overrule local governmental decisions that they did not like (see, e.g., M. Smith 2006, 23–24). In many ways, the Religious Right in these examples did not want the judges to make decisions based purely on legal reasoning; instead, religious conservatives wanted the judges to act more like political officeholders. The outcomes of the decisions were more important to the movement than were the decision-making processes used. As one lobbyist told me, "Schiavo and Kelo taken together demonstrate the primacy of outcomes over principles for these Religious Right groups."

Some social conservatives readily admit that they are calling for judges to be judicial activists, but with a conservative bent. For example, Mark Smith wrote, "Radical as it may sound to conservatives who have been taught that judicial activism is an inherent evil, our secret weapon—*conservative* judicial activism—in fact offers us the greatest opportunity to preserve and protect the rights, freedoms, and ideals that the Constitution was designed to protect and that America's Founders cherished" (M. Smith 2006, 9, emphasis in original). Thomas Keck (2004), of course, highlights conservative judicial activism by the current Supreme Court. As Wilcox and Larson (2006) remind us, almost all social movements are more concerned with policy outcomes than with broad philosophical debates such as the one concerning judicial activism and judicial restraint. The Religious Right is no exception.

Many argued that the Terri Schiavo episode would be the end of the conservative attacks on the courts, because the American public reacted so negatively to Congress's interference with the judicial process in that case. One poll reported that as many as 82 percent of Americans opposed the congressional action, and a majority agreed with the decision of the federal courts to uphold the ruling of the Florida state judges (see Geyh 2006, 274). As a Democratic staffer on the Senate Judiciary Committee told me, "The Schiavo episode backfired against the conservatives, and it ended Majority Leader Bill Frist's career." Members of the judiciary were clearly unhappy with the actions of Congress. Jeffrey Toobin reports that Congress's actions in the Schiavo case infuriated Justice Sandra Day O'Connor: "The Schiavo case marked only the latest outrage from the extremists whom she believed had hijacked her beloved Republican Party" (Toobin 2007, 249). Many then said that the Schiavo incident would remind members of Congress that they attacked the courts at their peril. The exact opposite, however, seems to have occurred. The anti-court rhetoric of the Religious Right has not cooled at all, and Congress actually enacted many anti-court measures after the Schiavo episode left the front pages of the daily papers (see chapter 5). If anything, the social conservatives may have changed their language a bit after the Schiavo affair, but they have not cut down on their assaults on the federal judiciary. The anti-court language and actions still play to the social conservative base of the Republican Party.

Reactions to the Religious Right

The constant attacks on the courts from the Religious Right have not gone unnoticed in the legal and political communities. Even Justice O'Connor declared that "lawmakers should not demand that a judge, under threat of impeachment, issue rulings that meet their nakedly partisan, result-oriented reasoning" (qtd. in Lash 2006b). Justice Ruth Bader Ginsburg has also expressed concern about threats to judicial independence and the use of judges as pawns in the culture wars: "Federal judges, whether appointed by Republican or Democratic Presidents, generally endeavor to administer justice impartially and to interpret law reasonably and sensibly, with due restrain and fidelity to precedent. Yet in some political circles, it is fashionable to criticize and even threaten federal judges who decide cases without regard to what the 'home crowd' wants" (2006, 7).

A direct response to the Religious Right attacks on the courts has come from the legal community, the American Bar Association, and especially from Justice at Stake, an organization that devotes its time to preserving judicial independence. As two spokespersons for Justice at

Stake have written, "Courts are not perfect. And some people of faith are honestly repelled when decision in controversial matters conflict with their deeply held tenets. But these good-faith believers are being abetted by political opportunists for whom the war on the courts is a way to harvest votes, donations and daily victories in the 24/7 culture wars. A rising outrage industry seeks to paint fidelity to the law as an assault on faith. Their mission, year in and out, is to chip away at our constitutional culture" (Brandenburg and Kay 2007, 2). As discussed in chapter 2, because of concerns over anti-judge rhetoric and actions in Congress, Representatives Adam Schiff (D-CA) and Judy Biggert (R-IL) created the Congressional Caucus on the Judicial Branch in order to further communication between Congress and the courts. They also introduced legislation in 2006 to increase judicial salaries.

Certainly the Religious Right has its political and academic opponents, and they have certainly fired back in the culture wars. For example, Alan Dershowitz attacks Christian Right revisionist history in *Blasphemy: How the Religious Right Is Hijacking Our Declaration of Independence* (2007). Chris Hedges's 2006 book is entitled *American Fascists: The Christian Right and the War on America.* In *Kingdom Coming: The Rise of Christian Nationalism* (2007) Michelle Goldberg argues that "the motivating dream of the movement is the restoration of an imagined Christian nation" (7). Catherine Crier, a former Republican elected judge in Texas and now a self-proclaimed independent with libertarian leanings, called her 2005 book attacking the Religious Right *Contempt: How the Right Is Wronging American Justice.* And Herman Schwartz published *Right Wing Justice: The Conservative Campaign to Take Over the Courts* in 2004.

Others focus on the radical nature of the Religious Right agenda regarding the federal courts. For example, Garber concludes that "the current Christian Right is built upon its 1970's precursor, but it has moved well beyond it to become a more radical movement in both style and substance. A centerpiece of this radicalism is a concerted, unabashed effort to make American courts—most obviously, and certainly not exclusively, the federal appellate courts—into conservative Christian adjuncts to the electoral, legislative, and administrative processes" (2006, 23). Charles Geyh argues that the Religious Right may have overplayed its hand in its attacks on the courts: "If conservative Christian efforts to control the courts are ultimately overtaken by a movement to restore respect for judicial independence and the rule of law, there is room for optimism. If, however, the political influence of Christian conservatives persists, or gives way to a new school of thought equally committed to bludgeoning the courts into submission to its views of the law, the post-realist free-fall will continue to accelerate" (2006, 272).

Partisan Differences in Approaches to the Courts

Congressional interactions with the federal courts may be just part of a larger partisan culture war being fought in Congress. Thomas Mann and Norman Ornstein (2006a, 2006b) argue that Congress has become "the Broken Branch" in large part because everything Congress does now is highly partisan and highly ideological. As these scholars wrote just before the November 2006 elections, "Partisanship [in Congress] particularly increased after the 1994 elections. . . . Now it is tribal warfare. The consequences are deadly serious. Party and ideology routinely trump institutional interests and responsibilities" (2006b). Others have also noted that institutional interests and the separation of powers are receiving far less attention in Congress today. According to Sidney Milkis, "Contemporary political activists engage in ideological and *institutional* confrontation that defies consensus and diminishes public trust in government" (2007, B9, emphasis added), and Keith Whittington notes that "partisan legislators are notoriously fickle in their views on institutional power" (2007, 168). A lobbyist told me in 2007 that the institutional culture on Capitol Hill had changed a great deal in the last decade and that judges especially did not understand these changes. "Judges don't see themselves as partisans," the lobbyist explained. "Judges don't see themselves as taking a side in the culture wars."

The courts have thus become a highly salient issue for both parties, although more so for the Republicans; thus they will remain a highly partisan and contentious issue. As one journalist commented, "Many conservatives see the courts as a bedrock counterweight to Democrats' inroads on Capitol Hill and their efforts to retake the White House" (Bumiller 2008). Further evidence of the importance of the courts in current political discourse comes from President Bush's 2007 State of the Union address. In this major address to the nation, President Bush said little of key interest to the Religious Right, but he did challenge the Senate to confirm his judicial nominees, implying that he would continue to nominate for the bench conservatives who were acceptable to this important constituency in the Republican Party. The *New York Times* journalist Carl Hulse reported, "The question of judicial appointments is a matter of fundamental concern to conservatives who see the courts as a counterbalance to the shifting politics of Congress and the executive branch" (2008). The Religious Right strategy seems to be working, because its members are urging President Bush to appoint more conservatives to the bench at the same time that they are raising a lot of money and political enthusiasm to fight the perceived liberal activist judges. Thus the Republican Party is benefiting from an increasingly conservative federal judiciary that is handing down an increasing number of conservative rulings, although the perception among conservative voters is that the courts remain far too liberal in their decisions. As Taylor describes the situation, "The transformation of judicial politics has brought dual bonanzas for the GOP, then. The courts have delivered the kinds of policy many conservatives want, while simultaneously providing them with a succinct and passionate rationale to persuade the public to vote Republican" (2005, 96).

The Democrats seem to have taken the position that they need to be the protectors and defenders of the courts under siege from the Religious Right. For example, former vice president Al Gore wrote in 2007: "Rarely in prior American history . . . has there been anything like the assault on the independence of the judiciary that we have seen in the Bush-Cheney years. Moreover, the administration has supported the assault on judicial independence that has been conducted by Republicans in Congress" (229). Gore is also highly critical of some of some of the actions of federal judges, but his concern is not generally with their increasingly conservative rulings. Instead, Gore is unhappy with the many conservative interest groups' practice of hosting what he calls corporate junkets for federal judges. He believes that these conservative groups are attempting to indoctrinate federal judges in key policy areas such as environmental regulation. He wants these judicial seminars to end (233–34). Sounding very supportive of the courts, Senator Patrick Leahy (D-VT), chairman of the Senate Judiciary Committee, stated publicly that "we need to do our part to ensure that the dedicated women and men of our judiciary have the resources, security, and independence necessary to fulfill their crucial responsibilities. Our independent Judiciary is the envy of the world, and we must take care to protect it" (U.S. Senate 2007). One Democratic member of Congress told me, "The courts are the last vestige of decency in our society."

The current conflicts between the courts and Congress have become part of this ideological and partisan battlefield. The Republican Party, at least in the House of Representatives, seems to have embraced the Religious Right's anti-court agenda, while almost all Democrats seemed to oppose it. Milkis even quotes Justice O'Connor as lamenting the "hyperpartisanship" that is clearly affecting the courts' relationship with other political actors (2007, B9). The irony of the situation is that the Republican Party's attacks on the courts have come at a time when the federal judiciary is becoming increasingly more conservative both in its makeup and in its decisions (see, e.g., Taylor 2005, 75–79). As Keck reminds us, "The contemporary [Supreme] Court was built almost entirely by Republican presidents, and some of the Court's decisions have been straightforward reflections of the national GOP platform" (2007a, 321).

Thus Religious Right attacks on the federal courts in general and on the U.S. Supreme Court in particular have occurred at a time when these courts reflect the values and positions of the Republican Party in many areas (see, e.g., Devins 2004, arguing that the Rehnquist Court in general protected majoritarian GOP concerns, especially on social issues; Clayton and Pickerill 2006, arguing that the Rehnquist Court's decisions on criminal-justice issues reflect the views of the GOP; and Pickerill and Clayton 2004, arguing that the Rehnquist Court rulings on federalism also reflect the needs of elites in the Republican Party). According to the Federal Judicial Center, of the total of 1,285 judges at all three levels of the federal judiciary in February 2008, 777, or just over 60 percent, were Republican appointees.

Republican judicial appointees have grown increasingly conservative over the last few years, especially those affiliated with the conservative Federalist Society for Law and Public Policy Studies. More than a third of President George W. Bush's appointees to the U.S. Courts of Appeals have been members of the Federalist Society, which has become an important force in evaluating other judicial nominees (see, e.g., Chaddock 2005; and Teles 2008). Founded in 1982, the Federalist Society grew out of conservatives' legal opposition to what they perceived as the liberal judicial activism dominating law schools and federal judicial decisions (see Toobin 2007, 12–14). The goals and purposes of the conservative Federalist Society are explained on the group's Web site. In explaining the group's point of view, the Web site states:

> Law schools and the legal profession are currently strongly dominated by a form of orthodox liberal ideology which advocates a centralized and uniform society. . . . The Federalist Society for Law and Public Policy Studies is a group of conservatives and libertarians interested in the current state of the legal order. It is founded on the principles that the state exists to preserve freedom, that the separation of governmental powers is central to

> our Constitution, and that it is emphatically the province and duty of the judiciary to say what the law is, *not what it should be.* (Federalist Society for Law and Public Policy Studies 2008, emphasis added)

The Federalist Society has become a potent political player in conservative legal circles. As one journalist described the group, "[The Federalist Society] has evolved into a powerful network for young conservatives looking for clerkships or jobs in Washington, fueling the buzz that one doesn't get a top legal job in government without a tie to the Federalist Society" (Chaddock 2005). Thus the attacks by social conservatives on the ever more conservative federal courts remain confusing. As one lobbyist told me, "The hostility of the Right toward the courts is puzzling because it is occurring simultaneously with the rise of Federalist Society judicial conservatives on the bench."

The views of the Religious Right clearly have affected how conservative members of Congress and especially the House Judiciary Committee approach the courts. Religious Right voters are a key component of the support for many Republican politicians, especially in the U.S. House of Representatives, and their influence cannot be underestimated. The Religious Right seems to want to silence the federal courts in the inter-institutional constitutional dialogue, even though those courts are mostly populated with judicial conservatives. Now the ideological and partisan demands from the Religious Right seem to trump the traditional respect for the courts that the House Judiciary Committee has always shown.

FOUR

The House Judiciary Committee: The Committee of Lawyers

When the Religious Right wanted to put its anti-court agenda into action, it turned to an unlikely source of anti-court sentiment, the House Judiciary Committee. In the late 1980s, when I first interviewed members of Congress about their attitudes toward the courts, Congressmen with law degrees and members of the House Judiciary Committee, regardless of their party and/or ideology, were the most supportive of the courts (see Miller 1992, 1993, 1995). At that time, almost all of those lawyer-legislators appreciated and valued the voice of legal reasoning and legal analysis that the courts bring to the inter-institutional conversational dialogue in the American system of government. Today, the attacks against the courts seem to be led by lawyer-legislators, especially—surprisingly—those who serve on the House Judiciary Committee. This indicates a clear change in the institutional culture of Congress, in particular the House of Representatives and even more particularly the House Judiciary Committee. Using a new institutionalist approach, in this chapter I examine these changes in the institutional culture of the House Judiciary Committee.

In examining the interactions between Congress and the federal courts, scholars and the media have focused much of their attention on the Senate Judiciary Committee because of its role in the judicial confirmation process (see, e.g., Binder and Maltzman 2002; and Walker 2004, 2007). However, in recent years much of the anti-court legislation considered by Congress has originated in the House Judiciary Committee, especially under the recent leadership of Chairman F. James Sensenbrenner

(R-WI). In many ways the Senate Judiciary Committee has served to block the most extreme proposals emanating from the House Judiciary Committee. This chapter examines how changes in the institutional culture of that House committee have bolstered the anti-court sentiment and recent anti-court actions of Congress as a whole.

The Committee of Lawyers

The House Judiciary Committee used to be known as the "Committee of Lawyers." Until relatively recently all of its members had law degrees. Congressman Sony Bono (R-CA) was among the first nonlawyers to sit on this committee, and after his death his wife, Mary Bono (R-CA), another nonlawyer, was appointed to the committee. The House Judiciary Committee has usually been classified, using Richard Fenno's (1973) typology of congressional committees, as a policy-oriented committee drawing lawyer members interested in legal issues (see., e.g., Deering and Smith 1997, 72–73) instead of one that members sought for purposes of reelection or power in the chamber. It was known for the attention it received from a variety of interest groups from both the Right and the Left. As Roger Davidson and Walter Oleszek explain, "The Judiciary Committees are buffeted by diverse and competing pressure groups that feel passionately on volatile issues such as abortion, school prayer, and gun control. The committees' chances for achieving agreement among their members or on the floor depend to a large extent on their ability to deflect such issues altogether or to accommodate diverse groups through artful legislative drafting" (2004, 218).

Although the House Judiciary Committee has not generally received a great deal of attention from academics, traditionally it has received more bills and resolutions than any other committee in the House (see Davidson 1988, 104). The committee was long known for its courtlike deliberative style and lawyerlike committee culture, in part because the vast majority of its members had practiced law or served as judges. It has drawn policy-oriented lawyer-legislators from both the far right and the far left of their respective political parties (see Davidson 1988, 105). Conservative members have long been attracted to the committee in order to advance a socially conservative agenda, while liberal members have sought to block such efforts (see, e.g., Cohodas 1980, 1982, 1986). Jackie Koszczuk and H. Amy Stern describe the House Judiciary Committee as a forum "where passionate and combative oratory is generally the order of the day" (2005, 797). The ideological polarization on the House Judiciary Committee may be due in part to self-selection among the members. As Davidson notes, "Ideologically committed members are drawn to arenas that allow them to voice their views and pursue their goals" (1993, 110). A lobbyist described the situation more bluntly, saying, "The true believers come to the House Judiciary Committee. There are bomb hurlers on both sides of that committee."

The House Judiciary Committee, which deals with some of the most divisive social issues of the day, has been known as one of the most partisan committees in Congress. Both parties have taken special care to put ideologically extreme members on the committee. As Davidson notes, "Partisan lines often are sharply drawn in legal and judicial controversies" (1993, 107). In the 1950s and 1960s the House Judiciary Committee was the arena for the civil rights battles in Congress. In the 1970s the Committee led the impeachment efforts against President Richard Nixon.

Also in the 1970s, the House Judiciary Committee, under the leadership of Peter Rodino (D-NJ), blocked legislation promoted by social conservatives on such issues as abortion, gun control, affirmative action, school prayer, flag burning, and the rights of criminal defendants. The Judiciary Committee became known as the graveyard for social conservative initiatives in the 1970s and 1980s, at least until Rodino stepped down as chair in 1989 and the Republican takeover of the House followed the 1994 elections. As Davidson reports, in the 1980s and early 1990s "House Democratic leaders made assignments that assured the Committee would kill constitutional amendments and other measures desired by conservatives on such subjects as school prayer, abortion, budget procedures, and term limits" (1993, 107). The committee eventually became less attractive to members because of its defensive posture on issues of constitutional interpretation, and the leadership of both parties had to change committee membership rules in order to attract members. With the Republican takeover of the House following the 1994 elections, the Judiciary Committee suddenly moved well to the right.

Although long made up of lawyer-politician members from the ideological extremes of both parties, nonetheless the committee was traditionally highly protective of the courts. As one member of Congress told me almost twenty years ago, "[House] Judiciary is special because there are so many lawyers there" (qtd. in Miller 1992, 953). While the membership is still overwhelmingly made up of lawyer-legislators, there are more nonlawyers on the committee now than in the past. Historically, its courtlike committee culture prevented the House Judiciary Committee from enacting anti-court legislation. As a committee staffer explained to me in the late 1980s, "Just like one can disagree with different schools of thought among legal scholars or other academics, Judiciary members disagree with the courts without attacking the courts as an institution. When Judiciary members disagree with a court's decision, they don't call for the impeachment of the judge; they file amicus briefs for the appeal" (qtd. in Miller 1995, 159–60). Given the recent attacks on the courts by the committee leadership, that statement seems quaint today.

Recently the House Judiciary Committee has been anything but the champion of the judiciary. For example, Lauren Bell and Kevin Scott (2006) found that members of the House Judiciary Committee were just as likely to introduce court-stripping legislation as were their colleagues who did not serve on the committee. Bell and Scott (2006) also found that members of Congress who were former practicing lawyers were just as likely to introduce court-stripping legislation as were non-lawyers. Most of the anti-court legislation recently considered by Congress has originated among the conservative Republican lawyers on the committee.

The number of requests to serve on the House Judiciary Committee has varied over the years. Certainly serving on the Judiciary Committee has been less desirable than serving on the committees that have jurisdiction over budgets, appropriations, taxes, commerce, and even foreign affairs (see, e.g., Barrow and Walker 1988, 253). In the 1960s and 1970s, membership on the Judiciary Committee was fairly desirable, but starting in the 1980s the party caucuses had to change their rules limiting the number of committees on which a single member could serve in order to recruit new members to the Judiciary Committee (see Deering and Smith 1997, 73). Lynette Perkins's interviews from the mid-1970s (1980, 1981) reveal that members of the House Judiciary Committee came to the committee with various goals in mind, but all of them felt comfortable with the highly legalistic subject matter the committee dealt with. Scott Frisch and Sean Kelly (2004) discovered that membership on the committee was sought more by Republicans than by Democrats from the 86th through the 101st Congress (1959–91).

Some consider membership on the committee important because the media pays a lot of attention to the issues it deals with (see Deering and Smith 1997, 92). However, service on the Judiciary Committee is a tough sell for many members. According to one employee of the judicial branch, "The Judiciary Committee is not the first choice for many members today. It's a tough committee because there is little fundraising potential from service on it and the issues are so controversial and divisive that there is no winning on Judiciary." Nevertheless, Davidson

(1993) notes that because the issues heard by the Judiciary Committee are important to key constituencies in both parties, the leadership of both parties choose their appointees to the committee carefully.

Although the Judiciary Committee has jurisdiction over issues affecting the day-to-day functioning of the courts, these issues have never been as attractive to members as have the broader issues of immigration, crime, civil rights, civil liberties, and even commercial law. Therefore, the "nuts and bolts of court operations" historically have received far less attention from the committee than the issues dividing the parties along ideological lines. Deborah Barrow and Thomas Walker write that "members of Congress, of course, are well aware of their responsibility to insure that the courts operate in a satisfactory manner. Because the political payoff for fulfilling this responsibility is relatively low, however, they tend to accommodate the needs of the judiciary with as little effort as possible" (1988, 253).

Lately the House Judiciary Committee has led the anti-court efforts in Congress, while the Senate Judiciary Committee has worked to block many of these anti-court bills. A federal judge remarked to me that the members of the Senate committee understand the day-to-day lives of federal judges better than the members of the House committee do. This judge expressed concern that the anti-judge rhetoric on the House Judiciary Committee had reached an alarming level, threatening judicial independence. Comparing the House and Senate Judiciary Committees, one lobbyist told me, "The Senate Judiciary Committee is more moderate and more helpful to judges." A former Republican Senate Judiciary Committee staffer said that "the Senate Judiciary Committee stops extreme measure passed by the House because of the threat of filibusters in that chamber. The House doesn't have to worry about filibusters. Their members can be as extreme as they choose to be."

Lawyer-Legislators and the Courts

This book is based in part on interviews with members of the House Judiciary Committee, its staff, lobbyists who pay special attention to that committee, and employees of the judicial branch (see the appendix). Almost twenty years ago I conducted similar interviews with members of three committees in the U.S. House of Representatives, as well as with members of the state legislatures of Ohio and Massachusetts. I found that congresspersons' differing views of the courts were due largely to whether the legislators were lawyers (the United States has a very high percentage of lawyer-legislators), as well as to the committees on which they served (see Miller 1992, 1993, 1995). Regardless of party and ideology, lawyer-legislators, especially those serving on the House Judiciary Committee, were the most protective of the courts. In fact, in my interviews from the mid-1980s more than 70 percent of the members of the House Judiciary Committee expressed extremely positive attitudes toward the federal courts (see Miller 1995, 105). Those lawyer-legislators appreciated the voice of the courts in the inter-institutional constitutional conversation. Things have changed dramatically since then. As an employee of the judicial branch told me in 2006, "The days when we could count on lawyers in the House to protect judicial independence are long over. Today ideology and party matter much more than whether a member has a law degree." It appears that today legislative attitudes toward the courts are driven much more by ideology and partisanship, with lawyers and nonlawyers in Congress being equally willing to attack judges and the courts as institutions.

The number of anti-court bills passed by the House Judiciary Committee in recent years is striking. These have included bills to strip the federal courts of jurisdiction over a variety of types of cases, to increase congressional oversight of the federal courts through such means as creating an inspector general for the courts, and threats of impeachment against federal judges because of their decisions. The House Judiciary Committee has also approved bills to limit legal fees in First Amendment Establishment of Religion cases, including a federal court ruling that a forty-three-foot cross had to be removed from the top of the Mt. Soledad National Veteran's Memorial. In addition to limiting attorney fees in such cases, Congress in 2006 responded specifically to this judicial ruling by enacting legislation that would transfer the property in question to federal control, thus changing the legal claims that the opponents of the cross could bring (see Brandenburg and Kay 2007, 8).

On the issue of attorney fees, the full House of Representatives approved a bill that would have barred judges from awarding attorney fees in any Establishment of Religion cases (see Cooperman 2006). It seemed that the bill was a clear attempt to stop the ACLU, the Americans United for Separation of Church and State, and other liberal interest groups from pursuing Establishment Clause cases against state and local governments. The bill later died in the Senate. Congressman Steve Chabot (R-OH), then chair of the House Judiciary Committee's Subcommittee on the Constitution, stated that the legislation was necessary to "prevent the use of the legal system in a manner that extorts money from State and local governments and inhibits their constitutional actions" (House

Committee on the Judiciary 2006a, 1) even though by definition these governmental bodies would not have paid attorney fees unless a court declared their actions to be unconstitutional. The sponsor of the bill, Congressman John Hostettler (R-IN), a member of the Judiciary Committee, said that the bill was important to conservatives because they did not "look kindly on the fact that their constitutional rights have become subject to the whims, literally, of unelected judges" (House Committee on the Judiciary 2006a, 5).

Another interesting fact is that almost all of the witnesses at the hearing who supported this legislation have appeared in a video used to raise funds for Religious Right groups. Opponents of the bill saw the effort as an attack on judicial independence. For example, Congressman Jerrold Nadler (D-NY) said at the hearings, "[Court] decisions defending the rights of unpopular minorities against the will of the majority have always inflamed passions. People have always questioned our system of checks and balances, and especially the role of the independent judiciary. But recourse to an independent judiciary is the bulwark of our liberties" (House Committee on the Judiciary 2006a, 3). Regarding this bill, one Democrat on the Judiciary Committee told me, "The attorney fees bill was clearly unconstitutional. It was done merely to make a statement. We have enough to do around here without making empty statements."

The Judiciary Committee also initiated legislation that eventually led the full House to express its disapproval of the Supreme Court's *Kelo* decision, in which the Court ruled that local elected officials could define "public use" for eminent-domain cases (see chapter 3). The congressional resolution opposing the *Kelo* ruling passed the House by a vote of 365-33. In a subcommittee hearing regarding potential congressional responses to the *Kelo* decision, Congressman Hostettler argued for a legislative-supremacy approach to constitutional interpretation when he stated that the Supreme Court did not have the last word on constitutional issues. Hostettler argued that Supreme Court rulings were "not the supreme law of the land, and in fact, Congress can in its constitutional authority go against the will of the United States Supreme Court" (House Committee on the Judiciary 2005b, 5). Congressman Trent Franks (R-AZ), another member of the House Judiciary Committee, went even further, claiming that the Supreme Court was diminishing Americans' liberty and their fundamental freedoms. Echoing the language of the Religious Right discussed in more detail in chapter 3, Congressman Franks proclaimed, "When we undermine those foundational constitutional rights, we essentially vitiate everything that the Founding

Fathers gave, everything they had to give us. And if a republic is anything, it is the rule of law. And when we find ourselves [oppressed] by a judicial oligarchy that simply ignores the law and writes it as they choose, it then becomes time . . . to board up the windows and go home, because there's no purpose in writing the law any further. The judges then write it for us" (House Committee on the Judiciary 2005b, 7–8).

The House Judiciary Committee has also held hearings on other anti-judge measures. For example, the Subcommittee on the Constitution held hearings in July 2005 on a resolution opposing the use of statements by foreign courts in U.S. judicial opinions. This issue was of particular importance to the Religious Right, which felt that the use of foreign precedents undermined the unique place of the American government on the world stage and reduced America's national sovereignty (see, e.g., Bork 2003; Posner 2005; and in opposition to this concern, e.g., Calabresi and Zimdahl 2005 and Tushnet 2006b, 2008). One of the main examples cited by the Religious Right was the Supreme Court's decision in *Lawrence v. Texas* (2003), which declared unconstitutional the Texas prohibition on homosexual sodomy. Justice Anthony Kennedy cited examples of how courts in other countries had approached this issue. Another case that drew the ire of the Religious Right on this issue was *Roper v. Simmons* (2005), in which the Supreme Court declared the death penalty for juvenile offenders to be unconstitutional. In that case the Court also invoked international judicial views on the issue. Likewise, the Christian Right was furious that the Supreme Judicial Court of Massachusetts had cited Canadian precedents in its *Goodridge v. Department of Public Health* (2003) decision, which declared a right to same-sex marriage in the state. As Congressman Chabot explained the problem from the Religious Right perspective, "By looking to and relying on the decisions of foreign courts in the interpretation of the Constitution of the United States, the judiciary not only is undermining the vision of our Founding Fathers but is chipping away at the core principles on which this country was founded, chipping away at our Nation's sovereignty and independence" (House Committee on the Judiciary 2005a, 2). Congressman Tom Feeney (R-FL) went even further. After declaring that six of the justices on the Supreme Court were "transnationalists" (see, e.g., Calabresi and Zimdahl 2005), Feeney proclaimed, "They have increasingly expressed essentially disappointment in our own U.S. Constitution as originally written by the Drafters and Framers of our Constitution by importing foreign laws, fads, constitutions, and political polls to somehow create or reinterpret . . . the very meaning of our Constitution"

(House Committee on the Judiciary 2005a, 4). Thus the anti-judge and anti-court rhetoric has run very high on the House Judiciary Committee. What is more disturbing is that the committee has actually taken actions against the federal courts as an institution.

The Committee under Chairman F. James Sensenbrenner Jr.

Former chairman of the House Judiciary Committee F. James Sensenbrenner Jr. (R-WI) often shepherded anti-court legislation through his committee in the six years that he chaired that committee (2001–6) and then through the larger House of Representatives. Although Sensenbrenner has a law degree from the University of Wisconsin, over his years as chairman he took a variety of anti-court and anti-judge positions. For example, in 2005 he sent a letter to the Seventh Circuit U.S. Court of Appeals complaining that a specific criminal sentence was too lenient. This action raised the anger of most of the legal community (see, e.g., Koszczuk and Angle 2007, 1112). Congressman Sensenbrenner has often called for the House Judiciary Committee and the full Congress to increase their oversight of the federal courts. As he explained one of his anti-court proposals, "This robust and aggressive oversight effort is aimed at improving the federal judiciary's operations and behavior. Efforts by Congress to fulfill its constitutional oversight responsibility over the federal judiciary do not threaten judicial independence, as some allege" (2005). However, it is not clear that the Sensenbrenner really was a fan of judicial independence. As one of his staff has argued, "There does seem to be this misunderstanding out there that our system was created with a completely independent judiciary" (qtd. in Gore 2007, 229). One should also note that Chairman Sensenbrenner led the fight for special legislation in the Terri Schiavo episode (see chapter 3).

In *Politics in America,* Koszczuk and Stern describe the former Judiciary Committee chairman as "opinionated and direct to a fault" (2005, 1122). In a later version of the book the authors were more blunt, saying, "Sensenbrenner doesn't suffer fools lightly. Known as much for his prickliness as his smarts, he can be downright ornery to colleagues, journalists, unprepared witnesses, and even constituents" (Koszczuk and Angle 2007, 1112). Thomas Mann and Norman Ornstein described Sensenbrenner as "heavy-handed" and "gratuitously partisan" (2006a, 175, 252). One Democratic member of the committee described the chairman as a "bulldog"; a lobbyist told me that Sensenbrenner was "spiteful and ignorant"; and a staffer for the Senate Judiciary Committee said, "Sensenbrenner is a partisan guy who wants to assert his power and always get his way."

Congressman Sensenbrenner was extremely unhappy when he lost the chairmanship of the House Judiciary Committee—"his dream job"—at the end of 2006. His prickly approach to his colleagues was clear at the end of his term as chairman. As the authors of *Politics in America* reported, "His final months as Judiciary chairman were pure Sensenbrenner theater. He defied President Bush on immigration policy, abruptly ended a hearing that displeased him by turning off the lights, and chastised a federal judge for his sentencing judgment—all par for the course for the gruff Midwesterner" (Koszczuk and Angle 2007, 1112).

There have been many critics of the way Chairman Sensenbrenner handled court-related issues. For example, the Alliance for Justice, a liberal advocacy group, filed a complaint with the House Ethics Committee in 2005 because of what they perceived as Chairman Sensenbrenner's improper interference with a case then being heard by the U.S. Court of Appeals for the Seventh Circuit (see Aron 2005). Others also noted this incident, stating that the perception in the legal community was that Sensenbrenner was attempting to interfere with judicial decision making in a specific case. The American Bar Association expressed its "vehement opposition to Representative Sensenbrenner's *ex parte* communication." Upset that he would not be the ranking member on the House Judiciary Committee in the 110th Congress, Chairman Sensenbrenner even blocked passage at the end of the 109th Congress of a relatively noncontroversial bill that would have improved the physical security and safety of federal judges. One interviewee even told me that in this instance Sensenbrenner was punishing judges for what he somehow perceived as a slight from them.

In many interviews with members of Congress, congressional staff, and lobbyists, I heard stories of Congressman Sensenbrenner's near hatred of the courts and his rude treatment of federal judges. I was told that federal judges, especially those appointed by Republican presidents, were shocked by their treatment when they would go to the Hill to talk to Republican members of the House Judiciary Committee, including Chairman Sensenbrenner. One lobbyist told me that "Sensenbrenner is unhappy with the courts on a number of fronts. He has a real animus towards the courts." Many pointed to Sensenbrenner's actions as one of the main reasons for the current friction between Congress and the federal courts. One Democratic member of the Judiciary Committee said, "Chairman Sensenbrenner wants to whip up the country against the courts, turning the judges into the enemy. Federal judges feel physically insecure right now." "Sensenbrenner just hates all judges," a Republican staffer in the House told me. Others echoed these strong feelings about Chairman Sensenbrenner. An employee of the federal courts described Sensenbrenner as "just evil, when it comes to his extreme mistrust of federal judges."

Federal judges have also publicly mentioned Congressman Sensenbrenner's strong dislike of them. The *New York Times* reported that Chairman Sensenbrenner "maintained an antagonistic stance toward judges" (Clemetson 2007). Judge Nancy Gertner, a Clinton appointee, described Sensenbrenner as being vindictive in the impeachment investigations against Judge James M. Rosenbaum, of the U.S. District Court in Minnesota (see chapter 5). "There was no question that judges were targeted under the Sensenbrenner committee for speaking out," Gertner said (qtd. in Clemetson 2007). As one lobbyist told me in 2006, "It is certainly harder to get attention in Congress for the needs of the federal courts today. The leadership of the House Judiciary Committee is clearly not receptive to hearing about the problems judges face today."

It is not clear whether Chairman Sensenbrenner's anti-court initiatives were due to his own personal views or whether he was just carrying water for the party leadership in the House. In general, Sensenbrenner has not been known as a champion of the Religious Right, although he certainly encouraged the House Judiciary Committee to further this movement's agenda, including his leadership in the Terri Schiavo incident. A congressional staffer told me that Chairman Sensenbrenner's actions merely reflected the priorities of the other Republican members of the committee. Another interviewee from a think tank explained that perhaps Sensenbrenner was using the anti-court legislation to gain attention in a large and crowded House of Representatives. Since there was little hope that the Judiciary Committee would be able to increase spending on pet projects for its members or to engage in oversight of an executive branch under Republican control, the only way to gain media attention was by passing the anti-court and anti-judge measures.

Other interviewees gave other explanations for Chairman Sensenbrenner's negative attitude toward the courts. One lobbyist told me that all of Sensenbrenner's anti-court attacks were due to a single committee staff member, who had been hired specifically to placate the Religious Right. This staff member was allegedly given free reign on the anti-court initiatives. Several lobbyists told me that there were more nonlawyer staffers on the Republican side of the House Judiciary Committee than in the past. Employees of the federal courts complained about dealing with nonlawyer staffers who did not understand the needs of the federal judiciary. Another lobbyist explained the situation on the House Judiciary Committee in this way: "The House Judiciary Committee is full of arch-conservatives. It is the most polarized committee in the Congress. There is a great deal of loyalty among the GOP on the Committee, especially since all the moderate Republicans left the committee a while ago." The clear implication is that Congressman Sensenbrenner was just advancing the preferences of the other Republican members of the committee. Thus the motives behind Chairman Sensenbrenner's positions remain murky, but it is clear that he was no friend of the federal judiciary while he was the leader of the House Judiciary Committee.

The Committee under Chairman Henry Hyde

Chairman Sensenbrenner's attitude toward the courts contrasted sharply with the approach taken by Congressman Henry Hyde (R-IL), who chaired the committee from 1995 to 2000. Hyde was the handpicked choice of Speaker Newt Gingrich to lead the House Judiciary Committee in the early years of the Republican Revolution in the mid-1990s, when the Republicans took control of the House for the first time in decades. Gingrich passed over several more senior members of the committee in choosing Hyde as chair (see Aldrich and Rohde 2001, 288). At the time, Hyde was seen as an "ideological loyalist" by the leadership (see Evans and Oleszek 1997, 200). Even though Chairman Hyde was chosen by the party leadership, he did not always see eye to eye with those at the top of his party's hierarchy. Hyde was viewed as an independent chair who refused to push some of the leadership's priorities through the committee. Often the party leaders just bypassed the Judiciary Committee when they felt that Hyde was not enough of a party loyalist. When asked why his committee was sometimes bypassed when party leaders were trying to push a bill to the floor of the House, Chairman Hyde revealed a great deal about what he saw as the committee's institutional culture when he replied, "We have a reputation of being deliberative" (qtd. in Aldrich and Rohde 2005, 258).

Although both Sensenbrenner and Hyde were strong conservatives from the Midwest, they viewed the courts very differently. While Sensenbrenner seemed to take great pride in attacking the courts whenever possible, Hyde actually led the effort to decouple judicial salaries from congressional salaries (see chapter 3). Several interviewees told me that federal judicial salaries are so low because the salaries of judges and those of members of Congress are linked. Congressman Hyde's attempts to improve the salaries of federal judges failed because then majority leader Tom DeLay (R-TX) refused to let the full House consider the Hyde proposal. In fact, the Republicans often bypassed the House Judiciary Committee when the leadership of the party was uncertain about how Chairman Hyde would respond to their priorities. Hyde was seen as an independent legislator who would sometimes oppose the leadership positions on key legislation, such as when he allowed constitutional amendments to impose term limits on members of Congress to come to the floor from the Judiciary Committee but then led the fight to defeat such measures. The leadership bypassed the Committee on legislation to repeal the assault-weapons ban because Chairman Hyde opposed the repeal (see Aldrich and Rhode 2005, 258). Likewise, Chairman Hyde would not allow anti-court legislation to come to the floor even when the leadership supported such proposals.

Although Hyde supported a variety of constitutional amendments to overturn Supreme Court decisions, he never allowed legislation that would attack the courts as an institution out of his committee. As one congressional staffer told me, "Congressman Hyde had an old-school approach to the courts, treating judges with the respect deserved for members of a co-equal institution. Sensenbrenner is a highly partisan guy who wants to assert his own power and impose his will on anyone who gets in his way, including federal judges." Another interviewee told me that "Hyde was an institutionalist who believed in the courts as an institution. Sensenbrenner is an ideologue who will gain notoriety in attacking the courts without concern for judicial independence issues."

Chairman Hyde always felt that members of Congress should not take a short-term, parochial view of their congressional duties and responsibilities. He believed that legislators should consider the long-term consequences of their actions and always be aware of what was good for the broader system of government. When it came to the role of the courts in the inter-institutional conversation, Chairman Hyde would never let his committee unduly restrict the independent voice of federal judges in the constitutional dialogue. He disagreed with many specific judicial decisions, most notably the ones allowing abortion, but he never attacked the courts as an institution. Hyde's broad, national-view approach to legislating permeated everything he did as chairman of the House Judiciary Committee. Speaking to a group of newly elected members of Congress in 1990, Congressman Hyde urged them to consider how their actions could serve the best interests of the broader system of government: "If you are here simply as a tote board registering the current state of opinion in your district, you are not going to serve either your constituents or the Congress well. . . . You must take, at times, a national view, even if you risk the displeasure of your neighbors and friends back home" (1990).

When Henry Hyde stepped down as chairman of the House Judiciary Committee in 2001, the U.S. Judicial Conference passed a resolution praising his assistance to the federal judiciary. *The Third Branch,* the newsletter of the Administrative Office of the United Stated Courts, reprinted the resolution upon Hyde's death in November 2007. The resolution read in part, "His record of accomplishments [in the House of Representatives] bears witness to an unwavering respect for the Constitution of the United States and an abiding belief in the rule of law. Henry Hyde is sensitive to the position of the Judicial Conference on legislation affecting the Judiciary, and on such matters, has been a source of wise counsel to judges. He recognizes the independence of the Judicial Branch, has vigorously supported improvements in the administration of justice, and has worked to provide appropriate and equitable compensation and benefits to judges and their staffs. The legacy of the Honorable Henry Hyde, as a Member of Congress, as a leader of the Committee on the Judiciary, and as a valued friend to the federal Judiciary will endure for many years to come" (Administrative Office of the United States Courts 2007b).

Changes in the Institutional Culture of the Committee

Congressman Sensenbrenner and his conservative Republican allies on the House Judiciary Committee were clearly able to transform the institutional culture of the committee from one that protected the courts under Chairman Hyde to one that used the courts as pawns in a broader partisan and ideological culture war. As one employee of the judicial branch explained to me, "Federal judges don't understand how the Hill has changed in the last 10 years." One should never forget that the House Judiciary Committee Republicans led the impeachment fight against President Bill Clinton under the reluctant leadership of Chairman Henry Hyde, a move that signaled that the extreme conservatives on the committee were attempting to change its institutional culture. When Hyde left the committee, the hard-core conservatives on the committee took over and transformed the institutional culture of the committee. This change in the committee culture has been noted by individuals who work in the judicial branch. As one judicial branch employee told me, "Formerly both parties on the House Judiciary Committee were very receptive to the needs of the judicial branch. They all would reach out to us. Now they don't want to hear from the courts or from individual judges, even on matters of vital interest to the judiciary."

Others also noted that overall communications between Congress and the courts have become more difficult lately. As one lobbyist told me, "The courts and Congress don't talk to each other very much. They really don't understand each other very well." Another lobbyist said, "The GOP won't talk to judges because they want to maintain their ability to attack activist judges, while the Democrats claim they are just too busy to talk to judges." A Republican staffer stated that his boss would welcome more communication from federal judges, as long as they were not liberal activists. A Democratic staffer countered, "The door is always open for judges to talk to Democrats in Congress."

The House Judiciary Committee has always drawn passionate members from the ideological extremes of their respective parties, but the most conservative elements were usually held at bay by Chairman Hyde. "The House Judiciary Committee is filled with conservative Republican and liberal Democratic *firebrands,*" reported Davidson and Oleszek (2004, 219, emphasis added). Although they were not successful under Chairman Hyde, eventually the most extreme conservative firebrands on the committee took control and transformed the committee's institutional culture with the assistance of Chairman Sensenbrenner. For our purposes, the most notable difference in the new committee culture is that conservative lawyer-legislators on the Republican side of the committee are leading the anti-court attacks, whereas formerly the lawyer-legislators on the committee were highly protective of the federal courts.

Former Congressman Steve Chabot, a hard-core movement conservative first elected in the Republican triumph of 1994, was the chair of the Subcommittee on the Constitution of the House Judiciary Committee from 2001 to 2006. This lawyer-legislator long supported a wide variety of constitutional amendments to overturn what he perceived as liberal judicial activist decisions from "rogue" federal judges. In criticizing the federal courts for citing decisions of non-American courts, Congressman Chabot stated, "Unfortunately, over the last several years, we have witnessed a trend, a dangerous trend I believe, in which the judiciary has strayed from its oath and duty to uphold the meaning of the Constitution" (House Committee on the Judiciary 2005a, 2). He has also been quoted as saying, for example, that "one way or another, we know the Constitution will be amended. The question is: Is it done the appropriate way, or is it done by unelected, activist judges?" (qtd. in Koszczuk and Stern 2005, 797).

In 2007 Congressman Lamar Smith (R-TX) became the ranking minority member on the House Judiciary Committee. This conservative lawyer "has been one of the foremost Republican critics of the federal judiciary and 'activist' judges" (Koszczuk and Stern 2005, 1006). He chaired the impeachment hearings against Judge Manuel L. Real (see chapter 5). He was also the cofounder and cochairman of the House Working Group on Judicial Accountability. According to a press release issued by the organization upon its founding in 2003, this group would educate members of Congress and the public about judicial abuses, especially the dangers of liberal judicial activism (L. Smith 2003). Congressman Chabot, who was also a founding member of the Working Group, defined judicial activism as follows: "Judicial activism occurs when judges exceed the authority given to them under Article III of the Constitution. When judges substitute their own political views for the law, the ramifications can be felt by communities across our nation" (qtd. in L. Smith 2003). Former majority leader of the House DeLay said at the time, "When it comes to judicial abuses, we are going to take no prisoners" (qtd. in Administrative Office of the United States Courts 2003).

Representative Howard Coble (R-NC), another conservative lawyer-legislator on the House Judiciary Committee, led the impeachment investigation against Judge Rosenbaum (see Koszczuk and Stern 2005, 768). Critics of this investigation said that the committee was retaliating against Rosenbaum for his testimony before the committee in favor of a proposal to reduce sentences in drug-trafficking cases, a position strongly opposed by the conservative Republicans who dominated the committee at the time.

Congressman Louie Gohmert (R-TX) is another conservative lawyer-legislator who sits on the House Judiciary Committee. When the U.S. Supreme Court ruled in *United States v. Booker* (2005) that the federal sentencing guidelines were merely advisory, Congressman Gohmert stated that the Court had ignored the Constitution and its own precedents in this decision, instead "following the fleeting whims of a daydreaming child" (qtd. in Koszczuk and Stern 2005, 971). He was also a strong critic of the Supreme Court's decision in the *Kelo* case, regarding who can define "public use" in eminent-domain cases. In attacking that ruling, Gohmert wrote that the Supreme Court made "it sound 'fair' that private property can be taken from one legitimate owner and forcibly transferred to one who offers greater financial rewards to the ruler" (qtd. in Koszczuk and Angle 2007, 951). What makes these attacks on the Court even more surprising is that Gohmert once served as the chief justice of the state appeals court in Texas, and he had served as a trial judge in the state for many years before that. In reference to his often harsh criticism of judges and his institutional attacks on the federal judiciary, Congressman Gohmert explained, "Former judges don't seem to have a problem having the courage to stand up and say what we believe is right" (qtd. in Koszczuk and Angle 2007, 951). Ross Baker notes that there are fewer former judges serving in Congress now than in the past (2007, 109–10).

Former Congressman Tom Feeney was another conservative lawyer-legislator who was not shy about attacking the courts. *Politics in America* describes him as "brash and ambitious" (Koszczuk and Angle 2007, 264). As a freshman member of Congress, Feeney authored an amendment that required the Department of Justice to monitor individual federal judges who deviated from the federal sentencing guidelines. Federal judges saw this move as a clear attack on judicial independence, because they perceived that the next step was impeachment for federal trial judges who deviated from the guidelines. The Feeney amendment was strongly opposed by the American Bar Association and the American Civil Liberties Union, and even Chief Justice William H. Rehnquist strongly criticized Congress for adopting such a blatant attack on judicial independence without even asking judges for their views on the legislation (see Rehnquist 2003, 2). Federal judges responded to the Feeney amendment on criminal sentencing with "anger, defiance, and action" (Geyh 2006, 270). As one federal judge said at the time, "They can have their blacklists, but we have life tenure" (qtd. in Geyh 2006, 270).

After the Supreme Court ruled in *United States v. Booker* (2005) that the federal sentencing guidelines were merely advisory, Feeney denounced the decision and launched new efforts to curb the discretion of federal judges (Koszczuk and Angle 2007, 264). Feeney continued his fervent attacks on the courts. In a hearing on the use of foreign legal sources by U.S. judges, Congressman Feeney said, "Six U.S. Supreme Court Justices . . . have increasingly expressed disappointment in the Constitution we inherited from the Framers and disdain for certain laws enacted by democratically elected representatives. . . . If foreign laws are imposed on Americans by five unelected Justices, then rule by 'philosopher kings' has replaced rule by 'We the People'" (House Committee on the Judiciary 2005a, 57). Feeney was also a leader in the Terri Schiavo episode (see chapter 3).

Other lawyer-legislators are now leading the attacks on the courts. Senator John Cornyn (R-TX) has often attacked liberal judges for their perceived activism. What makes the attacks from Senator Cornyn unusual is not only that he is a lawyer but also that he once served as a judge on the Texas Supreme Court (see, e.g., Murray 2007). Cornyn has been quoted as saying things like, "If the judiciary gets into the business of making blatantly political decisions, it pretty much does away with the need for a Congress" (qtd. in Koszczuk and Stern 2005, 969). He also said, "It causes a lot of people, including me, great distress to see judges use the authority that they have been given to make raw political or ideological decisions" (qtd. in Babington 2005). In 2005 Senator Cornyn even said that liberal judicial activism was the cause of physical threats and actual violence against federal judges (see Babington 2005). Thus movement conservatives, who are often lawyers, are leading the charge in Congress against the institution of the judiciary.

Why have the lawyer-legislators suddenly become the leaders in the anti-judge and anti-court efforts? Why has the institutional culture of the House Judiciary Committee changed so dramatically? In his seminal work on congressional committees, Richard Fenno (1973) wrote that members of Congress generally have four interdependent goals: reelection, making good public policy, power in the chamber, and perhaps attaining higher office. David Mayhew (1974) argued that reelection was the primary goal and that all actions by individual members of Congress could be explained by the need for reelection. Stressing the goal of making good public policy, Aage Clausen (1973) attempted to explain that the voting decisions of individual legislators were purely ideologically driven. John Kingdon (1989) argued that in their congressional voting decisions, members of Congress followed various cues, including the positions of trusted colleagues, interest groups, and the president. From my interviews, it has become clear that the conservative firebrands on the House Judiciary Committee are motivated by more than just reelection concerns, although some of the more strident members, such as Congressman John Hostettler, did lose their seats in the 2006 or 2008 elections. When asked, both liberals and conservatives felt that most of the Republican lawyer-legislators on the House Judiciary Committee were true believers in the Religious Right view that the courts were out of control and were corrupting American society. It is very difficult to discover the specific motivations of any particular member of Congress, but it appears that the policy-driven members of the House Judiciary Committee actually wanted to change the voice of the courts in the inter-institutional constitutional conversation. Some of them believed in the notion of legislative supremacy and judicial inferiority, but most just seemed to want to force the courts to render rulings that were acceptable to the social conservatives who followed the agenda of the Religious Right. Chairman Sensenbrenner's personal dislike of federal judges gave the extremists on the committee the opening they needed to transform its institutional culture.

From their statements and from their actions, it is clear that the controlling members of the House Judiciary Committee wanted to change the face of judicial policymaking. For some, this desire was motivated by the need for reelection, but for most it seemed to be policy driven. That powerful interest groups on the right also wanted a new judicial direction did not hurt matters. Under Chairman Sensenbrenner, attacking the federal courts was a way for individual committee members to enhance their reelection bids, to effect what they considered good public policy, and perhaps even to gain power in the chamber and potentially higher office all at once. All of these factors coalesced to make the anti-judge agenda of the Religious Right the anti-court actions of the House Judiciary Committee. The true believers of the Right took control of the committee, and the committee took a variety of actions that could be seen as threats to judicial independence. Thus the judges were the victims of the culture wars playing themselves out in the hearing rooms and on the chamber floors of Capitol Hill.

It is not the threats against the courts and judges perceived to be too liberal by those controlling the House Judiciary Committee that are remarkable. We have seen plenty of threats against the courts in American history, as chapter 1 indicates. What is remarkable is that the ultraconservative members of the House Judiciary Committee were able to persuade the full House to adopt some of these anti-court measures and that some of them were even enacted into law when they somehow passed the Senate too.

The House Judiciary Committee under Democratic Control

It is not clear how the Democratic control of the House Judiciary Committee that began after the 2006 elections will again change the culture of the committee, but it appears that the Democrats will not take any immediate anti-court actions. Certainly, the agenda of the new chair of the House Judiciary Committee, Congressman John Conyers (D-MI), is very different from his predecessor's. Conyers was extremely active in the civil rights movement, and as a cofounder of the Congressional Black Caucus he generally sees the courts as the protectors of minority interests. Conyers has consistently criticized actions of the Republicans that he thought would harm judicial independence. For example, he spoke out against federal legislation in the Terri Schiavo incident, claiming that the bill to force the federal courts to hear the case meant that "we are no longer a nation of laws but have been reduced to a nation of men" (qtd. in Koszczuk and Angle 2007, 534).

Congressman Conyers has often spoken out in defense of judicial independence and in favor of allowing the courts to have an independent voice in the inter-institutional constitutional conversation. At one hearing held when Republicans held the majority in Congress, Conyers argued, "Once again, we are considering proposed legislation that attacks the independence of the judiciary. Despite the fact that the Nation's founders meant for the judiciary to be free of partisan pressure and immune from political whims, this Administration and this Congress have pushed measures that subject courts to excessive oversight and strip them of their powers" (House Committee on the Judiciary 2006b, 8). One lobbyist predicted that Conyers would give special attention to the question of the constitutionality of presidential signing statements on legislation and to the scandals at the Department of Justice rather than to the anti-court measures favored by the Republicans on the Judiciary Committee: "Conyers will increase the Committee's oversight of the Executive Branch, rather than oversight of the Judicial Branch."

Other liberals on the House Judiciary Committee have spoken out to protect the courts from attack and in favor of more respect for judicial independence. For example, Congressman Jerrold Nadler (D-NY) said at one committee hearing when the Republicans controlled the committee, "Our main concern, Mr. Chairman, is that attacks on the judiciary in this Committee have crossed the dangerous and inappropriate line between acceptable commentary and response, and potentially destructive attempts to destroy our separation of powers, which have been one of our foundations of freedom. . . . While I realize that some issues before the Court arouse strong feelings, Congress has a duty to set a reasoned example to the Nation. Lambasting the courts as unelected judges—as if that were not the design of our Government—undercuts the protection of our liberties" (House Committee on the Judiciary 2005a, 3).

In interviews with me, liberals supported the courts. One Democratic member of the House Judiciary Committee took great exception to the anti-court tactics of the conservative Republicans on the committee: "Liberal groups will not attack judges, but instead will work to get better judges on the bench. The GOP message to their grassroots supporters is that it is acceptable to attack the courts as an institution.

I find that message to be sinister and cynical." Another Democrat on the committee told me, "We need independent courts. The courts must be allowed to remain free from politics so that they can do their job. The relationship between the courts and Congress must be one of mutual respect and independence." As a Democratic committee said to me, "There are a lot of practicing lawyers on the Democratic side of the committee who have a history of winning and losing cases in the courts. They have a better understanding of how the courts actually work. They won't attack the courts directly even if they work hard to overturn specific court decisions."

Some of the Democrats on the House Judiciary Committee see some tension between the courts and Congress as inevitable. "The courts and the Congress are equal branches, always jockeying for power," one Democratic committee member told me. "There will always be a back and forth and a constant dialogue with the courts on a wide range of issues. But the courts are clearly politicized today." The Democrats said that they would continue to act to change judicial decisions with which they disagree but that they would not attack the courts as institutions. As another Democratic member told me, "I think we should certainly consider legislation to overturn some of the more conservative rulings of the federal courts, such as the recent one allowing restrictions on late-term abortions. But I find the court-stripping proposals from the Republicans to be offensive and awful. They are just a power grab by the GOP."

Thus the liberal Democrats on the House Judiciary Committee seem to want to enhance the voice of the courts in the inter-institutional dialogue. As one Democratic staffer told me, "Liberals see the courts as a force for good. Liberals won't take their anger with specific court decisions out on the courts as institutions, but they will work to change those court rulings they don't like." The future patience of the Democrats with an increasingly conservative federal court system, however, is not at all clear.

Things have clearly changed in the twenty years that I have studied the relationship between Congress and the courts. While the U.S. Senate for the most part remains a very lawyerly body that refuses to enact most direct institutional attacks on the courts, the Republican-controlled House of Representatives and its Judiciary Committee used the courts as pawns in a larger partisan and ideological struggle. Since the Religious Right has recently increased its rhetorical attacks on the courts, politicians who depend on electoral support from those groups have also taken action against what they perceive to be liberal activist federal judges.

Thus the institutional culture and the institutional will in the House, and especially on the House Judiciary Committee, have changed over the years.

Whereas at one time the House Judiciary Committee was protective of the courts, now the conservative lawyer-legislators on that committee are leading the charge against the judiciary. These institutional attacks against the courts may subside now that the Democrats control Congress, although it may only be a matter of time before liberals grow weary of the conservative activism that the Rehnquist Court practiced (see, e.g., Keck 2004). Since the Roberts Court appears to be even more conservative than the Court was under Chief Justice Rehnquist, only time will tell whether the Democrats continue to protect the courts from institutional attacks.

FIVE

Three Recent Threats to Judicial Independence

Over the last several decades, conservatives in Congress have pushed for more congressional oversight of the judiciary and its decisions. Some have even claimed that the courts are inferior to Congress and that Congress should thus assert more authority over the courts and over specific court decisions. Congressional oversight of the executive branch is to be expected, since both branches make politically based decisions, but congressional oversight of the judicial branch might be seen as an attempt to make the courts subservient to the will of Congress and/or the president. Recently in Congress, and especially in the House of Representatives, there have been attempts to reduce judicial independence by increasing legislative oversight of the judicial branch and thus making federal judges more accountable to the majority view in Congress. These efforts could force enormous changes in the way the federal courts participate in the ongoing constitutional conversations among the institutions of government. This chapter discusses three such attempts to reduce judicial independence: court-stripping legislation, a proposed inspector general for the federal judiciary, and threats of impeachment of federal judges.

Court Stripping and Congressional Restrictions of the Jurisdiction of the Federal Courts

The U.S. Constitution in its Exceptions Clause seems to give Congress the ability to restrict the power of the federal judiciary to hear certain cases, although this power has been rarely used in U.S. history and its constitutionality remains in question. Limiting the power of the federal courts is often referred to as court stripping. In other words, it appears that Congress has the power to determine the jurisdiction of the federal courts, including the U.S. Supreme Court, but the extent of that power is unclear. Because such legislation has been enacted so rarely, there is a great deal of uncertainty about the extent of Congress's ability to strip the federal courts of jurisdiction in specific types of cases or for specific groups of people (see, e.g., Fisher and Adler 2007, 1042–51). Although it has threatened to do so many times in the nation's history, Congress has been hesitant to enact such anti-court measures until recently, when the number of court-stripping bills approved by Congress has reached an all-time high. Thus court stripping has gone from being extremely rare to being almost commonplace in the last few years. The speed of the change in congressional practice has been puzzling. A Congressional Research Service report to Congress on this issue concluded, "There appears . . . to be no direct legislative or judicial precedent for modern 'court-stripping' proposals" (Thomas 2005, 13). The heart of the issue is whether the federal courts should enjoy complete decisional and institutional independence or be accountable to the will of the elected branches of government and thus perhaps to the will of the people.

Historically, court stripping has often been threatened, for example by labor supporters and other progressives during the conservative activist era of the Supreme Court from the 1890s to the mid-1930s (see Ross 1994). Today, it is the conservatives who are acting to strip the federal courts of jurisdiction over a variety of types of cases. While their actions are controversial, some conservatives, such as former attorney general Edwin Meese, have clearly stated their preference that Congress strip the courts of jurisdiction under many circumstances. These conservatives often feel that too many federal judges take a liberal activist approach to judicial decision making and that court-stripping legislation is one clear way to reign in a judiciary in which federal judges improperly "legislate from the bench." In other words, these conservatives feel that the courts should reflect the will of the majority, and they perceive liberal judicial activism as counter-majoritarian. For example, overstating the historical record a bit Meese said, "Congress has in the past withdrawn jurisdiction from the lower federal courts when it became dissatisfied with their performance or concluded that state courts were the better forum for certain types of cases" (Meese and Dehart 1997, 181–82). In September 2004 the Senate Republican Policy Committee distributed a report entitled *Restoring Popular Control of the Constitution: The Case for Jurisdiction-Stripping Legislation.* The report states that "the American people must have a remedy when they believe that federal courts have overreached and interpreted the Constitution in ways that are fundamentally at odds with the people's common constitutional understandings and expectations" (Kyl 2004, 1). Thus court stripping is a method for changing the direction of federal judicial decisions and altering the independent voice of the courts in the inter-institutional constitutional dialogue.

The constitutional limits on how far Congress can go in stripping the federal courts of jurisdiction to hear certain types of cases are unclear (see, e.g., Thomas 2005). Supporters of court-stripping legislation usually cite *Ex Parte McCardle* (1869) for the proposition that there are few, if any, constitutional limits on the ability of Congress to change the jurisdiction of the federal courts. Opponents of court-stripping proposals usually cite *United States v. Klein* (1872), as well as equal-protection and due-process arguments, for the proposition that there are clear limits on congressional power in this area. Opponents also cite separation-of-powers arguments concerning judicial independence when they argue that court-stripping attempts are not constitutional.

In *Ex Parte McCardle* the Radical Republicans in control of Congress after the Civil War feared that the U.S. Supreme Court would rule that Reconstruction was unconstitutional (see chapter 1). McCardle was a Southern journalist who was highly critical of the Reconstruction efforts. He was arrested under the Reconstruction Acts and was awaiting trial before a military commission for publishing articles that had incited "insurrection, disorder, and violence." These articles were also considered incendiary and libelous. He filed a writ of habeas corpus to have his case heard in the regular federal courts instead of before a military tribunal. The U.S. Supreme Court accepted his petition and actually held oral arguments in the case. Then in 1868 Congress enacted legislation to withdraw the Supreme Court's jurisdiction in habeas corpus cases. A unanimous Supreme Court in *Ex Parte McCardle* then upheld the constitutionality of the court-stripping legislation, stating that the Court was "not at liberty to inquire into the motives of the legislature. We can only examine into its power under the Constitution; and the power to make exceptions to the appellate jurisdiction of this court is given by express words" (74 U.S. 506, 514). Given the Court's legitimate fear that the Radical Republicans in Congress would quickly move to attack the institutional power of the federal courts if the Supreme Court ruled against the court-stripping statute, it is understandable that the Court refused to confront Congress directly on this issue.

Just a few years later, however, in *United States v. Klein,* the Supreme Court seems to have come to the opposite conclusion about the constitutional limits on the power of Congress to restrict the ability of the Supreme Court to hear certain cases. Congress had attempted to use its appropriations power to nullify the president's pardon powers and to strip the federal courts of the ability to review such cases. Over the objections of the Radical Republicans, President Johnson in 1868 had issued a general pardon to former supporters of the Confederacy, which made it possible for former property owners in the South to file claims for the return of property seized by federal troops. Congress then had enacted legislation that prevented the Supreme Court under many circumstances from recognizing the president's general pardon or using the pardon as evidence in a lawsuit. Instead, Congress wanted each property owner to individually prove his loyalty to the Union. The statute was also intended to prevent the Supreme Court from hearing such property-seizure cases.

In *United States v. Klein* the Supreme Court, in a 7-2 opinion, struck down the statute as unconstitutional on the grounds, first, that Congress could not restrict the presidential pardon power granted by the Constitution and, second, that Congress could not prevent a presidential pardon from being admitted into evidence in court. Thus Congress had violated both presidential power and judicial power by enacting the statute. The majority of the Court stated that Congress, by stripping the Supreme Court of jurisdiction to hear this class of cases and by infringing upon the Court's decisional independence, "has inadvertently passed the limit which separates the legislative from the judicial power" (80 U.S. 128, 146–47). Thus *Klein* can stand for the proposition that Congress cannot strip the courts of jurisdiction for a group of cases or for a class of litigants.

The complicated set of precedents provided in these two opinions has left a great deal of confusion about the constitutional limits on Congress's power to strip the federal courts, and especially the Supreme Court, of power to hear certain cases (see, e.g., Epstein and Walker 2007, 97). On the one hand, Justice Felix Frankfurter followed the precedent in *McCardle* when he wrote in his dissent in *National Mutual Insurance v. Tidewater Transfer Co.* (1949) that "Congress need not give this Court any appellate power; it may withdraw appellate jurisdiction once conferred and it may do so even while a case [is pending before a judge]" (337 U.S. 582, 655). On the other hand, Justice William O. Douglas preferred to use the *Klein* precedent in his dissent in *Glidden Co. v. Zdanok* (1962), writing, "There is a serious question whether the *McCardle* case could command a majority view today" (370 U.S. 530, 606).

Many scholars remain uneasy about the precedents supporting court stripping. For example, Barry Friedman (2002) argues that *McCardle* cannot be divorced from its historical context, including the duress the Court faced from the Radical Republicans who controlled Congress at the time. Charles Geyh states that the precedent of *McCardle* remains "murky," noting that "uncertainty surrounding the durability of *McCardle* has never been resolved" (2006, 67). Thus the debate over the constitutionality of court-stripping measures continues to this day.

Many scholars feel that there are clear limits on the court-stripping powers of Congress, especially when Congress attempts to limit the ability of the U.S. Supreme Court to hear certain cases. The key question remains, can Congress use court-stripping legislation to prevent the Supreme Court from participating in the inter-institutional constitutional conversation? While stripping the lower federal courts of jurisdiction merely shifts those cases into the state courts, stripping the U.S. Supreme Court of jurisdiction may mean that no court would have the ability to standardize federal law on a specific topic (see, e.g., Fisher and Adler 2007, 1042–43). Thus it is not at all clear that later Supreme Courts would follow this line of precedent from *McCardle.*

One of the clearest statements of the limits on the power of Congress to strip the Supreme Court of jurisdiction came from one of the nation's leading experts on the federal courts and their jurisdiction. Professor Henry Hart wrote in 1953 that Article III of the Constitution prevents Congress from making exceptions to federal jurisdiction that "will destroy the essential role of the Supreme Court in the constitutional plan" (1953, 1402). Hart argued that concerns about separation of powers and judicial independence make court-stripping proposals, at least those involving the U.S. Supreme Court, unconstitutional. Other arguments in favor of limits on Congress's court-stripping powers center on issues of due process and equal protection. As the Supreme Court stated in *United States v. Bitty,* 208 U.S. 393, 399–400 (1908), Congress's power under the Exceptions Clause may be limited because Congress must exercise its jurisdiction limiting authority in a way that would give "due regard to all the provisions of the Constitution" (see also Fisher and Adler 2007, 1042). Although admitting that court-stripping proposals might be constitutional under some limited circumstances, William Ross argues that "there is widespread agreement that the power to curtail the jurisdiction of the lower federal courts must not be exercised in a manner that would interfere with the Constitution's supremacy clause, destroy the court's fundamental role, or deprive any person of life, liberty, or property without due process of law" (1994, 8).

Many scholars have noted that the Fourteenth Amendment was not yet in effect when the Supreme Court handed down its opinion in *McCardle* and that the Fourteenth Amendment's Due Process Clause may have limited the power of the *McCardle* precedent. For example, Harvard law professor and noted constitutional expert Lawrence Tribe supports the proposition that there are clear limits on Congress's power to restrict the jurisdiction of the federal courts, especially the U.S. Supreme Court: "The fact that federal jurisdiction over constitutional questions is not self-executing poses a potential danger that Congress may seek to circumvent the federal judiciary's accepted role as constitutional guardian by silencing it through removal of its jurisdiction over whole classes of cases" (2000, 271). Tribe continues, "Laws *designed* to hinder the exercise of constitutional rights are, to that degree, unconstitutional" (273, emphasis in original), and he says that the federal courts clearly have the right and duty to determine the constitutionality of any court-stripping statutes.

Louis Fisher also questions the constitutionality of court-stripping statutes. "An aggressive use of the Exceptions Clause by Congress," writes Fisher, "would make an exception the rule and deny citizens access to the Supreme Court to vindicate constitutional rights. Stripping the Supreme Court of jurisdiction to hear certain issues would vest ultimate judicial authority in the lower federal and state courts, producing contradictory and conflicting legal doctrines" (Fisher and Adler 2007, 1042–43). Thus Fisher argues that Congress cannot silence the voice of the Supreme Court in the inter-institutional constitutional dialogue. Some conservative Republicans have agreed with Fisher's analysis. For example, William French Smith, who served as attorney general in the Reagan administration, thought that court-stripping proposals, or at least those that prevented the U.S. Supreme Court from hearing certain cases, were unconstitutional. In 1982 Smith wrote to the Senate Judiciary Committee that "Congress may not . . . consistent with the Constitution, make 'exceptions' to Supreme Court jurisdiction which would intrude upon the core functions of the Supreme Court as an independent and equal branch in our system of separation of powers" (W. Smith 1982).

Lawrence Sager argued, using the governance as dialogue metaphor to make his point, that court-stripping proposals would violate the separation of powers: "Failed attempts to deprive the federal courts of jurisdiction can indeed be seen as conversation. But if Congress stops speaking softly and actually swings its jurisdictional club, our basic institutional arrangements will be badly unsettled" (1981, 21). Sager continued, "Congress' authority to shape federal jurisdiction cannot extend to shaving off discrete and disfavored constitutional claims with deep prejudice to judicially protected rights" (70). Thus he also agreed that Congress could not in effect prohibit the Supreme Court and the other federal courts from participating in the ongoing institutional conversation about how the Constitution shapes American society and government.

One practical argument against the court-stripping proposals is that the memberships of both Congress and the federal courts often change. Placing limits on the jurisdiction of the federal courts could prevent the courts from striking down as unconstitutional a statute that a new majority in Congress opposes or declaring a policy that a new majority in Congress would support (see, e.g., Pacelle 2002, 85–86).

For many decades, political scientists and other scholars argued that while Congress often threatened to strip the courts of jurisdiction over a variety of issues, it was prevented from actually enacting such restrictions for a number of reasons (see, e.g., Murphy and Pritchett 1961, 554–55). According to C. Herman Pritchett, "It may well be argued that the clause in the Constitution giving Congress control over the Court's appellate jurisdiction has in effect now been repealed by the passage of time and by the recognition that exercise of such power would be in the truest sense subversive of the American tradition of an independent judiciary" (Pritchett 1961, 122). Throughout American history, opponents of the courts have threatened to strip the courts of jurisdiction over various types, but these threats have rarely been carried out. Even at the height of congressional dissatisfaction with the Supreme Court, from 1890 to 1937, neither the Progressives nor the Populists enacted legislation to strip the courts of jurisdiction (see Ross 1994). However, the relationship between Congress and the federal courts seems to have changed over the last several years, and Congress seems far less circumspect about taking actions against the courts than it was previously.

The New Era of Court-Stripping Legislation

Beginning in the mid-1990s, Congress has passed a variety of laws that one could argue restrict judicial power. The nation generally had not seen these kinds of limits on the courts enacted into law since Reconstruction. The strongest supporters of most of these laws have been conservatives who feared what they perceived to be the liberal activist decisions of the federal judiciary. For example, the 1995 Prison Litigation Reform Act reduced the ability of federal judges to manage state prisons and force the early release of prisoners. The Anti-Terrorism and Effective Death Penalty Act of 1996 limited the ability of the federal courts to hear multiple habeas corpus appeals from death-row inmates (see Tarr 2006, 34). The 1996 Immigration Reform Act limited the number of appeals available to immigrants facing possible deportation. Other limits were placed on the discretion of the federal courts in a variety of circumstances in the mid-1990s (see, e.g., Greenhouse 1996). The Terrorism Risk Insurance Act of 2002 prohibited the federal courts from reviewing the U.S. secretary of the treasury's official designation of particular actions as "terrorist acts" (see Curry 2005). Some have even interpreted various sections of the 2001 Patriot Act as containing court-stripping measures (see, e.g., Brandenburg and Kay 2006, 2–8).

Some of these efforts to limit the discretion of the federal courts were supported by key federal judges, including the majority on the Supreme Court, who seemed to encourage Congress to limit the number of habeas corpus appeals the lower federal courts could hear. It seems that these measures were clearly intended to limit the discretion of the federal courts, although it is not entirely clear that the full Congress anticipated how these acts taken together could collectively harm the courts as an institution. As one employee of the judicial branch told me, "Court stripping is an easy fix for Congress. But it shows a lack of respect for the appellate process. The main problem is that court-stripping is not taken seriously by Members of Congress. They don't understand the long-term effects of their votes on court-stripping measures."

Court-stripping bills have also been supported by Democrats recently. In 2002 then Senate minority leader Tom Daschle (D-SD) quietly inserted language into an emergency appropriations bill that stripped all federal courts of jurisdiction over procedures governing timber projects in the Black Hills National Forest, in his home state of South Dakota (see Hudson 2002a; Munn 2002; and Kyl 2004, 7). As part of a compromise reached between timber interests and environmental groups, the legislation exempted a seven-hundred-acre portion of the Black Hills National Forest from environmental rules and lawsuits. The purpose of Daschle's language was to reach an accommodation among the various competing interests on the issue in order to help prevent forest fires (see Hudson 2002b). Congress then included similar provisions in the Healthy Forest Act. Opponents of the court-stripping measure said that it violated separation-of-powers principles; Representative Tammy Baldwin (D-WI) called it "a dangerous precedent in American legal standards" (qtd. in C. Smith 2003).

It is not at all clear that Senator Daschle intended to harm the courts through his actions or that he thought much about the broader implications for judicial independence when he inserted this language into the appropriations bill. It seems that he saw his amendment as a quick and easy solution to a purely local dispute. Republican critics at the time said that the maneuver was simply a ploy to assist Senator Tim Johnson (D-SD) in his difficult reelection bid that year (see, e.g., Boyer 2002; and Boyer and Hudson 2002). President Bush said that the South Dakota approach should be used for national forests nationwide, but Senator Daschle disagreed(see Sammon 2002). In a letter to the *Washington Times,* Daschle attempted to limit his proposal and its court-stripping provisions only to national-forest situations in which there was a consensus among "all local stakeholders—the federal government, community officials, environmental groups, and state government" (Daschle 2002).

The senator tried very hard to limit the precedent value of his amendment, both in the context of national forests and in the broader context of more general court-stripping efforts. Downplaying the importance of the Senate majority leader's court-stripping amendment, one lobbyist told me, "Stripping the courts of the ability to hear cases dealing with fundamental constitutional rights reaches a far different level than the minor interference with the courts that the Daschle amendment provided. The truly dangerous court-stripping proposals are coming primarily from the Right." Agreeing with this analysis, an employee of the judicial branch told me, "Some court-stripping proposals are anti-judge and some aren't." Republican supporters of court-stripping proposals, however, often cite Senator Daschle's actions to illustrate that court-stripping efforts garner bipartisan support.

One of the most important recent court-stripping actions occurred when Congress enacted the Military Commissions Act of 2006 (Public Law 109-366), which attempted to strip the courts of the right to hear habeas corpus appeals from any noncitizen designated as an "unlawful enemy combatant" by a military tribunal. It also prohibited federal judges from consulting foreign or international sources of law when interpreting Common Article 3 of the Geneva Convention, leaving that power to the president alone, and it banned the invocation of treaty rights by litigants in federal courts (see Wald and Kinkopf 2007, 69). One of the chief sponsors of the Military Commissions Act was Senator John McCain (R-AZ) (see Zernike 2008). Generally the Republican majority at the time supported the legislation, while most Democrats opposed it. The act therefore had Congress agreeing with the president that the executive branch alone should determine the fate and the constitutional rights of the detainees at Guantanamo Bay.

The court-stripping measures included in the legislation were in direct response to the Supreme Court's decisions in *Hamdi v. Rumsfeld* (2004), *Rasul v. Bush* (2004), and *Hamdan v. Rumsfeld* (2006). In these cases, the Supreme Court basically ruled that President Bush's proposals for trying accused terrorists being held at Guantanamo Bay were not constitutional, rejecting the Bush administration's assertions that "the detainees' fate was a question for the executive branch alone" (Greenhouse 2007b). More specifically, in *Hamdan* the Supreme Court held that the military tribunals set up to try accused terrorists were not constitutional, in part because they had not been properly approved by Congress. In *Rasul* the Supreme Court ruled 6-3 that detainees at Guantanamo Bay had habeas corpus rights, and in *Hamdi* the Court found that even U.S. citizens suspected of being terrorists have habeas corpus rights. In its 2006 legislation Congress attempted to strip the courts of the ability to continue to participate in this inter-branch constitutional conversation on the rights of accused terrorists, thus supporting the notion of executive supremacy on this issue. Louis Fisher (2008) and Jordan Paust (2007) have chronicled many recent instances in which the Supreme Court and other federal courts have disagreed with the president's constitutional assertions regarding suspected terrorists.

In passing the Military Commissions Act of 2006, the majority Republicans in Congress were supporting President Bush's position that he alone could determine how enemy combatants would be treated in the U.S. justice system. In September 2007, when the new majority Democrats and several liberal Republicans in the Senate attempted to repeal the court-stripping provisions of the Military Commissions Act of 2006, conservatives filibustered the repeal, and the Senate fell four votes short of ending the filibuster (see Weisman 2007). Senator Patrick J. Leahy (D-VT), the then chairman of the Senate Judiciary Committee, was clearly upset by the Senate's inability to end the filibuster, saying that the Senate's inaction on the repeal of the court-stripping measures "calls into question the United States' historic role of defender of human rights in the world." The Senator continued, "[The Military Commissions Act] accomplishes what opponents could never accomplish on the battlefield, whittling away our own liberties" (qtd. in Weisman 2007). Ultimately, five of the justices on the U.S. Supreme Court would agree with Leahy's position when the Court declared the Military Commissions Act to be unconstitutional by a 5-4 vote in *Boumediene v. Bush* (2008).

Before the Supreme Court issued its ruling in the *Boumediene* case, a variety of liberals, along with editorials in the *New York Times,* urged the Supreme Court to declare the court-stripping provisions unconstitutional. One *Times* editorial stated in 2007 that the Supreme Court had the chance "to redress an enormous wrong done by President Bush and Congress when they denied justice to a group of prisoners" (*New York Times* 2007b). Senator Arlen Specter (R-PA) also called on the Supreme Court to declare the court-stripping provisions of the Act unconstitutional, as well as to declare that the detainees had habeas corpus rights, even though he had voted for the original legislation: "To avoid an incongruous legal 'black hole' at Guantanamo, this Court should strike down the [Military Commissions Act's] illegal suspension of the Great Writ and allow Congress to establish procedures consistent with what national security and the Constitution require" (qtd. in R. Barnes 2007).

Five justices agreed with the liberal Senators Leahy and Specter when the Court in *Boumediene v. Bush* (2008) declared the Military Commissions Act to be unconstitutional, thus repudiating the position of President Bush and most of the Republicans in Congress on this issue (see, e.g., Greenhouse 2008a; R. Barnes 2008; and Biskupic and Gomez 2008). Although the Court did not address directly the general question of the constitutionality of all court-stripping measures passed by Congress, the majority of justices clearly said that in this instance Congress had crossed the line in attempting to prevent the federal courts from deciding cases dealing with the constitutional rights of the detainees at Guantanamo Bay. The Court clearly stated that Congress and the president could not silence the federal courts in the inter-institutional constitutional dialogue on this issue. As the majority opinion bluntly stated, "To hold that the political branches may switch the Constitution on or off at will would lead to a regime in which they, not this Court, say 'what the law is'" (128 S.Ct. 2229, 2259).

In declaring the Military Commissions Act of 2006 to be unconstitutional, Justice Anthony Kennedy's majority opinion thus stated, "Within the Constitution's separation-of-powers structure, few exercises of judicial power are as legitimate or as necessary as the responsibility to hear challenges to the authority of the Executive to imprison a person." Noting that the Court had the responsibility to protect fundamental constitutional rights, the Court continued, "The laws and Constitution are designed to survive, and remain in force, in extraordinary times. Liberty and security can be reconciled; and in our system they are reconciled within the framework of the law." In his concurring opinion Justice David Souter placed the principles of this case in a larger context, stating that "in this Court's exercise of responsibility to preserve habeas corpus something much more significant is involved than pulling and hauling between the judicial and political branches." After acknowledging the need for greater military intelligence in order to enhance U.S. security, Justice Kennedy concluded, "Security subsists, too, in fidelity to freedom's first principles. Chief among these are freedom from arbitrary and unlawful restraint and the personal liberty that is secured by adherence to the separation of powers." Chief Justice John Roberts and Justice Antonin Scalia both wrote strongly worded dissenting opinions, in which they were joined by Justices Samuel Alito and Clarence Thomas.

The reaction to the Court's opinion was predictable, with liberals praising the bravery of the majority opinion and conservatives lambasting the five majority justices for ignoring what they saw as heightened security needs in the era of the War on Terrorism. Clearly unhappy with the Court, President Bush declared, "We'll abide by the Court's decision—that doesn't mean I have to agree with it" (qtd. in Greenhouse 2008a). The Democratic leadership in Congress praised the decision (see Greenhouse 2008a), as did Senator Barack Obama (see Zernike 2008). Senator John McCain stated that he agreed with the views of the four dissenting justices in this case (see Zernike 2008). Senator Lindsey Graham (R-SC), another leading sponsor of the act, called the majority opinion "a tremendously dangerous and irresponsible ruling by the U.S. Supreme Court." Senator Graham continued, "The court has conferred upon civilian judges the right to make military decisions" (qtd. in R. Barnes 2008). On the other hand, an editorial in the *Washington Post* called the decision "a welcome victory for due process and the rule of law" (*Washington Post* 2008). A *New York Times* editorial praising this decision from a sharply divided Court, entitled "Justice 5, Brutality 4," described the ruling as "eminently reasonable" (*New York Times* 2008).

Since the Supreme Court in four different rulings has acted to limit presidential discretion in this area, the court-stripping provisions in the Military Commissions Act attempted to restrict the power of the courts and to increase the power of the presidency. This series of rulings is an example of when the Supreme Court, using legal reasoning, speaks with a different voice in the constitutional conversation than do the more political legislative and executive branches. As one journalist described the inter-institutional constitutional conversation on this issue:

> Each of the three branches of government has made a series of judgments on how to strike the balance between individual liberties and national security in the post-9/11 era. This latest Supreme Court confrontation, round three of the justices' encounter with the detainee questions, reflects an extraordinary interbranch drama, played out as a series of actions and reactions that has now cycled back to where it began: the role of the federal courts. This third round is potentially the most momentous, because at stake is whether the Supreme Court itself will continue to have a role in defining the balance or whether, as the administration first argued four years ago, the executive branch is to have the final word. (Greenhouse 2007b)

Thus the court-stripping legislation enacted in this case attempted to restrain a Supreme Court and other federal courts that viewed the issue of the rights of accused terrorists differently than did the legislative and executive branches at that time. After hearing the oral arguments in the *Boumediene* case, a highly respected journalist concluded that the bottom line from the Supreme Court would be that "when it comes to the rights of the detainees at Guantanamo Bay, the Supreme Court, and not the president or the Congress, will have the last word" (Greenhouse 2007c).

While it is extraordinary that the entire Congress has enacted these kinds of court-stripping restrictions on judicial power and thus attacked the courts as an institution, the U.S. House of Representatives, and especially its Judiciary Committee, has approved many more such limits on courts' ability to make decisions. The Republican-led House clearly had the institutional will to attack the courts as an institution and limit their voice in the inter-institutional constitutional dialogue. Thus even more court-stripping bills have recently passed in the House of Representatives, only to be killed in the Senate. For example, the House in 2005 passed legislation that would prevent the federal courts from hearing any cases arising from the proposed construction of a fence on the border between the United States and Mexico (see, e.g., Allen 2005a; and *Washington Post* 2005). In 2004 the House voted several times to strip the lower federal courts of jurisdiction to hear cases challenging the constitutionality of the Federal Defense of Marriage Act, which prohibited federal recognition of same-sex marriages, and of the Pledge of Allegiance. In both cases the votes were attempts to overturn specific decisions of the federal courts, but both later died in the U.S. Senate (see Fisher 2005, 1040–41). In 2006 the House again passed the Pledge Protection Act, and the Senate again killed it. The House has also considered legislation that would prevent the courts from hearing cases dealing with the Ten Commandments and prohibit the courts from citing international judicial decisions (see, e.g., Devins 2006).

Court-stripping legislation is clearly part of the strategy by social conservatives to assert legislative power over the courts. Lauren Bell and Kevin Scott (2006) found that most court-stripping measures were introduced by the most extreme conservatives in the House. Court-stripping measures are seen as another way for Congress to control what conservatives regard as federal courts out of control. As a staff member for a conservative Republican member of the Judiciary Committee told me, "The judiciary is not totally independent because Congress has the authority for oversight in order to narrow the focus of decisions where the judges have overreached."

Of course, court-stripping proposals have also been opposed by liberals who see the federal courts as protectors of individual rights. As one liberal member of the House Judiciary Committee told me, "I think court-stripping is offensive and awful. It's merely a power grab by the GOP." Another member of the House Judiciary Committee said, "We can't stop the federal courts from hearing cases and controversies prior to a lawsuit, but we can intervene after the fact to overrule an incorrect statutory interpretation decision or to attempt to alter a constitutionally based judicial ruling."

There has been opposition to these court-stripping proposals even from many conservatives. In his confirmation hearings, now Chief Justice Roberts repeatedly referred to court-stripping proposals as "bad policy" (see, e.g., Brandenburg and Kay 2007, 3), although he refused to say whether he thought these legislative proposals were constitutional or not. The late Senator Barry Goldwater, a frequent critic of many federal court decisions (see Clymer 1998), has nevertheless been quoted as calling court-stripping proposals "a frontal assault on the independence of the Federal courts [that] is a dangerous blow to the foundations of a free society" (qtd. in Brandenburg and Kay 2007, 3). The failed Supreme Court nominee and conservative icon Judge Robert Bork was also opposed to federal court-stripping proposals, in part because in his view "you'd have 50 different constitutions running around out there, and I'm not sure even the conservatives would like the results" (qtd. in Trippet 1981). Conservative Congressman Bob Inglis (R-SC) also decided to oppose court-stripping measures in Congress, saying, "I've come to the conclusion that court stripping is a dangerous concept. We citizens deserve the full protection of the Constitution, and we deserve a fully empowered federal court system to protect those rights. I'm also concerned that future liberal Congresses might use the court stripping concept to deny access to federal courts over claims that they might want to preclude" (2006).

Thus recently some court-stripping legislation has been enacted by Congress, with the U.S. House voting in favor of many more proposals that later died in the Senate. When Congress has enacted these court-stripping proposals, Congress and the president have agreed on this course of action, and they have agreed to curtail the discretion of the federal courts. While some would say that the court-stripping proposals of today are not very different from those proposed by Presidents Jefferson, Jackson, Lincoln, and the two Roosevelts, there is in fact a clear difference. Those presidents were almost always reacting to a Supreme Court dominated by the other party, and their threats against the Court never really became reality. They complained loudly about the courts, but then they moved to put loyalists from their own party on the bench in order to bring the courts more into line with their ideological preferences. Today, however, the Republican-controlled Supreme Court and the Republican-dominated lower federal courts are under attack from a Republican Congress and a Republican president. That the more majoritarian branches are taking action to limit the voice of a conservative Supreme Court is striking. Clearly, something has changed to make the more majoritarian branches unwilling to protect the independence of the federal courts in general and of the Supreme Court in particular. Only the future will determine whether Congress will continue to use such blunt mechanisms as court-stripping legislation to limit the decisional and institutional independence of the federal courts.

An Inspector General for the Federal Judiciary

In addition to stripping the courts of jurisdiction over a variety of cases, the House Judiciary Committee has discovered some novel ways to attack the courts. One example came in the form of a bill introduced by House Judiciary Committee Chair F. James Sensenbrenner Jr. (R-WI) that would have established an inspector general (IG) for the federal judiciary in order to oversee the courts, investigate ethical problems among federal judges, and conduct investigations into the issue of judges' overreaching their constitutional powers (see Allen 2005b; and Marcus 2005). At the 2006 hearings for the bill, neither federal judges nor representatives from the Administrative Office of the Federal Courts were allowed to testify. This legislation was approved by the House Judiciary Committee in September 2006 on a party-line vote (*Washington Post* 2006), although it then died at the end of the 109th Congress. Having an inspector general for the federal judiciary would skew the continuing dialogue between Congress and the courts, as well as potentially harm both the institutional and the decisional independence of the judiciary.

In September 2006 the U.S. House Judiciary Committee approved H.R. 5219, the Judicial Transparency and Ethics Enhancement Act, on a party-line vote. The committee's approval of this proposal came amidst extremely heightened tensions between Congress and the federal courts. The House Judiciary Committee had passed a variety of court-stripping bills, and there were threats of impeachment of federal judges coming from many committee members. Thus the inspector-general legislation was just one of several institutional attacks on the federal courts by the House Judiciary Committee when it was under Republican control. More alarming, the Judiciary Committee's actions occurred only a little more than a week after the Judicial Conduct and Disability Act Study Committee, chaired by Justice Stephen Breyer, had released to the chief justice its report *Implementation of the Judicial Conduct and Disability Act of 1980,* often referred to as the Breyer Report. The study committee had been appointed by Chief Justice Rehnquist in 2004, primarily to deal with Chairman Sensenbrenner's concerns about ethics in the judiciary.

IGs are usually executive-branch officials whose charge is to combat waste, fraud, and abuse in federal entities. Or in the words of Frederick Kaiser, "Statutory offices of inspector general consolidate responsibility for auditing and investigations within a federal department, agency, or other organization" (2003, 1). They generally have access to all records and information held by an agency, as well as subpoena powers to aid them in their investigations. Most IGs report their findings directly to Congress. Currently there are about sixty IGs in various federal entities, and almost all of them are governed by the Inspector General Act of 1978 and its 1988 amendments. The exceptions are the IGs for the Central Intelligence Agency, governed by the Intelligence Authorization Act of 1990, and for the Government Printing Office, governed by the GPO Inspector General Act of 1988 (see American Bar Association 2006, 3). The IGs for the U.S. House of Representatives is also exempt from the 1978 Inspector General Act. Almost all of these statutory IGs are appointed by the president or by the head of the parent agency and confirmed by the Senate, and they can be removed from office by the president or by the agency head. Each IG must submit an annual or more frequent report to his or her governing agency, and the agency must then forward that report to Congress, sometimes with additional comments from the parent agency (see Kaiser 2003).

Some entities have established their own IGs, for example, the Office of Inspector General for the U.S. House of Representatives, without a statutory requirement. There are quite a few differences between the statutory and nonstatutory IGs, so many that the American Bar Association report of 2006 calls these differences "striking" (5). For example, the IG for the House of Representatives is selected and appointed exclusively by the body it serves, and it does not have subpoena power (American Bar Association, 2006, 4–5). It does not report its findings beyond its parent agency. Unlike the statutory IG, the House IG thus does not share any information with anyone outside of the House leadership. The U.S. Senate has no inspector general.

Bills to create an inspector general for the federal judiciary were introduced by Congressman F. James Sensenbrenner, then chair of the House Judiciary Committee, and by Senator Charles Grassley (R-IA) in 2006; similar legislation had died in Congress a decade earlier (see Weinstein 2006a). Both Sensenbrenner's and Grassley's bills, H.R. 5219 and S. 2678, respectively, were formally introduced on 27 April 2006, although the concept had been discussed for several years prior to that. The most recent version seems to have originated in a 2004 meeting between Chairman Sensenbrenner and the Federal Judicial Conference, the policymaking body for the federal courts. In his 2004 appearance before the Judicial Conference, Chairman Sensenbrenner blasted federal judges in language that many attendees found to be disrespectful of the federal judiciary. Many of those whom I interviewed indicated that the federal judges present were shocked by Sensenbrenner's clear distain for them. In the press release announcing the introduction of the IG bill, Chairman Sensenbrenner noted that he had raised concerns with the Judicial Conference about "the Judicial Branch's lack of effort in recent years to police its Members' behavior" (2006, 1).

Chairman Sensenbrenner publicly raised the issue of an inspector general for the judiciary in May 2005, in a speech at Stanford University (see Allen 2005b; and MacLean 2005). The courts were on the alert for the attack, but it took Chairman Sensenbrenner and his staff almost a year to prepare the legislative language for the proposal. In introducing the new bill in the spring of 2006, Sensenbrenner said that the legislation was necessary because "integrity and accountability are the hallmarks of a public servant's trust with the people. It's my hope an independent

Inspector General for the Judicial Branch will help restore some of this trust with the public that has been damaged by the actions of some Federal Judges who have carelessly ignored the ethical guidelines established" (2006, 1). Senator Grassley was equally blunt: "An inspector general is just the right medicine the federal judiciary needs to ensure it is complying with its own ethical guidelines and to root out potential waste, fraud, and abuse in the system. Sunshine is the best disinfectant, and an IG can only help shed more light on the action of our judicial branch of government and keep it accountable to the American people" (qtd. in Lash 2006a).

Although both Sensenbrenner and Grassley said that the legislation was not intended to alter the case decisions of federal judges, others were less convinced. Following Sensenbrenner's Stanford speech, Professor Charles Geyh wrote that "context is everything. . . . The backdrop here is a fairly carnivorous House trying to hold judges accountable for the decisions they make. This proposal is not made in the context of judges spending lavishly. It is being used as a proxy for [congressional oversight of] their decisions" (qtd. in MacLean 2005). Justice Ruth Bader Ginsburg declared that "judges have good cause for concern" about the legislation, implying that Chairman Sensenbrenner's intent in the legislation was to force federal judges to issue decisions with which he agreed (2006, 8). Others wondered whether the legislation was introduced in order to shift public attention away from the many scandals then facing House Republicans (see, e.g., Lash 2006a). According to several of those whom I interviewed, the intent of the IG bill was clearly to influence the substantive decisions of the federal courts, not just to create more congressional oversight of the judiciary. As one lobbyist told me, "Having the IG report information to Congress is a clear form of intimidation of federal judges over the direction of their judicial decisions and a clear impeachment threat against them." Adding some force to this argument, Congressman Sensenbrenner said in his speech at Stanford, "The inspector general would be able to manage how we *punish* and who does the *punishing* for judges' misconduct" (qtd. in Yap 2005, emphasis added).

Many saw this legislation as just one more partisan attack on the federal courts. Congressman John Conyers (D-MI), then the ranking Democrat on the House Judiciary Committee and now chair of that committee, said about the proposed legislation, "It appears that an inspector general has been proposed as a means of intimidating judges into political compliance" (Judicial Transparency 2006, 8). Members of the bar, academics, and interest groups with an interest in protecting the independence of the courts mobilized in efforts to fight off the pending legislation. These efforts eventually found their way to national press outlets. For example, an editorial in the *Washington Post* suggested that the legislation "could serve to harass judges who issue politically unpopular opinions." The *Post* editorial continued, "Mr. Sensenbrenner's habit of using his committee's powers to investigate federal judges—some of whom merely acted in ways he did not like—creates a particularly troubling context" (*Washington Post* 2006). Several federal judges told me that they saw this bill as a clear attack on judicial independence, and the Judicial Conference and the American Bar Association took the rare step of opposing the legislation on the record (see Walter 2006).

The House and Senate IG bills were quite similar as introduced, although there were some key differences. For example, the Senate bill would have allowed the inspector general to investigate the activities of justices of the U.S. Supreme Court, while the House bill would have applied only to judges on the lower federal courts. Under both bills the IG for the judiciary would have been appointed by the chief justice of the United States, but only after consultation with the party leaders in both houses of Congress (see American Bar Association 2006, 6). The IG would have been required to report annually to the chief justice and to Congress on matters that might require their immediate attention. Violations of criminal laws by federal judges would have been reported directly to the U.S. attorney general. Thus the bills showed little respect for the fact that the judiciary is a separate and independent branch of the government. It seems clear that the legislation would have violated the constitutionally mandated notion of separation of powers, as well as the critical principle of judicial independence.

A *Washington Post* article on ethical lapses by federal judges, including questions involving stock holdings by judges and free trips sponsored by lobbyists, apparently prompted the immediate introduction of the legislation, but Congressman Sensenbrenner's long-standing conflicts with the federal courts certainly played a role in the House Judiciary Committee's approval of it. The lengthy *Washington Post* article and the investigations on which it was based raised concerns that some federal judges were refusing to recuse themselves from lawsuits in which they held a financial interest in one of the parties in the case. Other concerns were raised about judges traveling to fancy resorts for meetings with various interest groups, with the travel costs being paid by the groups. The main legal problem was that the judges had failed to list the free travel on their annual disclosure reports as required by law (see Stephens 2006).

The political problems these activities created were much more serious. Similar stories ran in other newspapers as well (see, e.g., Schaeffer 2006; and *USA Today* 2006).

Most ethical complaints against federal judges are handled by procedures spelled out in the Judicial Conduct and Disability Act of 1980. In general, the act created a complex system in which ethical complaints against judges are handled within the judiciary itself, often by a committee of other judges or by the chief judge of the federal circuit in which the accused judge sits. Both Senator Grassley and Congressman Sensenbrenner have long been critical of the way judges have policed themselves under this act. The September 2006 Breyer report attempted to address many of these concerns.

The House Judiciary Committee's Subcommittee on Crime, Terrorism, and Homeland Security held hearings on the IG legislation in June 2006. It seems a bit odd that this subcommittee had jurisdiction over the bill. Were the federal courts being accused of committing crimes, terrorism, or harming homeland security? It turns out that the chair of that subcommittee, Congressman Howard Coble (R-NC), had held similar oversight hearings in 2001, so the hearings were transferred out of the normal subcommittee of jurisdiction (see Judicial Transparency 2006, 7). At the June 2006 hearings, no federal judges, no representatives of the Judicial Conference, and no representatives of the Administrative Office of the U.S. Federal Courts were invited to testify. The refusal to allow judges to testify about this bill is further evidence of the extremely strained relationship between the committee and the federal courts. Two law professors, Ronald Rotunda of George Mason University and Arthur D. Hellman of the University of Pittsburgh law school, testified in favor of the bill, as did Senator Grassley. One law professor, Charles Geyh, of Indiana University, testified against it. Senator Grassley told the subcommittee, "Ever since I chaired the Senate Judiciary Subcommittee on Administrative Oversight and the Courts in the early 1990's, concerns have been raised about compliance with the judicial ethics rules and whether the judiciary can adequately policy itself on these matters. Concerns about alleged ethics violations, conflicts of interests, and appearances of impropriety by judges continue to be reported by the press" (Judicial Transparency 2006, 1).

The legislation was opposed by the Judicial Conference, by the American Bar Association, and by many federal judges speaking out individually. Justice Ginsburg called the legislation "a really scary idea" and compared it to the control of judges practiced in the former Soviet

Union (qtd. in Mauro 2006a). The Judicial Conference argued that the bill would harm judicial independence. The language used by the Judicial Conference was especially blunt for the usually reticent judges: "The proposal to create an IG is an entirely unnecessary and inappropriate imposition of control over the judiciary that creates precedents for further erosion of the fundamental constitutional principle of separation of powers" (Judicial Transparency 2006, 61). Even President Bush's then attorney general, Alberto R. Gonzales, spoke out against the proposed legislation in a speech to the American Enterprise Institute (Administrative Office of the United States Courts 2007a).

The House of Delegates of the American Bar Association passed a resolution opposing the pending legislation, as well as any legislation that would create an inspector general for the federal courts (see Walter 2006). The ABA said that the legislation was "unneeded and a threat to the constitutional separation of powers" (McMillion 2006). Other supporters of judicial independence persuaded a number of leading newspapers to oppose the bill on their editorial pages. For example, an editorial in the *Washington Post* called the proposed legislation "premature and ill-conceived" (*Washington Post* 2006). The *New York Times* ran an editorial saying that "an inquisitor of this kind would pose a threat to the independence of the judiciary", although the *Times* editors did want to see the judges do a better job of policing themselves (*New York Times* 2006b). A *Los Angeles Times* editorial called the bill "the latest attempt to muscle the courts" and said that it would "unnecessarily entangle the legislative branch in the day-to-day supervision of the judiciary" (*Los Angeles Times* 2006). Although Arthur Hellman had testified in favor of the bill in the June 2006 hearings, by December of that year even he opposed the legislation as unnecessary (see "Judiciary Moves to Soothe Congressional Concerns" 2006).

Others also opposed the bill, including all of the Democrats on the House Judiciary Committee who had voted at the September 2006 markup of the legislation (i.e., the meeting at which the committee considered amendments to the bill). The ranking Democrat on the subcommittee that held hearings on the bill, Congressman Robert C. Scott (D-VA), stated at the June 2006 hearing that he believed that the legislation violated the constitutional requirement of the separation of powers. Congressman Scott also noted that "we don't check with the executive or judicial branches when we select officers for the House, and it is insulting to think that they should have to consult with us when a judicial officer is appointed" (Judicial Transparency 2006, 7).

The judiciary also responded to the legislation, through indirect as well as direct means. Although it did not mention the legislative proposal by name, the Breyer Report made it clear that the judiciary would fight against the IG mechanism for handling ethical concerns among federal judges. The executive summary of the report from the Judicial Conduct and Disability Act Study Committee stated that any system for disciplining judges must take into account the need to protect judicial independence. In an oblique reference to the proposed legislation, the report stated, "A system that relies for investigation upon persons or bodies other than judges risks undue interference with the Constitution's insistence upon judicial independence, threatening directly or indirectly distortion of the unbiased handling of individual cases that Article III seeks to guarantee" (Breyer 2006, 1). As one lobbyist told me, "The Breyer report was masterful in stating the views of the judiciary on this issue."

Some of the opposition to the IG bill centered on broader concerns with inspector generalships in general. Although focusing on IGs in the executive branch, Steve Kelman, of Harvard University, raised a variety of concerns about "the Inspector General ideology" in an op-ed piece published in the *Washington Post:* "Most elected officials and journalists see inspectors general as nonideological fraud-busters whose only cause is protecting the taxpayer. Many therefore accept their pronouncements as truth-telling without fear or favor" (2007). Kelman challenged that conventional wisdom, arguing that inspectors general as a group focus on the negative instead of the positive aspects of government, preferring controls over creativity. The work of IGs often leaves federal employees discouraged and demoralized, creating "deep pain" among most honest and hard-working employees. Kelman concluded that "the IG culture . . . embodies an ideology about how public organizations should be managed that can make it harder, not easier, for government to perform well" (2007). Given the feeling of many federal judges that they are currently under attack, one wonders how creating an inspector general for the federal judiciary could harm the already low morale in the courts.

Partly in response to congressional pressure to clean up their act, the federal judiciary has taken steps to improve the handling of ethical concerns among judges. The Breyer Report found that the current system was working quite well, with only about 2–3 percent of the ethical complaints filed against federal judges being mishandled. The report stated, "The Committee is unanimous in its view that a processing error rate of 2% to 3% does not demonstrate a serious flaw in the operation of the system—given the number of complaints filed, their occasional lack of clarity, and the judgmental nature of the decisions as to whether further inquiry is required" (Breyer 2006, 5). However, the Breyer committee did find that the error rate for high-visibility cases, those that had received attention from Congress and/or from the media, was about 30 percent. While the absolute number of these cases was small (5 mishandled cases out of only 17 in this category), the Breyer committee did state that they could disproportionately shape the public's views on the proper functioning of the entire system.

Among its recommendations, the Breyer Report called for the formation of local committees of lawyers to give an outside point of view to the system. It also said that the Web pages of all federal courts should provide more information to the public about how the system of handing complaints actually works. The report also called for improved public reporting of the outcomes of ethical complaints against judges (Breyer 2006, 8–9). Chief Justice Roberts endorsed the recommendations of the Breyer report, and in his *2007 Year-End Report* he pledged to continue efforts to improve the handling of ethical concerns within the judicial branch. Roberts stated that "the Judiciary must relentlessly ensure that federal judges maintain the highest standards of integrity" (2008, 5). The chief justice did not mention or support oversight efforts carried out outside of the third branch, which an inspector general for the federal judiciary would have required.

The Judicial Conference has recently taken steps to improve self-policing among judges and to improve the public perception of the courts. For example, it has ruled that all judges on lower federal courts will be required to install "conflict checking" software on their computers in order to help them avoid participating in cases in which they might have a financial interest. Judges will be prohibited from having travel to seminars paid for by others unless the sponsor has filed a public disclosure statement on the content of the program and all sources of funding for the event. Judges will have to report their attendance at such seminars, and their information must be available on court Web sites (see Greenhouse 2006). A leading critic of the courts, Douglas T. Kendall, of the Community Rights Counsel, called the changes implemented by the judiciary "a dramatic change for the better" (qtd. in Greenhouse 2006). With these actions of the judiciary, Professor Hellman reversed his support for the IG legislation, saying, "I think the judiciary's latest recommendations and the Breyer Committee report went a long way toward doing what needed to be done" ("Judiciary Moves to Soothe Congressional Concerns" 2006). Both District Judge Thomas F. Hogan, the chair of the Judicial Conference's executive committee, and Justice Breyer acknowledged that the criticism from Congress had contributed to the actions taken by the judiciary. "Some criticisms in Congress have been taken to heart by the judiciary," stated Hogan, and Justice Breyer said, "We decided to respond directly to the criticism, and the criticism turned out to be constructive" (both qtd. in Lane 2006).

Despite these actions by the federal judges, the House Judiciary Committee on a party-line vote approved the bill creating an inspector general for the courts on 27 September 2006, just days after the Judicial Conference announced its new rule changes. This action was a clear attack on the independence on the judiciary, especially since the Judicial Conference had just taken appropriate actions to try to address congressional concerns. Thus the IG bill must be viewed in the larger context of relations between Congress and the courts. As one liberal member of the House Judiciary Committee told me, "I think the whole Inspector General notion is a poor idea. We need checks and balances, but the IG bill would upset the balance among the branches. Let judges police themselves." The IG legislation was never voted on by the full House, much less by the more lawyerly Senate. Thus the proposal died quickly after the House Judiciary Committee approved it, but not before the Republicans on the committee took one last parting shot at federal judges. As Frances Kahn Zemans reminds us, "With neither the power of the sword nor the power of the purse, the third branch has had an enduring vulnerability to attack" (1999, 625).

Threats of Impeachment of Federal Judges

In addition to court-stripping legislation and the proposed inspector general for the judiciary, the House Judiciary Committee has recently considered a variety of other attacks on the courts, even going so far as to initiate impeachment investigations and hold hearings on potential impeachments of federal judges (see Miller 2006). Under the U.S. impeachment process, first the House must vote articles of impeachment and then the Senate holds a trial to determine whether the judge or other impeached government official should be removed from office. Recall that the full House of Representatives actually impeached Presidents Andrew Johnson and Bill Clinton, but the Senate failed to remove these presidents from office. The House Judiciary Committee was close to bringing articles of impeachment against President Richard Nixon when he resigned from office. In each chamber it is the judiciary committee that initiates the congressional impeachment process.

Since the failed attempt to remove Justice Samuel Chase from the Supreme Court in 1803, impeachment of federal judges has almost never occurred because Congress objected to the decisions of the judge. Instead, federal judges have only been impeached for illegal or unethical behavior on the bench (see, e.g., Rehnquist 1992; and Volcansek 2001). Even though actual impeachments of federal judges have been extremely rare, the mere threat of impeachment has not been rare in American history. For example, angry members of Congress introduced two different proposals for the impeachment of Justice Douglas, the first in 1953, objecting to his willingness to stay the executions of Ethel and Julius Rosenberg, and the second in 1970, when then House minority leader Gerald Ford, among others, objected to his lifestyle (see Pacelle 2002, 96). Thus the threat of impeachment for federal judges remains real.

Recently, the attitude of some members of Congress regarding the propriety of impeaching judges merely because of disagreement with their decisions seems to have changed. For example, Justice at Stake, a group dedicated to protecting judicial independence, reports that there were fifty-eight impeachment threats against federal judges from 2002 to 2006 (Brandenburg and Kay 2007, 16–17). Concerned that threats of impeachment were being used to attempt to alter specific court decisions, in May 2005 almost two-thirds of the deans of U.S. law schools sent a letter to the leadership of both chambers of Congress opposing such actions. In part, the deans' letter stated, "It is irresponsible and harmful to our constitutional system and to the value of a judiciary that is independent, in fact and appearance, when prominent individuals and Members of Congress state or imply that judges may be impeached or otherwise punished because of their rulings" (Revesz et al. 2005, 2).

Others have also opposed the use of impeachment to change the direction of judicial decisions. As one Democratic member of the House Judiciary Committee told me, "Constitutional amendments and impeachment are meant to be extremely rare." Along the same lines, another Democrat on the committee said that "even threats of impeachment are rare. The thought of impeaching a judge because of their rulings is astonishing. Fortunately, cooler heads always prevail. Congress must be cautious with the use of this awesome power."

Many of the threats of impeachment come from legislators who support the agenda of the Religious Right. Many religious conservatives have called for the impeachment of judges who refused to follow their preferred ideological views. As early as 1997 former House majority leader Tom DeLay (R-TX) started calling for the impeachment of federal judges who handed down liberal activist decisions on issues such as affirmative action (see, e.g., Baum 2004). He would mention these threats throughout his years in Congress. Tom DeLay has long argued that Congress should take action against "judicial tyranny." DeLay reportedly said, "We can impeach judges who get drunk, so why not impeach those who get drunk with power?" (qtd. in Erbe and Shiner 1997).

Social conservative and Religious Right activists at a 2005 conference entitled "Remedies to Judicial Tyranny," organized by the Judeo-Christian Council for Constitutional Restoration, agreed that impeachment of federal judges was a valid way of gaining control of what they perceived to be the liberal activist federal courts. Michael P. Farris, chair of the Home School Legal Defense Association, stated at the conference, "If about 40 [federal judges] get impeached, suddenly a lot of these guys would be retiring" (qtd. in Milbank 2005). In addition to Congressman Tom DeLay, former Senator Rick Santorum (R-PA) and current U.S. Senator John Cornyn (R-TX) hinted that they would support using impeachment as a tool for influencing federal court decisions (see Marcus 2005). The conservative activist Phyllis Schlafly even called for the impeachment of the relatively conservative U.S. Supreme Court justice Anthony M. Kennedy because of his opinion for the Court forbidding the death penalty for juveniles in *Roper v. Simmons* (2005) (qtd. in Milbank 2005). Others have called for the impeachment of Justice Kennedy because of his habit of citing foreign law sources in his opinions (see, e.g., DeParle 2005; and Toobin 2007, 196–99). James Dobson, the founder of Focus on the Family, has called Justice Kennedy "the most dangerous man in America" (qtd. in Toobin 2007, 199). What is new is that the attitudes of the Religious Right toward the courts now play themselves out in the language and actions of the House Judiciary Committee.

Even politicians not usually associated with the Religious Right are echoing this movement's call for impeachment of federal judges who make decisions with which they disagree. For example, former Speaker of the House Newt Gingrich, at a conference on judicial independence held at Georgetown Law Center in September 2006, put it this way: "There are historical precedents for the nation to protect itself [from the courts], and that the legislative and executive branches . . . deserve equal respect from the court. And a court which asserts that it is supreme . . . and that there is judicial superiority is running I think both historically and legally a very, very dangerous track" (see "Fair and Independent Courts" 2006). Gingrich then implied that impeachment might be the proper tool for reigning in out-of-control courts.

In 2004 former Congressman Tom Feeney (R-FL), then a member of the House Judiciary Committee, called for the impeachment of federal judges who cited non-American or international precedents in their decisions (see Miller 2004, 66). Congressman Feeney has been quoted as saying, echoing the rhetoric of many Religious Right leaders, "Judicial independence does not equal judicial supremacy" (qtd. in Hulse and Kirkpatrick 2005). Former majority leader Tom DeLay agreed, and he often called for impeaching judges because he saw "a judiciary run amok" (qtd. in Hulse and Kirkpatrick 2005). Congressman Delay continued, "The failure is to a great degree Congress's. The response of the legislative branch has mostly been to complain. There is another way, . . . and that is to reassert our constitutional authority over the courts. . . . This era of constitutional cowardice must end" (qtd. in Hulse and Kirkpatrick 2005). Michael Schwartz, then chief of staff to Senator Tom Coburn (R-OK), agreed, saying, "I'm in favor of impeachment," even suggesting that "mass impeachment" of federal judges might be in order (qtd. in Hulse and Kirkpatrick 2005).

Some threats of impeachment from members of the House Judiciary Committee have caused great concern among federal judges. An example is the case of Chief Judge James M. Rosenbaum, of the U.S. District Court for Minnesota, and the aftermath of his testimony before a congressional committee in 2003 regarding the federal sentencing guidelines. Many federal judges feel that the threats of impeachment against Judge Rosenbaum have had a chilling effect on their work (see, e.g., Clemetson 2007). Judge Rosenbaum testified before the Crime Subcommittee of the House Judiciary Committee against a Republican-sponsored bill that would have overturned amendments to the federal sentencing guidelines authorizing shorter sentences for first-time drug defendants. Judge Rosenbaum, a Reagan appointee and former U.S. attorney, simply repeated criticisms of the sentencing guidelines for drug crimes that had often been voiced by prosecutors, defense attorneys, and even justices on the U.S. Supreme Court.

Conservatives on the House Judiciary Committee's subcommittee were so angered by Judge Rosenbaum's testimony that they tried to subpoena his records, eventually writing a twenty-page committee report critical of the judge that hinted that he might have committed perjury in his testimony before the subcommittee. Federal judges were uniformly outraged at the veiled threats of impeachment against Judge Rosenbaum. Whenever federal judges discuss the issue of judicial independence, this incident seems to come up. As one commentator characterized the situation, "The subcommittee, sensing a political opportunity, went after Judge Rosenbaum with a zeal once reserved for Cold War witch hunts. . . . This was not criticism of an individual judge's ruling but an attempt by two branches of government to use their official powers to muscle the third" (Wallance 2003).

Impeachment has been threatened against other federal judges as well. For example, the House Judiciary Committee held hearings in September 2006 on the potential impeachment of Federal District Judge Manuel L. Real (see Weinstein and Mendoza 2006). In another action, letters were sent from the House Judiciary Committee to Chief Judge Boyce F. Martin Jr., of the Sixth Circuit, in 2002 and 2003 investigating his role in panel assignments for certain affirmative-action cases in his circuit. No further actions were taken against these judges because the 109th Congress ended. Some members of Congress and congressional staff told me that they believed that these committee actions were clearly politically motivated, aimed at sending a clear message to liberal judges. Representative Zoe Lofgren (D-CA) has stated publicly that she found the impeachment hearings against Judge Real to be politically motivated. She tied the impeachment threats to legislative concerns over the perceived liberal activist decisions of the Ninth Circuit, which is a favorite focus of conservative ridicule because it is widely seen as the most liberal circuit court in the United States (see chapter 2). Congresswoman Lofgren said, "I believe we are here today because of the [Republican] majority's animosity toward the Ninth Circuit. For that I apologize" (qtd. in Weinstein and Mendoza 2006).

The actual impeachment of federal judges and their removal from the bench is extremely rare. For example, only two federal judges were impeached in the 1980s, both for allegedly committing federal crimes such as perjury and bribery. Nevertheless, the threats of impeachment have had a strong impact on federal judges, as many of them stated publicly and also told me privately. The mere threat of impeachment is an attempt to restrict the decisional and institutional independence of the federal courts in the United States. From the view of social conservatives, the relationship between Congress and the courts must be highly conflictual because the federal courts are currently usurping the proper role of the people and of the legislative branch. As one Republican member of the House Judiciary Committee told me in the early fall of 2006, "We need to increase impeachments of federal judges in order to reign in those judges who insist on legislating from the bench."

The three potential threats to judicial independence in the United

States discussed above—court-stripping legislation, a proposed inspector general for the federal judiciary, and threats of impeachment against federal judges because members of Congress disagreed with the ideological bent of their decisions—have been designed to increase congressional oversight of the federal judiciary as well as to influence the decisions of these judges. Such actions would clearly reduce the decisional and institutional independence of the federal judiciary. Even though the U.S. federal courts are seen as the most independent in the world, there are forces in U.S. politics that would like to restrict that independence. At the moment, it is conservatives who want to reign in what they see as a liberal activist federal judiciary. But it remains to be seen whether liberals will attempt to decrease the independence of the newly conservative federal courts. Liberal attacks on the conservative courts seem to be growing (see, e.g., Cohen 2007), but it is unclear whether that distrust of the courts will translate into institutional attacks on the federal courts.

SIX

The Need for Judicial Independence

If the Supreme Court and the other federal courts are to remain an important voice in the inter-institutional constitutional dialogue, judicial independence must be protected. It does not matter whether the threats to judicial independence come from the Right or from the Left. In the early twentieth century, most of the threats were from the Left; today most of them are from the Right. The courts have become a highly charged ideological and partisan issue in Congress, in part, as one employee of the judicial branch told me, "because the stakes are higher now as the role of the courts has grown in our society." The recent actions of the U.S. Congress, and especially the House Judiciary Committee under Republican control, may have threatened the independence of the judicial branch. This chapter explores in more detail why judicial independence is critical and how the current tense relationship between Congress and the federal courts may be eroding that foundational principle of the American system of government.

Currently we may be experiencing one of the periods of greatest conflict between Congress and the federal courts in the nation's history. Certainly the anti-court rhetoric of many members of Congress, especially Republicans on the House Judiciary Committee, has increased greatly both in tone and in frequency. What is more disturbing, in the last several years Congress has enacted a variety of court-stripping measures unheard of since Reconstruction. Congress has attempted to increase oversight of judicial decisions and of the other activities of judges, and the threats of impeachment against federal judges solely because of their decisions seem to be real. Federal judicial salaries have not kept pace with inflation; first-year lawyers in large law firms may earn more than federal judges. Thus there seems to be a general sense of disillusionment among federal judges. As an employee of the judicial branch told me, "It is harder to get the attention of the Congress today to even consider the needs of the federal courts."

Interest groups on the right are raising a great deal of money from their attacks on the courts, and it seems unlikely that these assaults will end in the near future. One academic commentator has observed, "Republicans in Washington are consequently exploiting the nexus between the elected and judicial branches to tap the energy of the religious right and its allies" (Taylor 2005, 95). Others have also noted that the relationship between Congress and the courts has changed. As one congressional staffer told me, "The natural institutional protections for the courts have broken down recently." Although most of the recent attacks on the courts have come from social conservatives, most of them affiliated with the Republican Party, it is not clear how long liberals and Democrats will continue to champion judicial independence as the federal courts become increasingly conservative in their decisions.

Journalists, judges, and politicians have all noted that the interactions between the courts and Congress are quite difficult at the moment. Recall that in my interviews conducted during the fall of 2006 various members of Congress and congressional staff described the relationship between Congress and the federal courts as "venomous," "hostile," "tense," "deteriorating," "contentious," "animosity," and "strained." Also recall that one liberal U.S. representative described the relationship as being "at an all time low."

Federal judges and employees in the judicial branch have certainly noticed that their relationship with the legislative branch is highly conflictual at the moment. In interviews, several employees of the judicial branch commented, "Recently there has been a holistic attack on the judiciary in general and on the lower federal courts in particular. The assaults on federal judges and the courts are more comprehensive today than in the past." These sentiments are also expressed by judges and even by justices on the Supreme Court. For example, in the summer of 2005, recently retired Justice Sandra Day O'Connor told a group of judges and lawyers gathered for the Ninth Circuit conference that "in all the years of my life, I don't think I've ever seen relations as strained as they are now between the judiciary and some Members of Congress" (qtd. in Kershaw 2005). And in an unprecedented appearance before the Senate Judiciary

Committee in February 2007, Justice Kennedy told the committee that "in more than three decades as a judge, I have not seen my colleagues in the judiciary so dispirited as at the present time" (A. Kennedy 2007).

Worrying that judicial independence may be eroding, various groups and individuals have recently come to the defense of the beleaguered federal courts. For example, the American Bar Association Web site states that "judicial independence exists for the benefit of the people, not for the personal benefit of the judge. . . . While there will always be interbranch conflict arising out of disputes over where to draw the line between judicial independence and judicial accountability, the key . . . is for each branch to act with mutual restraint, respect, and common purpose" (American Bar Association 2008).

Founded in 1998, the Constitution Project is a bipartisan group that seeks consensus on difficult constitutional issues. This group defines the importance of judicial independence as follows on its Web site: "From its beginning, our system of constitutional democracy has depended on the independence of the judiciary. Courts are able to protect the basic rights of individuals and decide cases fairly only when they are free to make decisions according to the law, without regard to political or public pressure. Similarly, the judiciary can maintain the checks and balances essential to preserving a healthy separation of powers only when judges are able to resist overreaching by the political branches" (Constitution Project 2008).

The Justice at Stake organization, which also sees its main purpose as protecting judicial independence, states on its Web site that "judicial independence means that judges are free to decide cases fairly and impartially, relying only on the facts and the law. It means that judges are protected from political pressure, legislative pressure, special interest pressure, media pressure, public pressure, financial pressure, or even personal pressure" (Justice at Stake Campaign 2008). Likewise, the American Judicature Society created its Center for Judicial Independence in 1997 "in response to an increase in unfair criticism and efforts to remove from the bench judges who have issued unpopular rulings" (American Judicature Society 2008).

Some judges worry that the current political climate has the potential to harm judicial independence and thus to harm America's constitutional democracy, because judicial independence is essential if the courts are to continue to participate as full and equal partners in the inter-institutional constitutional conversation. As Justice Kennedy stated in his testimony before Congress, "Separation of Powers instructs that each branch of our national government must have prerogatives that permit it to exercise its primary duties in a confident, forthright way, without over-reliance on the other branches. . . . Judicial independence is not conferred so judges can do as they please. Judicial independence is conferred so that judges can do as they must" (A. Kennedy 2007). Echoing this theme, Justice Ruth Bader Ginsburg has written, "Essential to the rule of law in any land is an independent judiciary, judges not under the thumb of other branches of Government, and therefore equipped to administer the law impartially" (2006, 1).

Others also assert that judicial independence is the key to the American system of constitutional democracy. As Gerald Rosenberg argues, "To laypeople, lawyers, and social scientists alike, judicial independence is central to American government" (1992, 369). Lawrence Friedman says of the need for judicial independence, "Independent judges are judges who are free from political interference as they go about their work. The government has no right to dictate their decisions" (2006, 141). Senator Patrick Leahy has taken up this theme, stating at a hearing on judicial security and independence that "in today's society, our independent Judiciary faces many and various types of threats. We have witnessed judges' physical security being threatened and their institutional security and independence under rhetorical attack by some affiliated with the political branches" (U.S. Senate 2007). And one Democratic member of the House Judiciary Committee told me, "The cornerstone of democracy is the independence of the judiciary. We cannot do anything to upset the balance of power among the branches. The courts are critical to democracy."

Interest Groups, Partisan Politics, and the Culture Wars

The context for the strained relationship between Congress and the federal courts is that interest groups vital to the Republican Party have adopted an anti-court stance. Thus the Republican agenda, at least in the House of Representatives when the Republicans held the majority in that chamber, included severe attacks on the courts. In other words, conservative Republican supporters of the Religious Right were simultaneously attacking the federal courts as too activist while spending a lot of time and money attempting to populate the courts with movement conservative judges (see, e.g., Greenburg 2007). They were also quietly using litigation sponsored by law firms associated with the Religious Right to change the direction of judicial rulings that they did not like. This three-pronged approach to reforming the courts found a clear voice on the House Judiciary Committee, many of whose members advocated a variety of methods to prevent federal judges from handing down what they perceived to be liberal activist decisions. Concerning this situation, one reporter observed that "congressional Republicans waged an intense and nonstop campaign against what they depicted as an overly activist federal judiciary" (N. Lewis 1997). These attacks against the courts have caused confusion among many federal judges. As one employee of the judicial branch explained, "Judges don't see themselves as taking a side in the culture wars."

Interest groups from the Religious Right are leading the charge against what they perceive to be out-of-control federal judges. These interest groups have managed to change the institutional culture on the House Judiciary Committee and perhaps in the House as a whole. As one lobbyist told me, "Recently the congressional culture has changed. The level of interest group activity is much higher now, and many of them in their appeals to their membership are getting lots and lots of money from attacking judges." When asked about the possibility that things could change in the future, this lobbyist responded, "These fundraising attacks on the courts are here to stay. These groups raise too much money from attacking the courts for it to stop any time soon." Another lobbyist told me that the conservative attacks against the courts would continue because "there is an increased focus on the courts as a political device. Groups use the attacks on the courts as a way to gin up their base. Attacks on federal judges are red meat for conservatives."

Many of my interviewees hinted that the culture in Congress has clearly changed regarding the relationship between Congress and the courts. Thomas Mann and Norman Ornstein (2006a, 2006b) have argued that the hyperpartisanship in Congress has led that institution to become "the Broken Branch." This hyperpartisanship has clearly affected the legislature's relationship with the courts. As one employee of the judicial branch told me, "There is so much fighting on the Hill today, and too much time spent on fundraising. Members don't work well together, and there is no mingling across party lines. There isn't even much socializing today among the members." Another change is that the media now seems to highlight judges as political decision makers. One employee of the judicial branch explained that "judges don't see themselves as partisans. But the media always identifies judges by party and their appointing president. This is new."

The traditions and norms in Congress that protected the courts from the most serious institutional attacks seem to have eroded recently. As one lobbyist told me, "There has been a shift in the discourse generally regarding the courts, and the tone has become so shrill." In budgetary terms, Congress has long seen the courts as just one more federal entity begging for money instead of treating the judiciary as an independent and coequal third branch of government. This notion that the courts are an ordinary player in the policymaking game and in the struggles among interest groups has led many politicians to feel that they can attack the courts as an institution without harming the traditional notion of separation of powers. Other factors are also at play. Since interest groups have spent so much time and money on judicial confirmation fights since the failed Bork nomination, many groups see no societal or institutional harm from attacking what they perceive to be overly political federal courts. As one employee of the federal courts told me, "The confirmation fights over Supreme Court justices have changed interest group behavior and their fundraising tactics."

The level of interest-group activity surrounding judicial nominations and confirmation struggles (see, e.g., Bell 2008) has affected the way that many members of Congress generally view the courts. Several lobbyists whom I interviewed said that they believe that the increased anti-court rhetoric has changed public perceptions of the courts. "The more fights the Right wins the more emboldened they become in their attacks on the courts." A liberal Democratic staffer in the House of Representatives agreed: "Conservatives have controlled the spin in the media on the courts, and we've got to change that."

Social conservatives thus remain highly skeptical that the federal courts will protect their interests without massive change among the federal judges. Thus anti-court and anti-judge proposals, including calls for impeachment of judges for ideological reasons, are quite common among social conservatives. As two conservative commentators have argued, "Raising the temperature of judicial politics is not a bad thing. By their actions, the judges have put themselves squarely in the political arena, and until they withdraw they are the proper subject of political battles. The goal of conservatives should be to provoke a constitutional crisis—or more accurately, to expose the one that judicial usurpation has already created" (George and Ponnuru 2000, 184). Social conservatives, including the Religious Right, are raising a lot of money and gathering a lot of support through their anti-court rhetoric and actions.

Will the new Democratic control of Congress make any difference in the relationship between Congress and the courts? Some argue that it will bring major changes in the interactions between Congress and the federal judiciary. One journalist summarized the differences between liberals and conservatives in their views of the courts in this way: "Reduced to the simplest terms, conservatives say judges should follow the law, and liberals say they should ensure that justice is done" (Savage 2008).

In almost all of my interviews with liberals, they came to the defense of the courts as institutions because they felt that the courts brought an important perspective to the inter-institutional constitutional conversation. Just as conservative groups are strident in their attacks on the courts, liberals are willing to discuss the courts in highly ideological and partisan terms. The following comments were typical. One Democratic member of Congress told me, "The right wingers in the House are so extreme today that they have created an abusive relationship between the courts and Congress now." Others were quick to criticize the anti-judge and anti-court rhetoric of the Right. Another Democratic member of Congress said, "I hate the term judicial activism. In today's discourse, the GOP doesn't apply the term activism to rulings they like. Judges merely interpret the law. Judges have an important role and purpose in our society, and we must respect the decision-making process of judges."

Liberal journalists have also come to the defense of the federal courts because they see the courts as the victims in the partisan culture wars. Concerned about all the anti-judge rhetoric and actions by Congress, a *New York Times* editorial observed, "One of the best ways Democratic and Republican leaders can set a new tone in Washington is by jettisoning the heated anti-judge posturing." The editorial went on to say that one benefit of the new Democratic control of Congress after the 2006 elections was that "the House is no longer led by Republicans who demonize judges for sport" (*New York Times* 2007a). Both a journalist and a professor, Jeffrey Rosen has even argued that the liberal position on many controversial issues reflects the needs and will of the majority in American society: "As the public sided with liberals rather than conservatives in the culture wars . . . so did the Court" (Rosen 2006, 3).

Thus liberal interest groups seem to see the federal courts as protectors of basic rights and freedoms. These positive feelings toward the courts are probably carry-overs from the 1950s, 1960s, and 1970s, when the courts expanded the protection of individual rights and issued other decisions so important to liberal groups. While the conservatives hated the Warren Court, the liberal groups continue to look to the courts to produce progressive change in America. "For a long time the courts have been the backstop of progressive causes," one lobbyist told me. "Liberals won't attack an institution that has done so much good for such a long time. The courts serve an important function in the system of government for liberals." "Both sides use their bully pulpit to criticize judicial opinions with which they disagree," said another lobbyist. "But the Left hasn't crossed the line yet to attack the courts as institutions or to use coercive measures that would ultimately harm judicial independence."

Another liberal theme was that liberals want to increase access to the courts because the courts are seen as the protectors of those in society who cannot protect themselves in the legislative or executive arenas. Many liberals used the phrase *access to justice* as shorthand for the notion that the courts should be available to protect the weak and less fortunate, much as they did when the Warren Court handed down *Brown v. Board of Education* and other liberal activist decisions. One Democratic staffer for a House Judiciary Committee member told me, "My boss opposes court-stripping measures because everyone deserves their day in court, regardless of class, culture, race, sex, or status." Another House Democratic staffer said, "Democrats focus on process issues and access to justice, while the Republicans focus on the outcomes of court rulings." One House Democratic staffer who formerly had worked as a lobbyist on legal issues put it more succinctly in January 2007: "The Republicans care most about the substance of court decisions, while the Democrats are more concerned about issues of access to justice." This theme was also picked up by a Republican House staffer, who told me, "There is a willingness among Republicans to intervene against court-created policies, but the Democrats are far less willing to interfere with the courts."

Liberal Democrats were quick to tell me that unlike their conservative counterparts, liberals would criticize specific court decisions without attacking the courts as institutions. The liberals painted themselves as the defenders of judicial independence, much as the conservatives had in the early twentieth century (see Ross 1994). "Liberal interest groups will not use the tactic of attacking judges," said one liberal member of Congress, "but instead will work hard to get better judges on the bench. The grass roots messages from the Right are sinister and cynical methods to attack the courts as institutions in an attempt to silence them." The theme that liberals would seek to change the direction of specific court decisions without harming the institutional role of the courts came up quite often in my interviews. For example, another liberal Democratic member of Congress told me, "Liberals won't attack the courts as institutions. We'll just find a way around specific court decisions we don't like." Thus liberals were not shy about attempting to change judicial rulings with which they disagreed, and they saw this attempt as legitimate; however, they viewed institutional attacks on the courts as illegitimate. "For example, the latest late term abortion decision from the Supreme Court is a poke in the eye of Congress," a liberal member of the House Judiciary Committee told me. "We're going to have to take legislative action to fix that one." Or as one Democratic member of Congress stated bluntly, "We like activist judges when we agree with them."

Other liberals hinted that their voting base still has a great deal of respect for the courts in general and for the U.S. Supreme Court in particular. These liberals also stated that frontal attacks on the courts would offend their voting base for reasons of style as much as substance. Thus one Democratic member of Congress complained that the Republicans have a long history of using personal attacks in their political campaigns, including personal attacks on federal judges, while the Democrats engage in a more policy-oriented debate. This member cited a *New York Times* article stating that the Republicans were preparing a "wave of negative advertisements against Democratic candidates" in the 2006 midterm elections, while the Democrats "intended to tie Republican incumbents to an unpopular Congress" (Nagourney 2006). This member concluded, "Democrats won't attack the courts directly because of our reformist and good government backgrounds."

Many liberals seemed quite sincere when they told me that the courts were key players in the inter-institutional dialogue. These members seemed to believe that protecting the courts was good public policy (see Fenno 1973) and the main reason they had run for Congress in the first place. For example, a Democratic member of the House Judiciary Committee told me, "Mutual respect and independence between the courts and Congress is what is needed in our relationship." Along these same lines, another Democratic member of the committee told me, "There should be deference from Congress to the courts. Congress can test the policy and limits of court opinions, but courts have a key role to play in our system of government." A Democratic Senate staffer complained, "It's such a shame that the natural institutional protections for the courts have broken down." Summarizing many of interviewees' comments, a staffer for a liberal member of the House said, "My boss just trusts courts and judges to do the right thing."

Some of the liberals whom I interviewed claimed that the liberal approach to the courts does not lend itself to easy explanations and bumper-sticker politics, again drawing clear distinctions between themselves and their social conservative colleagues. Two lobbyists told me that they agreed with many academics that the federal courts were practicing both liberal and conservative judicial activism. The problem for them was that it was easier rhetorically to attack liberal activism than to attack conservative judicial activism: "It is easier to demonize liberal activist judges than it is to explain the impact of Commerce Clause cases and conservative judicial activism," they said. "Understanding conservative judicial activism requires understanding complex legal concepts, while it is easy to defend the Pledge of Allegiance against attack from liberal judicial activists. The Right diverts the focus from the legal reasoning of the courts to hot button social and political issues."

Protecting judicial independence is difficult for liberals. As one lobbyist stated, "Liberal groups approach the courts carefully. Our more nuanced rhetoric makes it harder to rally the troops around the cause, especially a cause so difficult to explain as the need for judicial independence." Liberals also worry that the anti-court rhetoric from social conservatives makes their job much harder. "The champions of the courts as an institution are the best allies of the judiciary," another lobbyist noted, "but we worry about being labeled as promoters of judicial activism." The payoffs for liberal groups who defend judicial independence are not always clear. Thus it seems unlikely that the liberals in Congress saw themselves as defending the courts purely for reelection purposes. As still another lobbyist put it, "Protecting checks and balances doesn't get votes or dollars."

Given these difficulties, others are less sure that the relationship between Congress and the courts will improve any time soon, even with a more liberal Congress in place. A former judicial-branch employee told me, "I don't think the relationship between Congress and the courts will improve much after the 2006 midterm elections. The Democrats will just raise different issues." Some argue that the tension between Congress and the courts is inevitable and will continue long into the future. "Politicians running for re-election will always have issues with life termed federal judges because our decision-making approaches are so different," said one Democratic member of Congress. Another blamed Congress for the increased tensions with the federal courts: "Congress has been ducking the most difficult issues recently and forcing them into the courts. Then we blame the courts when they make a decision we don't like."

Liberals will certainly focus on different issues than the conservatives have when thinking about the courts, and many liberals are starting to raise questions about combating conservative judicial activism (see, e.g., Greenhouse 2008b). For example, in their confirmation hearings Senator Arlen Specter (R-PA) asked both Chief Justice John Roberts and Justice Samuel Alito about their views on conservative judicial activism. Liberals in Congress quickly held hearings to denounce the Supreme Court's decision in *Ledbetter v. Goodyear Tire and Rubber* (2007), in which the Supreme Court ruled 5-4 that tight time limits on filing sex-discrimination cases must be followed. As one journalist described the congressional reaction, "The decision led to Congressional hearings during which the Court was denounced as out of touch with the reality of women's working lives" (Greenhouse 2008b). Liberals in Congress immediately attempted, unsuccessfully, to overturn the Supreme Court's decision in this statutory-interpretation case.

Others are also raising the issue of conservative judicial activism. In a hearing held when the Republicans controlled Congress on the use of international sources of law in U.S federal courts, Congressman Jerrold Nadler (D-NY) said that the Subcommittee on the Constitution "has never taken the time to look into the Court's long and worrisome record of using the 11th Amendment contrary to its intent, limiting the reach of the commerce clause in undercutting Congress' powers to enforce the 14th Amendment in ways that have undercut our civil rights laws" (House Committee on the Judiciary 2005a, 3). Nadler was clearly expressing his unhappiness with the conservative judicial activism of the Rehnquist Court. It is unclear, however, whether he would ever take action to silence the courts in the inter-institutional constitutional dialogue.

There are other hints that liberals will continue to approach the courts with a cautious eye, especially federal courts that are now dominated by Federalist Society judges and are growing ever more conservative in their decisions. U.S. Senator Charles Schumer (D-NY), one of the more liberal members of the Senate, wrote a rather lengthy piece in the *Harvard Law and Policy Review* entitled "Under Attack: Congressional Power in the Twenty-first Century." In the piece, Senator Schumer strongly criticizes executive-branch encroachments on congressional power, as well as judicial limits on congressional decisions in the New Federalism line of opinions handed down by the U.S. Supreme Court starting with *United States v. Lopez* (1995). As Senator Schumer argued, "The relationship between Congress and the Court changed dramatically under Chief Justice William H. Rehnquist, particularly when Justice Clarence Thomas was elevated to the Supreme Court. . . . Perhaps most disturbingly, the Court made these changes with the rationale that it was better suited than Congress to make determinations about the extent of Congress's policymaking ability under the Constitution" (Schumer 2007, 26).

Thus Senator Schumer was quite critical of the Court's line of federalism decisions. He concluded with a stern warning against further limits on congressional power from the Supreme Court: "As Congress struggles to maintain its independence from the Executive, it is critical that we do not forget to vigilantly protect our legislative prerogatives from encroachment by the Judiciary" (Schumer 2007, 35). However, Schumer claimed that unlike the conservatives, he would not attack the courts as an institution. Instead, he favored having the Senate more closely scrutinize judicial nominees. In other words, he was calling for the rejection of conservative activist judges for ideological reasons, much as social conservatives have called for the rejection of liberal activist judicial appointees.

Thus the liberal Senator Schumer seemed to stop short of calling for institutional attacks on the conservative judiciary, but he did see Congress as having a legitimate role in shaping the ideological direction of judicial decisions. Time will tell whether liberals continue to be so patient with increasingly activist conservative judicial decisions.

Comparisons with Other Historical Eras

As discussed in chapter 1, there have always been periods of intense conflict between the federal courts and the other branches of government in the United States. "It is an old story: the courts get in the way and make politicians angry," one journalist noted slyly (Greenhouse 1996, 5). Most of these conflicts have stayed at the rhetorical level, and Congress and/or the president have rarely taken concrete steps to reign in the judicial branch. Instead, presidents and more recently Congress have used the judicial confirmation process to attempt to change the direction of judicial rulings. As much as the Jeffersonians mistrusted the Federalist-dominated Supreme Court, they took no real action to lessen its independent voice in the inter-institutional constitutional conversation. Presidents Jackson and Lincoln ignored the Supreme Court and refused to implement its rulings, but both presidents understood that they needed an independent judiciary to help them with other parts of their political agendas. The Radical Republicans after the Civil War took the most obvious actions to reduce the independence of the Supreme Court and to prevent it from declaring Reconstruction unconstitutional, through passage of court-stripping legislation and manipulation of the number of justices on the Court. But even they refrained from limiting the independence of the lower federal courts, because they needed their assistance in other political matters.

The rhetorical attacks against the courts from liberals in the period 1890–1937 did not lead to any real anti-court actions, and it is noteworthy that Congress steadfastly refused to approve FDR's Court-Packing Plan. The American people saw criticism of specific court decisions and even of the courts as a whole as proper and expected political discourse, but they rejected as illegitimate more serious institutional attacks that would harm judicial independence. Presidents and Congress could influence the courts through the nomination and confirmation processes, but they could not attack the foundation of the courts as institutions. Thus William Ross concluded that throughout American history, "critics of the federal courts have attempted to use every conceivable means—some of highly questionable constitutionality—to curtail the power of the courts. . . . [However], critics of the courts have tended to accept the reality of judicial power and to work within the system [instead] by influencing the nomination and confirmation processes" (Ross 1994, 9).

Some argue that the courts themselves have recognized the threats from Congress and have backed down from the most difficult fights. Certainly during Reconstruction the Supreme Court quickly reversed its Legal Tender decisions in part due to strong opposition from Congress, and the Supreme Court backed away from limiting congressional investigations during the McCarthy era in response to enormous pressures from Congress. But the Supreme Court seemed quite willing to reduce congressional prerogatives in its *Boerne* and *Dickerson* decisions.

Charles Geyh has argued that the courts have promoted the congressional norm of protecting customary judicial independence by refraining from attacking too many congressional prerogatives over the nation's history. As Geyh notes, "The tradition of restraint [from the judiciary] serves to establish a reservoir of goodwill that preserves independence norms and thereby enables the Court to uphold the law by making the occasional, countermajoritarian decision without fear of retaliation" (2006, 244). "Perpetuation of norms that guard against 'inappropriate' or 'improper' congressional intrusions upon the judiciary's autonomy," writes Geyh, "has been aided by the courts' timely sensitivity and deference to Congress and the political process, which has made such intrusions largely unnecessary" (2006, 19). Likewise, Keith Whittington (2005), among others, has argued that the mere threat of congressional attack on the courts has caused judges to alter their judicial behavior. It does not seem likely, however, that the present Supreme Court will back down from fights with Congress or with the president any time soon.

The conventional wisdom is that the courts were protected from attack by a public reverence for their decisions. Evidence for this reverence is found in the constitutional prohibitions on reducing federal judicial salaries and in their life terms. Lawrence Friedman, however, argues that judicial independence goes beyond life tenure and salary protections, saying that American culture in general protects the courts from the most severe attacks against them: "Actually, independence is much more than a matter of structure. Culture, perhaps, play an even more important role. Judging is an honorable profession. . . . Judges have about them an aura of dignity and fairness" (2006, 147).

Many scholars argue that institutional norms and traditions are very important in the relationship between Congress and the courts (see, e.g., L. Friedman 2006). For example, John Drobak writes that "norms guide human conduct and social interaction as much as formal legal rules. . . . The prevailing views of a society act as a constraint on both judge-made and statutory law because social norms influence judges and legislators alike" (2006, 1). Other scholars have noted that the American people consider institutional attacks against the courts to be constitutionally improper. Because the voters find such institutional attacks objectionable, Congress throughout its history has generally refused to enact such restrictions on the judiciary, even in periods when the anti-judge and anti-court rhetoric has been most intense. As Geyh observed, "To the extent that Congress has, as a matter of 'constitutional custom', declined to impeach unpopular judges, to impose litmus tests on judicial nominees, or to court pack or jurisdiction strip because it has long regarded such practices as antithetical to Article III independence, the stature and stability of Congress's self-restraint is logically enhanced. Although Congress remains free to overlook or override its customs and precedents, decisions to do so must first overcome the presumption that such action is contrary to the Constitution as Congress has traditionally construed it" (2002, 163; see also Geyh 2006, 10–14).

What is different today about the relationship between Congress and the federal courts? One obvious difference between the current anti-court climate in Congress and the climate in earlier periods when Congress and/or the president severely criticized the courts is that for the first time since Reconstruction, Congress has actually enacted court-stripping measures, and threats to impeach federal judges because of their decisions have seemed real. What makes the current tense interactions between Congress and the federal courts even more striking is that social conservatives in a Republican-controlled Congress and a conservative Republican president were attacking a federal judiciary also controlled by Republican appointees and members of the legally conservative Federalist Society. Previously, presidents and Congress had taken aim at federal courts controlled by the other party, but during the period focused on in this study, Republicans controlled all of the apparatus of government. Thus Republicans were attacking their own.

Some have claimed that the recent attacks on the courts from social conservatives are very similar to the complaints liberals made before and during both Roosevelt presidencies. The difference is that, except during Reconstruction, Congress always stopped short of taking direct action that would harm the independence of the judiciary. The House of Representatives impeached Justice Samuel Chase in 1803, but the Senate refused to remove him from office. While Andrew Jackson and Abraham Lincoln refused to implement decisions of the Supreme Court justices, they took no steps to curtail the legitimacy of the judiciary. Populists, Progressives, and labor-union supporters rejected the pro–big business decisions of the Supreme Court during the years 1890–1937, but they took no actions to silence the courts in the inter-institutional dialogue.

Countless academic studies have examined why the conservative attacks on the Warren Court led to no concrete actions to reduce the power of the judiciary. The difference today is that the Religious Right and other social conservatives have never really accepted the legitimacy of legal reasoning and judicial decision making, and like-minded politicians are taking concrete steps to reduce the voice of the courts in the inter-institutional constitutional dialogue.

There are many reasons why the courts must remain an independent voice in the constitutional conversation. Throughout the nation's history, lawyers, academics, and others have come to the defense of beleaguered judges and courts that were unable to protect themselves from political assault. It did not matter whether these attacks came from the Right or the Left. Today the Right is attacking the federal courts, but in the future the Left may take up the fight against an increasingly conservative federal judiciary. It is important that the courts remain a key player in the inter-institutional constitutional conversation. The courts bring a unique perspective to that dialogue, and the other two branches must always act to protect the judiciary's unique voice.

The Courts as Umpires

The U.S. notion of separation of powers really means that interdependent but separate institutions of government share duties, responsibilities, and powers. The idea of checks and balances is key to the separation of powers in America. In the United States there is a continuous constitutional dialogue among the governmental institutions about how the Constitution and other sources of law will shape the future of American society. The power of judicial review is an important component of this institutional conversation, because it is clearly a form of policymaking. As Cornell Clayton and J. Mitchell Pickerill describe it, "Rather than a mechanism for protecting minorities or the disempowered, judicial review is conceptualized as an institutional instrument for policymaking like others in the legislative or administrative process. From an empirical standpoint, judicial review is used by political actors, both powerful and weak, on all sides of policy issues, to advance policy agendas" (Clayton and Pickerill 2006, 1391).

The courts are key voices in this constitutional conversation. Although the federal courts and especially the Supreme Court are clearly political bodies, with their membership chosen through political selection processes (see, e.g., Comiskey 2008), they are nonetheless different from the elected branches because their decisions must be based on both politics and legal reasoning. The appellate courts must explain to the public and to other judges how their decisions are based on the law and legal reasoning in a way that the more political branches do not. In addition to their reliance on legal analysis, the courts also serve as umpires or referees in the struggles between other political actors. Robert Kagan (2001, 2004) has labeled this phenomenon, which is key to understanding the policymaking process in the United States, "adversarial legalism."

There are times in the constitutional conversation among the institutions of government and other political actors that all three branches of the federal government will be in agreement, as the regime-politics movement among political scientists and law professors has attempted to show (see, e.g., Klarman 1997; Gillman 2004; and Clayton and Pickerill 2006). Judicial deference to federal agencies' interpretations of statutory language is one such example (see, e.g., Melnick 1994, 2004). Thus, at time the courts support the needs of the political parties, interest groups, or the governmental institutions in the political regime and especially its governing coalition (see, e.g., Dahl 1957; Gillman 2004; and Keck 2007b). The courts' power of judicial review does not upset the balance in the inter-institutional constitutional conversation, but it does alter the nature of the dialogue. Using a regime-politics approach, Mark Graber defines the benefits of judicial review in this way:

> Adjudication is one of many means politicians and political movements employ when seeking to make their constitutional visions the law of the land. Elected officials provide vital political foundations for judicial power by creating constitutional courts, vesting those courts with jurisdiction over constitutional questions, staffing those courts with judges prone to exercising judicial power, assisting or initiating litigation aimed at having those courts declare laws unconstitutional, and passing legislation that encourages justices to make public policy in the guise of statutory or constitutional interpretation. Judicial review does not serve to thwart or legitimate popular majorities; rather that practice alters the balance of power between the numerous political movements that struggle for power in a pluralist democracy. (Graber 2005, 425)

There are times, however, as Graber hints, when Congress and the president disagree on their institutional prerogatives, and the courts must step in to settle that dispute. The Watergate-era Supreme Court decision in *United States v. Nixon* (1974) comes to mind. In that case, the Supreme Court ruled that criminal prosecutors and the U.S. Congress had the right to hear the so-called Watergate tapes, tapes illegally made by President Nixon of every conversation that occurred in the Oval Office. That case could be seen as a clear institutional fight between Congress and the president over who controlled access to the tapes. Of course, one direct result of the Supreme Court's decision in *United States v. Nixon* was the resignation of President Nixon. A more recent example concerns the potential legal effects of presidential signing statements, added by the president when he or she signs legislation into law (see, e.g., Devins 2007; Fisher 2007; and Krent 2007). Will the Supreme Court settle future disputes between Congress and the president regarding these presidential signing statements?

There are times when the legislative and executive branches are united in their policy position but courts bring a different institutional perspective to the question (see, e.g., Keck 2007a). As Clayton and Pickerill note, "Judges may be expected to deviate further from the specific policy preferences of the dominant political coalition than many other policymakers because of the unique institutional feature of courts" (2006, 1393). Along these lines, Rosen has even argued that "unelected Supreme Court justices sometimes express the views of popular majorities more faithfully than the people's elected representatives" (2006, 4). For instance, who should have the last word on the legal rights of detainees at Guantanamo Bay? President George W. Bush has argued that he should determine the legal rights of these detainees, and in the Military Commissions Act of 2006 the then majority in Congress agreed with him. The Supreme Court, however, has consistently ruled that there are clear limits on presidential power in this area. In response, Congress stripped the federal courts of their ability to hear such cases. The majority in Congress appeared ready to repeal these court-stripping provisions but was unable to do so because of filibusters in the Senate. Thus the majority in Congress hoped that the Supreme Court would strike down these court-stripping measures. This is a clear example of the courts bringing a different legal and institutional perspective to the constitutional conversation. It is important that the courts remain independent in order to be able to protect this unique judicial voice.

The notion of the courts as umpires in the struggles between and among various political actors came up many times in the interviews I conducted. Even though the Supreme Court was dominated by Republican appointees, many of the Democrats interviewed looked to the Court to serve as a check on the Republican majority in Congress and on the Republican president. Many expressed worry that there had been a real shift in the balance of power and that the notion of separation of powers itself was under attack. A Democratic member of Congress told me, "The separation of powers is currently out of whack." Discussions about the need to protect the separation of powers do not score many political points for the politicians making those arguments.

Echoing this concern that the courts are the only ones able to check undue executive power, another Democratic member of Congress said, "The balance of power is out of balance. The executive is getting too powerful at the moment, and the courts are under attack if they try to reign in that excessive Executive power." Claiming that the courts are important referees in the constitutional dialogue, a lobbyist complained, "Congress doesn't pay enough attention to issues of constitutionality and to how their actions harm the esteem of the judiciary."

There are practical reasons for legislators to support judicial independence. One such reason is that an independent judiciary can bolster legislative goals in the long run (see, e.g., Gillman 2002). As Ross notes about the failure of anti-court measures in the late nineteenth and early twentieth century, "Despite all of their protestations about the dangers of 'judicial oligarchy', many progressives and union leaders recognized that a powerful judiciary could serve their interests. By helping to make government more orderly, stable and rational, the judiciary helped to implement fundamental progressive goals" (1994, 320). Seeing judicial independence as the best way to fight Republican domination, many liberals whom I interviewed were pinning their hopes on an assertive judiciary. As one Democratic staffer told me, "There is a concern around here that the Executive has too much power. The courts and Congress must work together to reign in the President's abuse of his powers. The courts are the liberals' only hope against one party government."

Judicial independence is important so that the Supreme Court and the other federal courts will be able to settle disputes between Congress and the president. As one interviewee told me, "The courts need to be a neutral umpire between Congress and the President. But in the fight between Congress and the courts, there is no neutral third party to protect the courts' interests." Thus the bar, academics, and others must defend the courts against attacks, because they cannot always defend themselves. It may also be in the best interests of Congress to defend an independent judiciary's voice in the inter-institutional constitutional conversation. "Congress has the duty to act as a balance between the president and the courts," said one Democratic staffer in the House.

Some have argued that congressional attacks against the courts are counterproductive. As Patricia Wald and Neil Kinkopf have argued, "Congress needs independent judges to preserve congressional power and to enforce demands for information from a recalcitrant executive. . . . Congress wants and deserves independent judges who will umpire constitutional disputes in a fair and sensitive manner, will interpret laws as Congress passed them, and will, as a last resort, aid Congress in asserting its constitutional prerogatives" (2007, 70–71).

The Courts as Protectors of Individual and Fundamental Rights

Another reason to guard against restrictions on judicial power is that independent courts are necessary to protect human rights and other individual rights against what John Stuart Mill termed the "tyranny of the majority." In other words, courts can at times serve a counter-majoritarian function in a rights-based constitutional democracy. As Justice Stephen Breyer of the U.S. Supreme Court and Robert Badinter, a former judge and president of France's Conseil Constitutionnel, remind us, "Today almost all Western democracies have come to believe that independent judiciaries can help to protect fundamental human rights through judicial interpretation and application of written documents containing guarantees of individual freedom" (Badinter and Breyer 2004, 3). And as the Supreme Court said in *West Virginia State Board of Education v. Barnette* (1943), "The very purpose of a Bill of Rights was to withdraw certain subjects from the vicissitudes of political controversy, to place them beyond the reach of majorities and officials and to establish them as legal principles to be applied by the courts. One's right to life, liberty, and property, to free speech, a free press, freedom of worship and assembly, and other fundamental rights may not be submitted to vote; they depend on the outcome of no elections" (319 U.S. 624, 638–39). Jeffrey Rosen cites a recent poll stating that 73 percent of the American public believes that "the role of the courts is to protect minorities from the tyranny of the majority and that judges, as a result, should be shielded from outside pressures" (2006, xi–xii).

This counter-majoritarian theme is quite familiar to those who look fondly on the Warren Court's protection of individual and minority rights. Thus judicial independence and the power of judicial review allow courts in the United States to "stand as the ultimate guardians of our fundamental rights" (Horsky 1958, 1111). This theme was also prevalent in the interviews I conducted. As one lobbyist told me, "Issues facing the courts should not be subject to majoritarian rules." Liberals, of course, were quick to mention this anti-majoritarian role of the courts. A staffer for a liberal member of Congress put it this way: "The Constitution is fundamental for Americans. The Democrats want to avoid discussing certain issues because we saw the Republicans limit civil liberties through the actions of the House Judiciary Committee." The fact that the courts could serve as a counter-majoritarian protector of individual rights was one reason why none of the court-curbing proposals of the early twentieth century ever passed. As Ross concludes, "Many Americans cherished the courts as bulwarks of personal liberties and property rights" (1994, 320).

It is not difficult to think of Supreme Court decisions that seem counter-majoritarian in nature and serve to protect individual rights and freedoms. Most would immediately cite *Brown v. Board of Education* (1954), although some recent scholarship has questioned the anti-majoritarian nature of that decision (see, e.g., Klarman 2004). The Court's privacy decisions, such as *Griswold v. Connecticut* (1965), in which the Court struck down as unconstitutional a state statute prohibiting the use of contraceptives, is clearly a statement of fundamental rights and freedoms. It is also hard to see the Court's flag-burning decisions as anything but anti-majoritarian, especially given the intense pressure in Congress to pass a constitutional amendment to overturn the decisions. In fact, Thomas Keck argues that most of the modern free-speech rulings from the Supreme Court "are best understood as the product of the divergent institutional missions of the Court and Congress, with the legislators acting to promote popular public policy demands . . . and the justices acting to defend inherited jurisprudential traditions" (Keck 2007b, 532; see also Keck 2007a).

Recent controversial decisions such as *Lawrence v. Texas* (2003), in which the Court declared homosexual antisodomy laws to be unconstitutional, seem to be quite anti-majoritarian in nature. Although some academic literature tries to portray this decision as falling squarely within the policy preferences of the governing elites (see, e.g., Balkin 2004, 1554; B. Friedman 2004, 1301; Tushnet 2006a, 156; and Klarman 2005, 443), it is hard to imagine such a progressive outcome coming from the U.S. Congress or from most state legislatures. Thus it seems highly unlikely that the victors in these cases could have prevailed in the legislative or executive branches.

While the general public and political elites may eventually come to see these decisions as reasonable protections of individual rights and freedoms, it seems that the Court led public and elite opinion to these conclusions rather than the other way around. It seems that when the Supreme Court acts to protect fundamental and individual rights, it is often leading public opinion rather than following it and/or the views of the elites in the political regime.

Will liberals always see the courts as the defenders of individual rights? Some argue that in the future liberals and Democrats might not protect the courts in the same way that they have protected them recently. As the federal courts grow progressively more conservative and issue increasingly conservative activist decisions, will the Left move to restrict judicial power? As Geyh argues, "Liberals have long regarded the federal courts as countermajoritarian champions for the rights and liberties of the politically frail. That view is seemingly contradicted by the Rehnquist Court's recent campaign that has overturned legislation protecting the rights of groups that liberals hold dear. Insofar as those decisions disillusion an independent judiciary's most reliable defenders by convincing them that the Court is less interested in following the law (as embodied in sixty years of precedent) than in implementing a conservative political agenda, the long-term prospects for customary independence become uncertain" (2006, 245).

Legal Reasoning and the Courts

A final reason that a independent judiciary brings a different perspective to the inter-institutional constitutional conversation is that appellate judges must explain their decisions using legal reasoning and legal analysis (see, e.g., Sunstein 1998; Baum 2004, 1; and Carter and Burke 2004). While law professors have often stressed legal reasoning in writings (see Graber 2002; and Keck 2007b), political scientists have often downplayed this important aspect of the judiciary (see, e.g., Richards and Kritzer 2002). My point is not that judges, especially Supreme Court justices, rely only on legal reasoning and analysis in their decision making; clearly, courts and judges are political institutions in the American system of government. Rather, the key idea is that an individual will almost certainly make different decisions in his or her role as a judge than he or she would as a legislator or an executive-branch official. As noted in the introduction, various Supreme Court justices have said that they felt bound by the law and would make different policy choices if they were elected officials.

Some political-science work in the regime-politics mode has tended to downplay the importance of legal reasoning in judicial decision making. As Keck argued, "From Dahl forward, the chief weakness in the regime politics literature has been a tendency to overstate the influence of external political pressure in a way that implies that the justices' actual decisions were inevitable and neglects the possibility of relatively independent institutional action by the Court" (2007b, 513).

This notion of legal reasoning and the explanation of decisions through legal analysis is what makes the institutional judicial voice in the constitutional conversation so different from the voice of the purely political branches. Only the courts bring this legal reasoning component to the policymaking process. Mark Richards and Herbert Kritzer label this form of judicial decision making a "jurisprudential regime." Recall the conclusion of these scholars quoted earlier in this work: "The Supreme Court is not simply a small legislature. Law matters in Supreme Court decision making in ways that are specifically jurisprudential" (Richards and Kritzer 2002, 315). Thus judges make decisions based on the law.

This theme of the courts making their decisions based on matters of law came up often in my interviews. Many used the term *legal ideology* to explain the unique decision-making style of the courts. A Democratic member of Congress put it this way: "The conservatives don't understand the courts and the legal ideology of the courts very well. They don't really know the impact of the opinions of the courts and they don't bother to try to understand judicial rulings. They just attack the courts. Lawyers must stand up for the courts when they can't stand up for themselves." Some drew parallels between judicial rulings based on law and the need of the courts to champion individual rights. As a lobbyist told me, "Judicial decisions should be apolitical and anti-majoritarian, and thus the courts have to be protected from partisan politics."

Others mentioned that while legal reasoning is a unique purview of the courts, the political debate often draws attention away from the legal basis for a court decision. "The Right diverts focus from legal reasoning to the hot button issues important to their base," one lobbyist said. Another interviewee noted that the rhetorical attacks on the federal courts were an effort to undermine the legitimacy of the judiciary. As another lobbyist told me, "The Right claims that *Marbury* was wrongly decided and that the courts shouldn't have the power of judicial review. This is an extremely cynical view, and it's just their only response to the fact that there is a lack of legal basis for the Right's arguments." Some stressed the legal nature of judicial decision making as an important component of the American system of government. Another Democratic member of Congress said, "Conservatives don't understand the courts and the legal ideology of the courts. They just don't bother to understand court rulings based on the law and not on politics."

Many worry that the courts cannot adequately defend themselves against congressional assaults because judges will not engage in direct political confrontation. As one interviewee put it, "Today judges have become caricatures. The judiciary is defenseless to protect itself against these attacks." As one lobbyist told me, "Judges are restricted in their communication by ethical concerns, and they can't really defend themselves without crossing that ethical line." Again stressing the legal-reasoning side of what judges do, one lobbyist stated the view of several lobbyists that "protecting the day to day work of judges just isn't sexy. The more nuanced rhetoric from judges and lawyers makes it hard to rally the troops around the cause. The Right can attack the monolith of an unelected judiciary without having to worry about nuance or subtleties."

Finally, interviewees stressed the need to educate the American people about the importance of legal reasoning and its effects on judicial decision making. For example, some members of Congress took exception to the notion that federal judges are too activist today. A Democratic member of Congress told me, "The term activism doesn't seem to apply to the rulings the GOP likes. There is a myth of judicial activism out there. In reality, federal judges just interpret the law like someone trained in the law should. We must respect the decision-making processes of judges." Others also highlighted the need for new language in the political dialogue to describe the work of the courts. One Democratic staffer on the Senate Judiciary Committee said that "liberals cling to the lingering notion that law and politics are separate. There is fear that the conservatives have captured the discourse in this country on the courts. We need to develop progressive ways of talking about courts and legal reasoning."

The Courts as an Independent Voice in the Inter-Institutional Constitutional Dialogue

Preserving judicial independence is crucial to maintaining the important contributions that the courts can and do make in the inter-institutional constitutional dialogue. The courts must be protected from assaults from both the Left and the Right. Keck concludes, "The active use of judicial review does not seem hard to justify. After all, it represents a longstanding practice, consistent with original understandings of the constitutional order, and widely supported by mass publics and political elites alike" (2007b, 540).

The courts' active use of their powers of judicial review benefits American society in many ways. Judicial independence allows the courts to serve as referees in the struggles between other political actors. It provides a mechanism for protecting fundamental and individual rights, which probably would not be carried out by the political branches alone. And most important, the courts bring the essential voice of legal reasoning and legal analysis to the constitutional dialogue. While it is true that the courts have a political component to their decision-making process, nonetheless it is crucial to remember that the judiciary is the only institutional actor that uses legal reasoning and legal analysis as part of its decision-making process. H. W. Perry and Lucas Powe (2004) have argued that although the constitutional debate has been polarized along partisan lines for many years, the Supreme Court has tried to voice a "third way" alternative in its contributions to the institutional dialogue. This third way may be termed the *legal ideology*. The courts also bring their own institutional needs to the inter-institutional conversation, of course, but they also serve as crucial arbiters of the rule of law in America's constitutional democracy.

Will Congress and the president, who throughout the nation's history have criticized the courts and specific court decisions, come to the realization that the courts must be protected in the inter-institutional dialogue? The American people have accepted the courts' actions. They also consider it legitimate for the executive and legislative branches to attempt to change the direction of judicial decisions by putting like-minded jurists on the bench through careful attention to the judicial nomination and confirmation processes.

Until very recently, however, the American people clearly rejected attempts to weaken the courts as institutions. Direct assaults on judicial independence have been quite rare in American history. There has always been a line that Congress and the president dared not cross in their interactions with the courts. The relationship between Congress and the courts has grown more confrontational recently; it remains to be seen whether the American people will force the legislative and executive branches to reverse their attempts to weaken the courts as an institution. As former senator Barry Goldwater said, "The frontal assault on the independence of the federal courts is a dangerous blow to the foundations of a free society" (qtd. in Greenhouse 1996, 5).

The relationship between Congress and the courts remains one of a permanent conversation or an inter-institutional constitutional dialogue. At times the conversation is pleasant; at other times the interactions between Congress and the courts are fraught with tension and mutual suspicion. At present the dialogue between Congress and the courts seems to have begun to break down, with each institution trying to force the other to change its institutional perspective, its institutional culture, and its institutional will. Social conservatives in Congress and the interest groups that support them want to change the way that courts and judges approach the decision-making process. Liberals seem to want to protect the independence of the courts, but it is unclear how long liberals can support an increasingly conservative activist federal judiciary. Clearly, judicial independence is crucial if the courts are to be meaningful participants in the institutional constitutional dialogue. As Keck concludes, "The [Supreme Court] justices are political people with political preferences, placed on the bench for political reasons. But they are also—most of them—legal professionals, committed to maintaining the Court's independence and autonomy. Thus, they will ever be pulled in two directions, and the outcome of their internal struggle is of great consequence to the rest of us" (2007b, 540–41).

This work has attempted to clarify how Congress views the courts and how it will approach its interactions with the judicial branch. Many have gained politically both from rhetorical attacks against the courts and from actually taking action to harm the courts as institutions. They have attempted to restrict the judicial voice in the inter-institutional constitutional conversation. These assaults on the federal courts, however, may result in the loss of judicial independence. Many in the legal and academic communities consider this too high a price to pay. Although the courts and Congress have very different institutional perspectives and cultures, these two branches of government must find ways to work together for the good of the country. The dialogue between the branches continues, but in a new context. The interactions between the federal courts and Congress in this new context deserve greater scrutiny in future research endeavors.

APPENDIX

The Interviews

The research for this book is supplemented by interviews with a variety of individuals having an interest in the interactions between Congress and the federal courts. During the 2006–7 academic year I was a visiting scholar at the American Political Science Association's Centennial Center for Political Science and Public Policy, in Washington, D.C. During that period I interviewed members of Congress, key congressional staff, federal judges, employees of the judicial branch, lobbyists, and others. The interviews were mostly loosely structured conversations that varied in length depending on the circumstances. All of the interviews were conducted with the understanding that my sources would remain anonymous so that those being interviewed could speak freely. Thus I do not attribute the quotations from the interviews used in this book.

Congressional staff members whom I interviewed were responsible for judiciary issues, and all spoke on behalf of their congressional employers. Many of these staff members had previously worked in the judicial branch or as lobbyists on behalf of the courts. Therefore, I asked them to distinguish between their own views and the views of their employers where those views might diverge. I did not draw a distinction between personal staff and committee staff, because all of the staff handled judiciary-related issues and all were authorized to speak on behalf of their employers.

All of these staff members were "professionals" as defined by Barbara Romzek and Jennifer Utter (1997). As Romzek and Utter noted, "Congressional legislative staff, those individuals who work directly for elected

Members of Congress, oftentimes represent a thread of continuity, institutional memory, and expertise within the institution" (1252). I used the congressperson as an enterprise model (see Loomis 1979; Salisbury and Shepsle 1981; Whiteman 1995; and Hammond 1996), treating statements from congressional staff as statements on behalf of their employers. As Romzek and Utter note, "Staff's professional norms emphasize deference and loyalty vis-à-vis Members of Congress and as such appear to define professionalism, at least in part, as responsiveness to members" (1997, 1275). However, I always indicate whether a quotation is from a member of Congress or from a staff person so that readers can draw their own conclusions.

Similarly, I treat the comments of employees of the judicial branch as reflective of the needs of the judiciary as a whole because they were authorized to speak on behalf of the judicial branch collectively, although of course they could not speak for individual federal judges. Throughout the book I supplement quotations from the interviews with public statements made by various members of Congress and federal judges.

Interviews by Category

Current or former House Judiciary Committee Republican members: 5 (1 member and 4 staff)
Current or former House Judiciary Committee Democratic members: 8 (5 members and 3 staff)
Current or former Democratic members of Congress (not Judiciary Committee members): 6 (3 members and 3 staff)
Current or former Republican members of Congress (not Judiciary Committee members): 1 (0 members and 1 staff)
Current or former Senate Judiciary Committee Republican staff: 2
Current or former Senate Judiciary Committee Democratic staff: 3
Federal judges: 2
Current or former employees of the judicial branch: 9
Lobbyists: 6
Think-tank employees: 2

REFERENCES

Published Sources

Administrative Office of the United States Courts. 2003. "Judiciary under Attack." *Third Branch* 35:1.

———. 2007a. "Attorney General Opines on the Proper Role of Judges." *Third Branch* 39:12.

———. 2007b. "Former Representative Henry J. Hyde Dies." *Third Branch* 39:2.

Aldrich, John H., and David W. Rohde. 2001. "The Logic of Conditional Party Government: Revisiting the Electoral Connection." In *Congress Reconsidered,* edited by Lawrence C. Dodd and Bruce I. Oppenheimer. 7th ed. Washington, D.C.: CQ Press.

———. 2005. "Congressional Committees in a Partisan Era." In *Congress Reconsidered,* edited by Lawrence C. Dodd and Bruce I. Oppenheimer. 8th ed. Washington, D.C.: CQ Press.

Allen, Mike. 2005a. "GOP Seeks More Curbs on Courts; Sensenbrenner Proposes an Inspector General." *Washington Post,* 12 May, A3.

———. 2005b. "House Bill Tightens Border Controls." *Washington Post,* 11 February, A4.

American Bar Association. 2006. *Report on the Inspector General for the Judiciary.* Washington, D.C., August.

———. 2008. Home page. http://www.abanet.org/.

American Judicature Society. 2008. Home page. http://www.ajs.org/.

Aron, Nan. 2005. Letter to the chairman and ranking member of the House Committee on Standards of Official Conduct. 27 July.

Babington, Charles. 2005. "Senator Links Violence to 'Political' Decisions; 'Unaccountable' Judiciary Raises Ire." *Washington Post,* 5 April, A7.

Badinter, Robert, and Stephen Breyer. 2004. *Judges in Contemporary Democracy: An International Conversation.* New York: New York University Press.

Baker, Ross K. 2007. *Strangers on a Hill: Congress and the Court.* New York: W. W. Norton.

Balkin, Jack M. 2004. "What *Brown* Teaches Us about Constitutional Theory." *Virginia Law Review* 90:1537–77.

Balkin, Jack M., and Sanford Levinson. 2001. "Understanding the Constitutional Revolution." *Virginia Law Review* 87:1045–1104.

Banks, Christopher P., and David M. O'Brien. 2008. *Courts and Judicial Policymaking.* Upper Saddle River, NJ: Pearson Prentice Hall.

Barak, Aharon. 2006. *The Judge in a Democracy.* Princeton, NJ: Princeton University Press.

Barnes, Jeb. 2004a. "Adversarial Legalism, the Rise of Judicial Policymaking, and the Separation of Powers Doctrine." In Miller and Barnes, *Making Policy, Making Law.*

———. 2004b. *Overruled? Legislative Overrides, Pluralism, and Court-Congress Relations in an Age of Statutes.* Palo Alto, CA: Stanford University Press.

Barnes, Jeb, and Mark C. Miller. 2004a. "Governance as Dialogue." In Miller and Barnes, *Making Policy, Making Law.*

———. 2004b. "Putting the Pieces Together: American Lawmaking from an Interbranch Perspective." In Miller and Barnes, *Making Policy, Making Law.*

Barnes, Robert. 2007. "Justices Weigh Courts' Role in Detainee Cases." *Washington Post,* 5 December, A20.

———. 2008. "Justices Say Detainees Can Seek Release." *Washington Post,* 13 June, 1A.

Barone, Michael, Richard E. Cohen, and Grant Ujifusa. 2005. *The Almanac of American Politics, 2006.* Washington, D.C.: National Journal Group.

Barrow, Deborah J., and Thomas G. Walker. 1988. *A Court Divided: The Fifth Circuit Court of Appeals and the Politics of Judicial Reform.* New Haven, CT: Yale University Press.

Barrow, Deborah J., Gary Zuk, and Gerald S. Gryski. 1996. *The Federal Judiciary and Institutional Change.* Ann Arbor: University of Michigan Press.

Baum, Lawrence. 1997. *The Puzzle of Judicial Behavior.* Ann Arbor: University of Michigan Press.

———. 2001. *American Courts: Process and Policy.* 5th ed. Boston: Houghton Mifflin.

———. 2004. *The Supreme Court.* 8th ed. Washington, D.C.: CQ Press.

Baum, Lawrence, and Lori Hausegger. 2004. "The Supreme Court and Congress: Reconsidering the Relationship." In Miller and Barnes, *Making Policy, Making Law.*

Bauman, Richard W., and Tsvi Kahana, eds. 2006. *The Least Examined Branch: The Role of Legislatures in the Constitutional State.* New York: Cambridge University Press.

Bell, Lauren Cohen. 2002a. "Senatorial Discourtesy: The Senate's Use of Delay to Shape the Federal Judiciary." *Political Research Quarterly* 55:589–608.

———. 2002b. *Warring Factions: Interest Groups, Money and the New Politics of Senate Confirmation.* Columbus: Ohio State University Press.

———. 2008. “In Their Own Interest: Pressure Groups in the Federal Judicial Selection Process.” In Miller, *Exploring Judicial Politics.*

Bell, Lauren Cohen, and Kevin M. Scott. 2006. “Policy Statements or Symbolic Politics? Explaining Congressional Court-limiting Attempts.” *Judicature* 89: 196–201.

Benesh, Sara C. 2006. “Understanding Public Confidence in American Courts.” *Journal of Politics* 68:697–707.

Bergara, Mario, Barak Richman, and Pablo T. Spiller. 2003. “Modeling Supreme Court Strategic Decision Making: The Congressional Constraint.” *Legislative Studies Quarterly* 28:247–80.

Berman, Howard. “An Interview with Representative Howard Berman.” *Third Branch* 39:1–3.

Bickel, Alexander M. 1962. *The Least Dangerous Branch: The Supreme Court at the Bar of Politics.* Indianapolis: Bobbs-Merrill.

Binder, Sarah A., and Forrest Maltzman. 2002. “Senatorial Delay in Confirming Federal Judges, 1947–1998.” *American Journal of Political Science* 46:190–99.

Biskupic, Joan. 2007. “Justice Pleads with Senate: No Cameras in High Court.” *USA Today,* 14 February.

Biskupic, Joan, and Alan Gomez. 2008. “Ruling Lays Path from Guantanamo to U.S. Courts.” *USA Today,* 13 June, 1A.

Blum, John Morton. 1991. *Years of Discord: American Politics and Society, 1961–1974.* New York: W. W. Norton.

Bork, Robert H. 2003. *Coercing Virtue: The Worldwide Rule of Judges.* Washington, D.C.: AEI Press.

Boyer, Dave. 2002. “Case Talking in South Dakota Race; GOP Challenger Complains of Power Play by Daschle.” *Washington Times,* 24 August, A1.

Boyer, Dave, and Audrey Hudson. 2002. “Daschle Waiver Helps a Colleague; Challenger Calls Protection Political, Not Environmental.” *Washington Times,* 31 July, A4.

Bragaw, Stephen G., and Mark C. Miller. 2004. “The City of Boerne: Two Tales of One City.” In Miller and Barnes, *Making Policy, Making Law.*

Bragaw, Stephen G., and Barbara A. Perry. 2002. “The ‘Brooding Omnipresence’ in Bush v. Gore: Anthony Kennedy, the Equality Principle, and Judicial Supremacy.” *Stanford Law and Policy Review* 13:19–32.

Brandenburg, Bert, and Amy Kay. 2006. *Courting Danger: How the War on Terror Has Sapped the Power of Our Courts to Protect Our Constitutional Liberties.* Washington, D.C.: Justice at Stake Campaign.

———. 2007. *Crusading against the Courts: The New Mission to Weaken the Role of the Courts in Protecting Our Religious Liberties.* Washington, D.C.: Justice at Stake Campaign.

Breyer, Stephen. 2006. *Implementation of the Judicial Conduct and Disability Act of 1980: A Report to the Chief Justice from the Judicial Conduct and Disability Act Study Committee.* Washington, D.C.: Administrative Office of the United States Courts.

Brigham, John. 1987. *The Cult of the Court.* Philadelphia: Temple University Press.

Bright, Stephen B. 1997. "Political Attacks on the Judiciary: Can Justice Be Done amid Efforts to Intimidate and Remove Judges from Office for Unpopular Decisions?" *New York University Law Review* 72:308–31.

Brodie, Ian. 2002. *Friends of the Court: The Privileging of Interest Group Litigants in Canada.* Plattsburgh: State University of New York Press.

Brown, Steven P. 2002. *Trumping Religion: The New Christian Right, the Free Speech Clause, and the Courts.* Tuscaloosa: University of Alabama Press.

Brownback, Sam. 2004. Statement on the Partial Birth Abortion Ruling. 108th Cong., 2nd sess. *Congressional Record,* daily ed. (3 June), S6444.

Bryce, James. 1891. *The American Commonwealth.* 2nd ed. Vol. 1. London: Macmillan.

Bumiller, Elisabeth. 2005. "War Rooms (and Chests) Ready for a Supreme Court Vacancy." *New York Times,* 20 June, A13.

———. 2008. "McCain Assures Conservatives of His Stance on Judges." *New York Times,* 7 May, A22.

Burack, Cynthia. 2003. "Getting What 'We' Deserve: Terrorism, Tolerance, Sexuality, and the Christian Right." *New Political Science* 25:329–49.

Burbank, Stephen B., and Barry Friedman, eds. 2002. *Judicial Independence at the Crossroads: An Interdisciplinary Approach.* Thousand Oaks, CA: Sage.

Burke, Thomas F. 2004. "The Judicial Implementation of Statutes: Three Stories about Courts and the Americans with Disabilities Act." In Miller and Barnes, *Making Policy, Making Law.*

Calabresi, Steven G., and Stephanie Dotson Zimdahl. 2005. "The Supreme Court and Foreign Sources of Law: Two Hundred Years of Practice and the Juvenile Death Penalty Decision." *William and Mary Law Review* 47:743–910.

Caldeira, Gregory A., and James L. Gibson. 1992. "The Etiology of Public Support for the Supreme Court." *American Journal of Political Science* 36:635–64.

Campbell, Colton C., and John F. Stack Jr., eds. 2001. *Congress Confronts the Court: The Struggle for Legitimacy and Authority in Lawmaking.* Landham, MD: Rowman & Littlefield.

Canellos, Peter S. 2006a. "Amid the Abortion Rifts, a History of Court Shifts." *Boston Globe,* 28 February, A3.

———. 2006b. "The Religious Right Faces Its Purgatory." *Boston Globe,* 10 January, A3.

Carter, Lief, and Thomas F. Burke. 2004. *Reason in Law.* 7th ed. Old Tappen, NJ: Longman.

Chaddock, Gail Russell. 2005. "A Judicial Think Tank—or a Plot?" *Christian Science Monitor,* 4 August, 1.

Chemerinsky, Erwin. 2003. "Understanding the Rehnquist Court: An Admiring Reply to Professor Merrill." *Saint Louis University Law Journal* 47:659–75.

———. 2004. "In Defense of Judicial Review: A Reply to Professor Kramer." *California Law Review* 92:1013–25.

Choudhry, Sujit, and Claire E. Hunter. 2003. "Measuring Judicial Activism on the

Supreme Court of Canada: A Comment on Newfoundland (Treasury Board) v. Nape." *McGill Law Journal* 48:525–58.

Clausen, Aage. 1973. *How Congressmen Decide: A Policy Focus.* New York: St. Martin's.

Clayton, Cornell W. 1992. *The Politics of Justice: The Attorney General and the Making of Legal Policy.* Armonk, NY: M. E. Sharpe.

———. 1999. "The Supreme Court and Political Jurisprudence: New and Old Institutionalisms." In Clayton and Gillman, *Supreme Court Decision-Making.*

Clayton, Cornell W., and Howard Gillman, eds. 1999. *Supreme Court Decision-Making: New Institutionalist Approaches.* Chicago: University of Chicago Press.

Clayton, Cornell W., and David A. May. 1999. "A Political Regimes Approach to the Analysis of Legal Decisions." *Polity* 32:233–52.

Clayton, Cornell W., and J. Mitchell Pickerill. 2006. "The Politics of Criminal Justice: How the New Right Regime Shaped the Rehnquist Court's Criminal Justice Jurisprudence." *Georgetown Law Journal* 94:1385–1425.

Clemetson, Lynette. 2007. "Judges Look to New Congress for Changes in Mandatory Sentencing Laws." *New York Times,* 9 January, A12.

Clymer, Adam. 1998. "Barry Goldwater Is Dead at 89; Conservatives' Standard-bearer." *New York Times,* 30 May, A1.

Cohen, Adam. 2007. "Last Term's Winner at the Supreme Court: Judicial Activism." *New York Times,* 9 July, 16.

Cohodas, Nadine. 1980. "Kennedy and Rodino: How Two Very Different Chairmen Run Their Panels." *Congressional Quarterly Weekly Report,* 2 February, 267–71.

———. 1982. "House Judiciary Committee Bottles Up the Tough Ones." *Congressional Quarterly Weekly Report,* 17 April, 863–64.

———. 1986. "House Judiciary Looks to Post-Rodino Era." *Congressional Quarterly Weekly Report,* 7 June, 1307.

Comiskey, Michael. 2004. *Seeking Justices: The Judging of Supreme Court Nominees.* Lawrence: University Press of Kansas.

———. 2008. "Is There Really a Countermajoritarian Problem?" In Miller, *Exploring Judicial Politics.*

Constitution Project. 2008. Home page. http://www.constitutionproject.org/.

Cooperman, Alan. 2006. "House Passes Measure on Religion Suits." *Washington Post,* 27 September, A4.

"The Courts, the Legislature, and the Executive, Separate and Equal? Issues at the Federal Level." 2004. *Judicature* 87:220–29.

Crier, Catherine. 2005. *Contempt: How the Right Is Wronging American Justice.* New York: Rugged Land.

Culp, Maurice S. 1929. "A Survey of the Proposals to Limit or Deny the Power of Judicial Review by the Supreme Court of the United States." *Indiana Law Journal* 4:386–98.

Curry, Brett. 2005. "The Courts, Congress, and the Politics of Federal Jurisdiction." PhD diss., Ohio State University.

Cushman, Barry. 1998. *Rethinking the New Deal Court: The Structure of a Constitutional Revolution.* New York: Oxford University Press.

Dahl, Robert A. 1957. "Decision-Making in a Democracy: The Supreme Court as a National Policy-Maker." *Journal of Public Law* 6:279–95.

Daschle, Tom. 2002. "Senator Daschle's 'Misunderstood' Amendment." Letter to the editor. *Washington Times,* 30 July, A16.

Davidson, Roger H. 1988. "What Judges Ought to Know about Lawmaking in Congress." In Katzmann, *Judges and Legislators.*

———. 1993. "Elected Branch Influences in Constitutional Decisionmaking." *Law and Contemporary Problems* 56:99–119.

Davidson, Roger H., and Walter J. Oleszek. 2004. *Congress and Its Members.* 9th ed. Washington, D.C.: CQ Press.

Deering, Christopher J., and Steven S. Smith. 1997. *Committees in Congress.* 3rd ed. Washington, D.C.: CQ Press.

DeFigueiredo, John M., and Emerson H. Tiller. 1996. "Congressional Control of the Courts: A Theoretical and Empirical Analysis of Expansion of the Federal Judiciary." *Journal of Law and Economics* 39:435–62.

Den Dulk, Kevin R. 2006. "In Legal Culture, But Not of It: The Role of Cause Lawyers in Evangelical Legal Mobilization." In *Cause Lawyers and Social Movements,* edited by Austin Sarat and Stuart Scheingold. Stanford, CA: Stanford University Press.

Den Dulk, Kevin R., and Dennis Hoover. 2003. "Christian Conservatives Go to Court: Religion and Legal Mobilization in the U.S. and Canada." *International Journal of Political Science* 25:9–34.

Den Dulk, Kevin R., and J. Mitchell Pickerill. 2003. "Bridging the Lawmaking Process: Organized Interests, Court-Congress Interaction, and Church-State Relations." *Polity* 35:419–40.

DeParle, Jason. 2005. "In Battle to Pick Next Justice, Right Says Avoid a Kennedy." *New York Times,* 27 June, 1.

Dershowitz, Alan. 2007. *Blasphemy: How the Religious Right Is Hijacking Our Declaration of Independence.* Hoboken, NJ: John Wiley & Sons.

Devins, Neal. 2004. "Is Judicial Policymaking Countermajoritarian?" In Miller and Barnes, *Making Policy, Making Law.*

———. 2006. "Should the Supreme Court Fear Congress?" *Minnesota Law Review* 90:1337–62.

———. 2007. "Signing Statements and Divided Government." *William and Mary Bill of Rights Journal* 16:63–80.

Devins, Neal, and Keith E. Whittington, eds. 2005. *Congress and the Constitution.* Durham, NC: Duke University Press.

Diamond, Sara. 1998. *Not by Politics Alone: The Enduring Influence of the Christian Right.* New York: Guilford.

Dobson, James. 2004. *Marriage under Fire: Why We Must Win This Battle.* Sisters, OR: Multnomah.

Dodd, Lawrence C. 1981. "Congress, the Constitution, and the Crisis of Legitimation." In *Congress Reconsidered,* edited by Lawrence C. Dodd and Bruce I. Oppenheimer. 2nd ed. Washington, D.C.: CQ Press.

Drobak, John N., ed. 2006. *Norms and the Law.* New York: Cambridge University Press.

Durham, Martin. 2006. "Evangelicals and the Politics of Red America." In Morgan and Davies, *Right On?*

Easton, David. 1965. *A Systems Analysis of Political Life.* New York: Wiley.

———. 1975. "A Re-Assessment of the Concept of Political Support." *British Journal of Political Science* 5:435–57.

Edsall, Thomas Byrne, and Mary Edsall. 1991. *The Impact of Race, Rights, and Taxes on American Politics.* New York: W. W. Norton.

Edwards, Harry T. 2006. "Judicial Norms: A Judge's Perspective." In Drobak, *Norms and the Law.*

Eilperin, Juliet. 2008. "McCain Says He Would Put Conservatives on Supreme Court." *Washington Post,* 7 May, A9.

Elliott, Shelden D. 1958. "Court-Curbing Proposals in Congress." *Notre Dame Lawyer* 33:597–616.

Ellis, Richard E. 1971. *The Jeffersonian Crisis: Courts and Politics in the Young Republic.* New York: Oxford University Press.

———. 1987. *The Union at Risk: Jacksonian Democracy, States' Rights, and the Nullification Crisis.* New York: Oxford University Press.

Entin, Jonathan L., and Erik M. Jensen. 2006. "Taxation, Compensation, and Judicial Independence." *Case Western Reserve Law Review* 56:965–1015.

Epstein, Lee. 1985. *Conservatives in Court.* Knoxville: University of Tennessee Press.

Epstein, Lee, and Jack Knight. 1998. *The Choices Justices Make.* Washington, D.C.: CQ Press.

Epstein, Lee, Jack Knight, and Andrew D. Martin. 2004. "Constitutional Interpretation from a Strategic Perspective." In Miller and Barnes, *Making Policy, Making Law.*

Epstein, Lee, and Jeffrey A. Segal. 2005. *Advice and Consent: The Politics of Judicial Appointments.* New York: Oxford University Press.

Epstein, Lee, and Thomas G. Walker. 2007. *Constitutional Law for a Changing America: Institutional Powers and Constraints.* Washington, D.C.: CQ Press.

Erbe, Bonnie, and Josetts Shiner. 1997. "Rights before the Bench." *Washington Times,* 17 May, D3.

Eskridge, William. 1991a. "Overriding Supreme Court Statutory Interpretation Decisions." *Yale Law Journal* 101:331–417.

———. 1991b. "Reneging on History? Playing the Court/Congress/President Civil Rights Game." *California Law Review* 79:613–84.

Evans, C. Lawrence, and Walter J. Oleszek. 1977. "Congressional Tsunami? The Politics of Committee Reform." In *Congress Reconsidered,* edited by Lawrence C. Dodd and Bruce I. Oppenheimer. 6th ed. Washington, D.C.: CQ Press.

Fagan, Amy. 2005. "House Panel OKs Provision to Divide the 9th Circuit Court." *Washington Times,* 4 November, A2.

"Fair and Independent Courts: A Conference on the State of the Judiciary." 2006. Georgetown Law Center, 28–29 September. http://www.law.georgetown.edu/judiciary/index.html. Many of the presentations have been reprinted in *Georgetown Law Journal* 95 (April 2007).

Federalist Society for Law and Public Policy Studies. 2008. Home page. http://www.fed-soc.org/.

Fehrenbacher, Don E. 1978. *The Dred Scott Case.* New York: Oxford University Press.

Feldman, Noah. 2008. "What Is It about Mormonism?" *New York Times Magazine,* 6 January, 34.

Fenno, Richard. F. 1973. *Congressmen in Committees.* Boston: Little, Brown.

Ferejohn, John A., and Larry D. Kramer. 2006. "Judicial Independence in a Democracy: Institutionalizing Judicial Restraint." In Drobak, *Norms and the Law.*

Ferejohn, John A., and Charles Shipan. 1990. "Congressional Influence on Bureaucracy." *Journal of Law, Economics, and Organization* 6:1–20.

Ferejohn, John A., and Barry Weingast. 1992. "A Positive Theory of Statutory Interpretation." *International Review of Law and Economics* 12:263–79.

Fisher, Louis. 1988. *Constitutional Dialogues: Interpretation as Political Process.* Princeton, NJ: Princeton University Press.

———. 2004. "Judicial Finality or an Ongoing Colloquy?" In Miller and Barnes, *Making Policy, Making Law.*

———. 2005. *American Constitutional Law.* 6th ed. Durham, NC: Carolina Academic Press.

———. 2007. "Signing Statements: Constitutional and Practical Limits." *William and Mary Bill of Rights Journal* 16:183–211.

———. 2008. "The Federal Courts and Terrorism." In Miller, *Exploring Judicial Politics.*

Fisher, Louis, and David Gray Adler. 2007. *American Constitutional Law.* 7th ed. Durham, NC: Carolina Academic Press.

Fitzpatrick, Brian T. 2007. "Disorder in the Court: The 9th Circuit is Overturned More Than Any Other Appeals Court." *Los Angeles Times,* 11 July, A15.

Franklin, Charles H. 2002. "Behavioral Factors Affecting Judicial Independence." In Burbank and Friedman, *Judicial Independence at the Crossroads.*

Friedman, Barry. 1990. "A Different Dialogue: The Supreme Court, Congress, and Federal Jurisdiction." *Northwestern University Law Review* 85:1–61.

———. 1991. "Federal Jurisdiction and Legal Scholarship: A (Dialogic) Reply." *Northwestern University Law Review* 85:478–94.

———. 1993. "Dialogue and Judicial Review." *Michigan Law Review* 91:577–681.

———. 2002. "The History of the Countermajoritarian Difficulty, Part II: Reconstruction's Political Court." *Georgetown Law Journal* 91:1–66.

———. 2004. "The Importance of Being Positive: The Nature of and Function of Judicial Review." *University of Cincinnati Law Review* 72:1257–1303.

Friedman, Lawrence M. 2006. "Judge the Judges: Some Remarks on the Way Judges Think and the Way Judges Act." In Drobak, *Norms and the Law.*

Frisch, Scott A., and Sean Q. Kelly. 2004. "Self-Selection Reconsidered: House Committee Assignment Requests and Constituency Characteristics." *Political Research Quarterly* 57:325–36.

Garber, Judith A. 2006. "The Christian Right, the Federal Courts, and the Constitution of the United States." *Constitutional Forum* 15:23–35.

Gely, Rafael, and Pablo T. Spiller. 1990. "A Rational Choice Theory of Supreme Court Statutory Decision with Applications to the State Farm and Grove City Cases." *Journal of Law, Economics, and Organization* 6:263–300.

George, Robert P., and Ramesh Ponnuru. 2000. "Courting Trouble: Only a Frontal Assault on the Power of the Courts Can Restore American's Constitutional Balance." In *21 Debated Issues in American Politics,* edited by Gregory M. Scott and Loren Gatch. Upper Saddle River, NJ: Prentice Hall.

Gerhardt, Michael J. 2000. *The Federal Appointments Process: A Constitutional and Historical Analysis.* Durham, NC: Duke University Press.

———. 2005. "The Federal Appointments Process as Constitutional Interpretation." In Devins and Whittington, *Congress and the Constitution.*

Geyh, Charles G. 2002. "Customary Independence." In Burbank and Friedman, *Judicial Independence at the Crossroads.*

———. 2006. *When Courts and Congress Collide: The Struggle for Control of America's Judicial System.* Ann Arbor: University of Michigan Press.

Gibson, James L., and Vanessa A. Baird. 1997. "The Legitimacy of the United States Supreme Court: A Conceptual and Empirical Analysis." In *Perspectives on American and Texas Politics,* edited by Donald S. Lutz, Kent L. Tedin, and Edward P. Fuchs. 5th ed. Dubuque, IA: Kendall/Hunt.

Gibson, James L., Gregory A. Caldeira, and Vanessa A. Baird. 1998. "On the Legitimacy of National High Courts." *American Political Science Review* 92:343–58.

Gibson, James L., Gregory A. Caldeira, and Lester Kenyatta Spence. 2003. "The Supreme Court and the US Presidential Election of 2000: Wounds, Self-Inflicted or Otherwise?" *British Journal of Political Science* 33:535–56.

Gillman, Howard. 1993. *The Constitution Besieged: The Rise and Demise of Lochner Era Police Powers Jurisprudence.* Durham, NC: Duke University Press.

———. 1996. Review of *A Muted Fury,* by William G. Ross. *Journal of Interdisciplinary History* 26:736–37.

———. 1999. "The Court as an Idea, Not a Building (or a Game): Interpretive Institutionalism and the Analysis of Supreme Court Decision-Making." In Clayton and Gillman, *Supreme Court Decision-Making.*

———. 2002. "How Political Parties Can Use the Courts to Advance Their Agendas: Federal Courts in the United States, 1875–1891." *American Political Science Review* 96:511–24.

———. 2004. "Elements of a New 'Regime Politics' Approach to the Study of Judicial Politics." Paper presented at the annual meeting of the American Political Science Association, Chicago, 2–5 September.

———. 2006a. "Party Politics and Constitutional Change: The Political Origins of

Liberal Judicial Activism." In Kahn and Kersch, *Supreme Court and American Political Development.*

———. 2006b. "Regime Politics, Jurisprudential Regimes, and Unenumerated Rights." *University of Pennsylvania Journal of Constitutional Law* 9:107–19.

Gillman, Howard, and Cornell Clayton. 1999. "Beyond Judicial Attitudes: Institutional Approaches to Supreme Court Decision-Making." In Clayton and Gillman, *Supreme Court Decision-Making.*

Ginsburg, Ruth Bader. 1995. "Communicating and Commenting on the Court's Work." *Georgetown Law Journal* 83:2119–29.

———. 2006. "Judicial Independence: The Situation of the U.S. Federal Judiciary." *Nebraska Law Review* 85:1–15.

Ginsburg, Tom, and Robert A. Kagan, eds. 2005. *Institutions and Public Law: Comparative Approaches.* New York: Peter Lang.

Goldberg, Michelle. 2007. *Kingdom Coming: The Rise of Christian Nationalism.* New York: W. W. Norton.

Goldman, Sheldon. 1997. *Picking Federal Judges: Lower Court Selection from Roosevelt through Reagan.* New Haven, CT: Yale University Press.

Gore, Al. 2007. *The Assault on Reason.* New York: Penguin.

Graber, Mark A. 1993. "The Non-Majoritarian Difficulty: Legislative Deference to the Judiciary." *Studies in American Political Development* 7:35–73.

———. 1998. "Establishing Judicial Review? Schooner Peggy and the Early Marshall Court." *Political Research Quarterly* 51:21–39.

———. 2002. "Constitutional Politics and Constitutional Theory: A Misunderstood and Neglected Relationship." *Law and Social Inquiry* 27:309–33.

———. 2005. "Constructing Judicial Review." *Annual Review of Political Science* 8:425–51.

———. 2006. "Legal, Strategic or Legal Strategy: Deciding to Decide during the Civil War and Reconstruction." In Kahn and Kersch, *Supreme Court and American Political Development.*

Green, John C. 1995. "The Christian Right and the 1994 Elections: An Overview." In *God at the Grassroots: The Christian Right in the 1994 Elections,* edited by Mark Rozell and Clyde Wilcox. Lanham, MD: Rowman & Littlefield.

Green, John C., and Nathan S. Bigelow. 2005. "The Christian Right Goes to Washington: Social Movement Resources and the Legislative Process." In Herrnson, Shaiko, and Wilcox, *Interest Group Connection.*

Greenburg, Jan Crawford. 2007. *Supreme Conflict: The Inside Story of the Struggle for Control of the United States Supreme Court.* New York: Penguin.

Greenhouse, Linda. 1996. "How Congress Curtailed the Courts' Jurisdiction." *New York Times,* 27 October, 5.

———. 2005a. "The Court v. Congress: Specter's Questioning Reflects Recent Battle as Justices Move to Curb Lawmakers' Powers." *New York Times,* 15 September, A1.

———. 2005b. "Justice Weighs Desire v. Duty (Duty Prevails)." *New York Times,* 25 August, A1, A23.

———. 2005c. "Rehnquist Resumes His Call for Judicial Independence." *New York Times,* 1 January, 10.

———. 2006. "Federal Judges Take Steps to Improve Accountability." *New York Times,* 20 September, A20.

———. 2007a. "The Focus on the Effects of Life Tenure." *New York Times,* 10 September, A20.

———. 2007b. "For Justices, Another Day on Detainees." *New York Times,* 3 December, 1.

———. 2007c. "Justices Ready to Answer Detainee Rights Question." *New York Times,* 6 December, 32.

———. 2008a. "Detainees in Cuba Win Major Ruling in Supreme Court." *New York Times,* 13 June, A1.

———. 2008b. "In Latest Term, Majority Grows to More than 5 of the Justices." *New York Times,* 23 May, 1.

———. 2008c. "A Second Case on Detainees Complicates Supreme Court Deliberations." *New York Times,* 6 February, 14.

Guth, James L., Lyman A. Kellstedt, John C. Green, and Corwin E. Smidt. 2002. "A Distant Thunder? Religious Mobilization in the 2000 Elections." In *Interest Group Politics,* edited by Allan J. Cigler and Burdett A. Loomis. 6th ed. Washington, D.C.: CQ Press.

Hacker, Hans J. 2005a. *The Culture of Conservative Christian Litigation.* Lanham, MD: Rowman & Littlefield.

———. 2005b. "Defending the Faithful: Conservative Christian Litigation in American Politics." In Herrnson, Shaiko, and Wilcox, *Interest Group Connection.*

Hall, Peter A., and Rosemary C. R. Taylor. 1996. "Political Science and the Three New Institutionalisms." *Political Studies* 94:936–57.

Hallow, Ralph Z., and Stephen Dinan. 2008. "Activists Refusing to Back McCain; A Straw Poll of Conservatives Finds Opposition to GOP Candidate Unabated." *Washington Times,* 10 February, A1.

Hammond, Susan Webb. 1996. "Recent Research on Legislative Staffs." *Legislative Studies Quarterly* 21:543–76.

Hart, Henry M., Jr. 1953. "The Power of Congress to Limit the Jurisdiction of Federal Courts: An Exercise in Dialectic." *Harvard Law Review* 66:1362–1402.

Hausegger, Lori, and Lawrence Baum. 1998. "Behind the Scenes: The Supreme Court and Congress in Statutory Interpretation." In *Great Theatre: The American Congress in the 1990s,* edited by Herbert F. Weisberg and Samuel C. Patterson. New York: Cambridge University Press.

———. 1999. "Inviting Congressional Action: A Study of Supreme Court Motivations in Statutory Interpretation." *American Journal of Political Science* 43:162–85.

Hedges, Chris. 2006. *American Fascists: The Christian Right and the War on America.* New York: Free Press.

Henschen, Beth. 1983. "Congressional Response to the Statutory Interpretations of the Supreme Court." *American Politics Quarterly* 11:441–59.

Herrnson, Paul S., Ronald G. Shaiko, and Clyde Wilcox, eds. 2005. *The Interest Group Connection: Electioneering, Lobbying, and Policymaking in Washington.* 2nd ed. Washington, D.C.: CQ Press.

Hiebert, Janet L. 2002. *Charter Conflicts: What Is Parliament's Role?* Montreal: McGill-Queen's University Press.

Hogg, Peter W., and Allison A. Bushell. 1997. "The Charter Dialogue between Courts and Legislatures: (Or Perhaps the Charter of Rights Isn't Such a Bad Thing After All)." *Osgoode Hall Law Journal* (York University) 35:75–124.

Holley, Joe. 2007. "Jerry Falwell, 1933–2007: Harnessed the Political Power of Evangelicals." *Washington Post,* 16 May, A1, A6.

Horsky, Charles A. 1958. "Law Day: Some Reflections on Current Proposals to Curtail the Supreme Court." *Minnesota Law Review* 42:1105–11.

Huckabee, Mike. 2008. "Mike Huckabee for President Web Site: Family, Faith, Freedom." http://www.mikehuckabee.com (accessed 20 February 2008).

Hudson, Audrey. 2002a. "Daschle Seeks to Exempt His State; Wants Logging to Prevent Fires." *Washington Times,* 24 July, A1.

———. 2002b. "GOP Reverses Course on Daschle Ploy; Logging in Wildfire States at Issue." *Washington Times,* 25 July, A4.

Hughes, Charles Evans. 1928. *The Supreme Court of the United States.* New York: Columbia University Press.

Hulse, Carl. 2008. "Distrust of McCain Lingers over '05 Deal on Judges." *New York Times,* 25 February, A1.

Hulse, Carl, and David D. Kirkpatrick. 2005. "DeLay Says Federal Judiciary Has 'Run Amok,' Adding Congress Is Partly to Blame." *New York Times,* 8 April, A21.

Hyde, Henry J. 1990. "Advice to Freshmen: 'There Are Things Worth Losing For.'" *Roll Call,* 3 December, 5.

Ignagni, Joseph, and James Meernik. 1994. "Explaining Congressional Attempts to Reverse Supreme Court Decisions." *Political Research Quarterly* 47:353–71.

Inglis, Bob. 2006. "Judiciary: Pledge Protection Act." www.inglis.house.gov/issues .asp?content=sections/issues/current/pledge_protection.

Irons, Peter H. 1982. *The New Deal Lawyers.* Princeton, NJ: Princeton University Press.

Jackson, Derrick Z. 2006. "The Antigay Obsession." *Boston Globe,* 18 November, A11.

Jackson, Robert H. 1955. *The Supreme Court in the American System of Government.* Cambridge, MA: Harvard University Press.

James, Patrick, Donald E. Abelson, and Michael Lusztig, eds. 2002. *The Myth of the Sacred: The Charter, Courts, and the Politics of the Constitution in Canada.* Montreal: McGill-Queen's University Press.

Johnsen, Dawn E. 2004. "Functional Departmentalism and Nonjudicial Interpretation: Who Determines Constitutional Meaning?" *Law and Contemporary Problems* 67:105–47.

Jones, Charles O. 1994. *The Presidency in a Separated System.* Washington, D.C.: Brookings Institution.

———. 1995. "A Way of Life and Law." *American Political Science Review* 89:1–9.

"Judiciary Moves to Soothe Congressional Concerns." 2006. *BCD News and Comment,* 12 December.

Justice at Stake Campaign. 2008. Home page. http://www.justiceatstake.org/.

Kagan, Robert A. 2001. *Adversarial Legalism: The American Way of Law.* Cambridge, MA: Harvard University Press.

———. 2004. "American Courts and the Policy Dialogue: The Role of Adversarial Legalism." In Miller and Barnes, *Making Policy, Making Law.*

Kahn, Ronald, and Ken I. Kersch, eds. *The Supreme Court and American Political Development.* Lawrence: University Press of Kansas.

Kaiser, Frederick M. 2003. *Statutory Offices of Inspector General: Establishment and Evolution.* CRS Report 98–379. 5 March.

Kamisar, Yale. 2006. "Dickerson v. United States: The Case That Disappointed Miranda's Critics—and Then Its Supporters." In *The Rehnquist Legacy,* edited by Craig M. Bradley. New York: Cambridge University Press.

Kaplan, Esther. 2004. *With God on Their Side.* New York: New Press.

Kasindorf, Martin. 2003. "The Court Conservatives Love to Hate." *USA Today,* 7 February, 3A.

Katzmann, Robert A., ed. 1988. *Judges and Legislators: Toward Institutional Comity.* Washington, D.C.: Brookings Institution.

———. 1995. "Judiciary and Congress." In *The Encyclopedia of the United States Congress,* edited by Donald C. Bacon, Roger H. Davidson, and Morton Keller. New York: Simon & Schuster.

———. 1997. *Courts and Congress.* Washington D.C.: Brookings Institution Press.

Keck, Thomas. 2004. *The Most Activist Supreme Court in History: The Road to Modern Judicial Conservatism.* Chicago: University of Chicago Press.

———. 2007a. "Party, Policy, or Duty: Why Does the Supreme Court Invalidate Federal Statutes?" *American Political Science Review* 101:321–38.

———. 2007b. "Party Politics or Judicial Independence? The Regime Politics Literature Hits the Law Schools." *Law and Social Inquiry* 32:511–44.

Kelman, Steve. 2007. "The IG Ideology." *Washington Post,* 4 April, A13.

Kennedy, D. James. 2003. *What If America Were a Christian Nation Again?* Nashville: Thomas Nelson.

Kershaw, Sarah. 2005. "O'Connor Sees Strains between the Judiciary and Some in Congress." *New York Times,* 22 July, A1.

Kingdon, John W. 1989. *Congressmen's Voting Decisions.* 3rd edition. Ann Arbor: University of Michigan Press.

Klarman, Michael J. 1997. "Majoritarian Judicial Review: The Entrenchment Problem." *Georgetown Law Journal* 85:491–553.

———. 2004. *From Jim Crow to Civil Rights: The Supreme Court and the Struggle for Racial Equality.* New York: Oxford University Press.

———. 2005. "Brown and Lawrence (and Goodridge)." *Michigan Law Review* 104: 431–89.

Klein, Rick. 2005. "DeLay Apologized for Blaming Federal Judges in Schiavo

Case, But House Leader Calls for Probe of 'Judicial Activism.'" *Boston Globe,* 14 April, A9.

Kornhauser, Lewis A. 2002. "Is Judicial Independence a Useful Concept?" In Burbank and Friedman, *Judicial Independence at the Crossroads.*

Koszczuk, Jackie, and Martha Angle. 2007. *CQ's Politics in America 2008: The 110th Congress.* Washington, D.C.: CQ Press.

Koszczuk, Jackie, and H. Amy Stern. 2005. *Politics in America 2006: The 109th Congress.* Washington, D.C.: CQ Press.

Kramer, Larry D. 2004. *The People Themselves: Popular Constitutionalism and Judicial Review.* New York: Oxford University Press.

Krent, Harold J. 2007. "Fee Shifting as a Congressional Response to Adventurous Presidential Signing Statements." *William and Mary Bill of Rights Journal* 16:211–31.

Kritzer, Herbert M. 2001. "The Impact of Bush v. Gore on Public Perceptions and Knowledge of the Supreme Court." *Judicature* 85:32–38.

Kyl, Jon. 2004. *Restoring Popular Control of the Constitution: The Case for Jurisdiction-Stripping Legislation.* Report from the U.S. Senate Republican Policy Committee, 28 September.

Lane, Charles. 2006. "Judges Alter Rules for Sponsored Trips." *Washington Post,* 20 September 2006, A23.

Lash, Steve. 2006a. "Bill Would Establish Inspector General for Judiciary." *Chicago Daily Law Bulletin,* 2 May, 1.

———. 2006b. "O'Connor: Lawyers Must Come to Defense of Judicial Independence." *Chicago Daily Law Bulletin,* 9 March, 1.

Lawson, Gary, and Christopher D. Moore. 1996. "The Executive Power of Constitutional Interpretation." *Iowa Law Review* 81:1267–1331.

Levin, Mark R. 2005. *Men in Black: How the Supreme Court Is Destroying America.* Washington, D.C.: Regnery.

Levinson, Sanford V. 2003. "Why I Do Not Teach *Marbury* (Except to Eastern Europeans) and Why You Shouldn't Either." *Wake Forest Law Review* 38:553–78.

Lewis, Anthony. 1999. "An Independent Judiciary." *St. Louis Law Journal* 43:285–96.

Lewis, Neil A. 1997. "Impeach Those Liberal Judges! Where Are They?" *New York Times,* 18 May, D5.

Lewis, Ron. 2005. "Accountability for Judicial Activism Act Introduced in House: Rep. Lewis Introduces Legislation to Override Certain SCOTUS Decisions." Press release, 30 June. http://www.house.gov/list/press/kyoz_lewis/scotus.html.

Lithwick, Dahlia. 2007. "Justice's Holy Hires." *Washington Post,* 8 April, B2.

Loomis, Burdett A. 1979. "The Congressional Office as a Small Business: New Members Set Up Shop." *Publius* 9:35–55.

Los Angeles Times. 2006. "Judging Congress." Editorial. 7 June, B12.

Lovell, George I. 2003. *Legislative Deferrals: Statutory Ambiguity, Judicial Power, and American Democracy.* Cambridge: Cambridge University Press.

Luo, Michael. 2007. "Romney, Eye on Evangelicals, Defends His Faith." *New York Times,* 7 December, 1.

———. 2008. "Challenges and Miscalculations Dogged Romney from the Start." *New York Times,* 8 February, 17.

MacKay, A. Wayne. 2001. "The Legislature, the Executive, and the Courts: The Delicate Balance of Power or Who Is Running the Country Anyway?" *Dalhousie Law Journal* 24:37–74.

MacLean, Pamela A. 2005. "Does the Judiciary Need a Watchdog?" *National Law Journal,* 23 May.

Maltese, John Anthony. 1995. *The Selling of Supreme Court Nominees.* Baltimore: Johns Hopkins University Press.

Maltzman, Forrest, James Spriggs, and Paul Wahlbeck. 2000. *Creating Law on the Supreme Court: The Collegial Game.* New York: Cambridge University Press.

Manfredi, Christopher P., and James B. Kelly. 1999. "Six Degrees of Dialogue: A Response to Hogg and Bushell." *Osgoode Hall Law Journal* (York University) 37:513–27.

Mann, Thomas E., and Norman J. Ornstein. 2006a. *The Broken Branch: How Congress Is Failing America and How to Get It Back on Track.* New York: Oxford University Press.

———. 2006b. "Congress as 'The Broken Branch.'" *Washington Post,* 11 October, A17.

Marcus, Maeva, and Emily Van Tassel. 1988. "Judges and Legislators in the New Federal System, 1789–1800." In Katzmann, *Judges and Legislators.*

Marcus, Ruth. 2005. "Boot the Bench: There's New Ferocity in Talk of Firing Activist Judges." *Washington Post,* 11 April, A19.

Marks, Brian A. 1989. "A Model of Judicial Influence on Congressional Policymaking: Grove City v. Bell." PhD diss., Washington University in St. Louis.

Marshall, Bryan W., Richard L. Pacelle Jr., and Christine Ludowise. 2008. "A Court of Laws or a Super Legislature? An Integrated Model of Supreme Court Decision Making." In Miller, *Exploring Judicial Politics.*

Martin, Andrew D. 2006. "Statutory Battles and Constitutional Wars: Congress and the Supreme Court." In Rogers, Flemming, and Bond, *Institutional Games and the U.S. Supreme Court.*

Martin, Robert. 2003. *The Most Dangerous Branch: How the Supreme Court of Canada Has Undermined Our Law and Our Democracy.* Montreal: McGill-Queen's University Press.

Martinek, Wendy L. 2008. "Appellate Workhorses of the Federal Judiciary: The U.S. Courts of Appeals." In Miller, *Exploring Judicial Politics.*

Mauro, Tony. 2006a. "Justices Fight Back." *USA Today,* 20 June, A13.

———. 2006b. "Roberts, Gonzales Speak on Judicial Independence." *Legal Times,* 2 October.

———. 2007. "Justice Kennedy: Yes to Judicial Pay Hikes, No to Cameras at High Court." *Legal Times,* 15 February.

Mayhew, David R. 1974. *Congress: The Electoral Connection.* New Haven, CT: Yale University Press.

McCloskey, Robert G. 1960. *The American Supreme Court.* Chicago: University of Chicago Press.

———. 1972. *The Modern Supreme Court.* Cambridge, MA: Harvard University Press.

———. 1994. *The American Supreme Court.* 2nd ed. Chicago: University of Chicago Press.

McClusky, Tom. 2006. "Rein in Activist Judges." *USA Today,* 2 August, 8A.

McCubbins, Mathew D., Roger G. Noll, and Barry R. Weingast. 1995. "Politics and the Courts: A Positive Theory of Judicial Doctrine and the Rule of Law." *Southern California Law Review* 68:1631–83.

McGinty, Brian. 2008. *Lincoln and the Court.* Cambridge, MA: Harvard University Press.

McKeever, Robert. 2006. "Constitutional Issues, Rights and Supreme Court Appointments." In Morgan and Davies, *Right On?*

McMahon, Kevin J. 2004. *Reconsidering Roosevelt on Race: How the Presidency Paved the Road to Brown.* Chicago: University of Chicago Press.

McMillion, Rhonda. 2006. "A Firm Stand: ABA Opposes Bills to Create Inspector General for Federal Courts." *American Bar Association Journal,* December, 64.

Meckler, Laura. 2008. "McCain Speech to Shed Light on Judicial Philosophy." *Wall Street Journal,* 6 May, A8.

Meese, Edwin, III, and Rhett DeHart. 1997. "Reining in the Federal Judiciary." *Judicature* 80:178–83.

Melnick, R. Shep. 1994. *Between the Lines: Interpreting Welfare Rights.* Washington, D.C.: Brookings Institution Press.

———. 1995. "Statutory Reconstruction: The Politics of Eskridge's Interpretation." *Georgetown Law Journal* 84:91–121.

———. 2004. "Courts and Agencies." In Miller and Barnes, *Making Policy, Making Law.*

Mikva, Abner. 1992. "How Should We Select Our Judges in a Free Society?" *Southern Illinois University Law Journal* 16:547–56.

Milbank, Dana. 2005. "And the Verdict on Justice Kennedy Is: Guilty." *Washington Post,* 9 April, A03.

Milkis, Sidney M. 2007. "Partisan Rancor and Representative Democracy." *Chronicle of Higher Education,* 2 March, B6–B9.

Miller, Mark C. 1992. "Congressional Committees and the Federal Courts: A Neo-Institutional Perspective." *Western Political Quarterly* 45:949–70.

———. 1993. "Courts, Agencies, and Congressional Committees: A Neo-Institutional Perspective." *Review of Politics* 55:525–66.

———. 1995. *The High Priests of American Politics: The Role of Lawyers in American Political Institutions.* Knoxville: University of Tennessee Press.

———. 2004. "The View of the Courts from the Hill: A Neoinstitutional Perspective." In Miller and Barnes, *Making Policy, Making Law.*

———. 2006. "When Congress Attacks the Federal Courts." *Case Western Reserve Law Review* 56:1015–30.

———, ed. 2008a. *Exploring Judicial Politics.* New York: Oxford University Press.

———. 2008b. "The Interactions between the Federal Courts and the Other Branches." In Miller, *Exploring Judicial Politics.*

Miller, Mark C., and Jeb Barnes, eds. 2004. *Making Policy, Making Law: An Interbranch Perspective.* Washington, D.C.: Georgetown University Press.

Moen, Matthew C. 1989. *The Christian Right and Congress.* Tuscaloosa: University of Alabama Press.

Mondak, Jeffrey J., and Shannon Ishiyama Smithey. 1997. "The Dynamics of Public Support for the Supreme Court." *Journal of Politics* 59:1114–42.

Morgan, Iwan, and Philip Davies, eds. *Right On? Political Change and Continuity in George W. Bush's America.* London: Institute for the Study of the Americas.

Morton, F. L. 2001. "Dialogue or Monologue?" In *Judicial Power and Canadian Democracy,* edited by Paul Howe and Peter H. Russell. Montreal: McGill-Queen's University Press.

Morton, F. L., and Rainer Knopff. 2000. *The Charter Revolution and the Court Party.* Peterborough, ON: Broadview.

Munn, Michelle. 2002. "Plan to Curb Forest Fires Wins Support." *Los Angeles Times,* 2 August, A16.

Murphy, Walter F. 1962. *Congress and the Court.* Chicago: University of Chicago Press.

———. 1964. *Elements of Judicial Strategy.* Chicago: University of Chicago Press.

———. 1986. "Who Shall Interpret? The Quest for the Ultimate Constitutional Interpreter." *Review of Politics* 48:401–23.

Murphy, Walter F., and C. Herman Pritchett. 1961. *Courts, Judges, and Politics: An Introduction to the Judicial Process.* New York: Random House.

Murphy, Walter F., C. Herman Pritchett, Lee Epstein, and Jack Knight. 2006. *Courts, Judges, and Politics: An Introduction to the Judicial Process.* 6th ed. Boston: McGraw-Hill.

Murray, Shailagh. 2007. "Texas Senator Bucks Trend, Stands Solidly by Bush." *Washington Post,* 17 February, A5.

Nagel, Stuart S. 1965. "Court-Curbing Periods in American History." *Vanderbilt Law Review* 18:925–44.

Nagourney, Adam. 2006. "New Campaign Ads Have a Theme: Don't Be Nice." *New York Times,* 27 September, A1.

Nather, David. 2005. "Race against the Nuclear Clock." *Congressional Quarterly Weekly Report,* 30 May, 1440–43.

Nelson, Michael. 1988. "The President and the Court: Reinterpreting the Court-Packing Episode of 1937." *Political Science Quarterly* 103:267–93.

Nemacheck, Christine L. 2007. *Strategic Selection: Presidential Nomination of Supreme Court Justices from Herbert Hoover through George W. Bush.* Charlottesville: University of Virginia Press.

Neustadt, Richard E. 1980. *Presidential Power: The Politics of Leadership from FDR to Carter.* New York: Macmillan.

New York Times. 2006a. "A Bad Court-Splitting Plan." Editorial. 23 September, A10.

———. 2006b. "Judges Should Police Themselves." Editorial. 18 May, A28.

———. 2007a. "Better Security for Judges." Editorial. 2 February, A18.

———. 2007b. "A Key Moment for Justice." Editorial. 5 December, 30.

———. 2008. "Justice 5, Brutality 4." Editorial. 13 June, A26.

O'Brien, David M. 1988. "The Reagan Judges: His Most Enduring Legacy." In *The Reagan Legacy,* edited by Charles O. Jones. Chatham, NJ: Chatham House.

———. 2001. "How the Republican War over 'Judicial Activism' Has Cost Congress." In Campbell and Stack, *Congress Confronts the Court.*

———. 2003. *Storm Center: The Supreme Court in American Politics.* 6th ed. New York: W. W. Norton.

———. 2005. *Storm Center: The Supreme Court in American Politics.* 7th ed. New York: W. W. Norton.

O'Connor, Sandra Day. 2006. "The Threat to Judicial Independence." *Wall Street Journal,* 27 September, A18.

Orren, Karen, and Stephen Skowronek. 2004. *The Search for American Political Development.* New York: Cambridge University Press.

Pacelle, Richard L., Jr. 2002. *The Role of the Supreme Court in American Politics: The Least Dangerous Branch?* Boulder, CO: Westview.

Parker, Tom. 2005. "Alabama Justices Surrender to Judicial Activism." *Birmingham News,* 1 January, B4.

Paschal, Richard A. 1991. "The Continuing Colloquy: Congress and the Finality of the Supreme Court." *Journal of Law and Politics* 8:142–226.

Paulsen, Michael Stokes. 1994. "The Most Dangerous Branch: Executive Power to Say What the Law Is." *Georgetown Law Journal* 83:217–345.

Paust, Jordan J. 2007. *Beyond the Law: The Bush Administration's Unlawful Responses to the "War" on Terror.* New York: Cambridge University Press.

Peretti, Terri Jennings. 1999. *In Defense of a Political Court.* Princeton, NJ: Princeton University Press.

———. 2002. "Does Judicial Independence Exist? The Lessons of Social Science Research." In Burbank and Friedman, *Judicial Independence at the Crossroads.*

———. 2005. "An Empirical Analysis of Alexander Bickel's *The Least Dangerous Branch.*" In *The Judiciary and American Democracy: Alexander Bickel, the Countermajoritarian Difficulty, and Contemporary Constitutional Theory,* edited by Kenneth D. Ward and Cecilia R. Castillo. Albany: State University of New York Press.

Perine, Keith. 2004. "Heightened Tensions Fray Judicial-Legislative Relations." *Congressional Quarterly Weekly Report,* 18 September, 2148–53.

———. 2005. "In Letter to Nominee Roberts, Specter Criticizes Court's Federalism Decisions." *Congressional Quarterly Weekly Report,* 15 August, 2254.

Perkins, Lynette P. 1980. "Influences of Members' Goals on Their Committee Behavior: The U.S. House Judiciary Committee." *Legislative Studies Quarterly* 5: 373–93.

———. 1981. "Member Recruitment to a Mixed Goal Committee: The House Judiciary Committee." *Journal of Politics* 43:348–64.

Perry, Barbara A. 1999. *The Priestly Tribe: The Supreme Court's Image in the American Mind.* Westport, CT: Praeger.

Perry, H. W., and Lucas A. Powe Jr. 2004. "The Political Battle for the Constitution." *Constitutional Commentary* 21:641–96.

Petter, Andrew. 2006. "Look Who's Talking Now: Dialogue Theory and the Return to Democracy." In Bauman and Kahana, *Least Examined Branch.*

Phillips, Kevin P. 1970. *The Emerging Republican Majority.* New York: Anchor.

Pickerill, J. Mitchell. 2004. *Constitutional Deliberation in Congress: The Impact of Judicial Review in a Separated System.* Durham, NC: Duke University Press.

Pickerill, J. Mitchell, and Cornell W. Clayton. 2004. "The Rehnquist Court and the Political Dynamics of Federalism." *Perspectives on Politics* 2:233–48.

Pierson, Paul, and Theda Skocpol. 2001. "Historical Institutionalism in Contemporary Political Science." In *Political Science: State of the Discipline,* edited by Ira Katznelson and Helen V. Milner. New York: W. W. Norton.

Posner, Richard A. 2005. "Foreword: A Political Court." *Harvard Law Review* 119: 31–103.

Powe, Lucas A., Jr. 2000. *The Warren Court and American Politics.* Cambridge, MA: Harvard University Press, Belknap Press.

Preyer, Kathryn. 1992. "Judiciary Acts of 1801 and 1802." In *The Oxford Companion to the Supreme Court of the United States,* edited by Kermit L. Hall. New York: Oxford University Press.

Pritchett, C. Herman. 1948. *The Roosevelt Court: A Study in Politics and Values, 1937–1947.* New York: Macmillan.

———. 1961. *Congress versus the Supreme Court, 1957–1960.* Minneapolis: University of Minnesota Press.

Quaid, Libby. 2008. "McCain Castigates Obama on Judges." *Boston Globe,* 6 May.

Rae, Nicol C. 1989. *The Decline and Fall of Liberal Republicans: From 1952 to Present.* New York: Oxford University Press.

Ransom, William L. 1912. *Majority Rule and the Judiciary.* New York: Scribner.

Rawls, John. 1971. *A Theory of Justice.* Cambridge, MA: Harvard University Press.

Reed, Ralph. 1994. *Politically Incorrect: The Emerging Faith Factor in American Politics.* Dallas: Word.

———. 1996. *Active Faith: How Christians Are Changing the Soul of American Politics.* New York: Free Press.

Rehnquist, William H. 1992. *Grand Inquests: The Historic Impeachments of Justice Samuel Chase and President Andrew Johnson.* New York: Quill William Morrow.

———. 1996. "Keynote Address: Symposium on the Future of the Federal Courts." *American University Law Review* 46:267–74.

———. 1998. *All the Laws But One: Civil Liberties in Wartime.* New York: Alfred A. Knopf.

———. 2001. *The Supreme Court.* New York: Alfred A. Knopf.

———. 2003. *2003 Year-End Report on the Federal Judiciary.* Washington, D.C.: Supreme Court of the United States.

———. 2004. *The Year-End Report on the Judiciary, 2004.* Washington, D.C.: Supreme Court of the United States.

Remini, Robert V. 1988. *The Legacy of Andrew Jackson: Essays on Democracy, Indian Removal, and Slavery.* Baton Rouge: Louisiana State University Press.

Resnik, Judith. 2000a. "The Problematic Judiciary: Lobbying, Judging, and Invalidating the Violence Against Women Act." *Southern California Law Review* 74:269–94.

———. 2000b. "Trial as Error, Jurisdiction as Injury: Transforming the Meaning of Article III." *Harvard Law Review* 113:924–1037.

Resnik, Judith, Danny J. Boggs, and Howard Berman. 2004. "The Independence of the Federal Judiciary." *Bulletin of the American Academy of Arts and Sciences,* Winter, 17–28.

Reston, Maeve. 2008. "What McCain Expects from Federal Judges." *Los Angeles Times,* 7 May.

Revesz, Richard, et al. 2005. Letter from Deans of U.S. Law Schools to the Leadership of Both Chambers of Congress. 4 May. http://www.nyu.edu/public.affairs/releases/detail/647.

Reynolds, Maura. 2006. "A Stark Division in Vote for Alito." *Los Angeles Times* 1 February, A1.

Richards, Mark J., and Herbert M. Kritzer. 2002. "Jurisprudential Regimes in Supreme Court Decision Making." *American Political Science Review* 96:305–20.

Rishikof, Harvey, and Barbara A. Perry. 1995. "Separateness but Interdependence, Autonomy but Reciprocity: A First Look at Federal Judges' Appearances before Legislative Committees." *Mercer Law Review* 46:667–76.

Roach, Kent. 2001a. "Constitutional and Common Law Dialogues between the Supreme Court and Canadian Legislatures." *Canadian Bar Review* 72:481–533.

———. 2001b. *The Supreme Court on Trial: Judicial Activism or Democratic Dialogue.* Toronto: Irwin Law.

———. 2005a. "Constitutional, Remedial, and International Dialogues about Rights: The Canadian Experience." *Texas International Law Journal* 40:537–76.

———. 2005b. "The Rule of Law/The Rule of Judges: Common Law Bills of Rights as Dialogue between Courts and Legislatures." *University of Toronto Law Journal* 55:733–66.

Roberts, John G., Jr. 2006. *2005 Year-End Report on the Federal Judiciary.* Washington, D.C.: Supreme Court of the United States.

———. 2007. *2006 Year-End Report on the Federal Judiciary.* Washington, D.C.: Supreme Court of the United States.

———. 2008. *2007 Year-End Report on the Federal Judiciary.* Washington, D.C.: Supreme Court of the United States.

Robertson, Pat. 2004. *Courting Disaster: How the Supreme Court Is Usurping the Power of Congress and the People.* Brentwood, TN: Integrity.

Rogers, James R. 2001. "Information and Judicial Review: A Signaling Game of Legislative-Judicial Interaction." *American Journal of Political Science* 45:84–99.

Rogers, James R., Roy B. Flemming, and Jon R. Bond, eds. 2006. *Institutional Games and the U.S. Supreme Court.* Charlottesville: University of Virginia Press.

Romzek, Barbara S., and Jennifer A. Utter. 1997. "Congressional Legislative Staff: Political Professionals or Clerks?" *American Journal of Political Science* 41:1251–79.

Rosen, Jeffrey. 2006. *The Most Democratic Branch? How the Courts Serve America.* New York: Oxford University Press.

———. 2007. "The Dissenter." *New York Times Magazine,* 23 September.

Rosenberg, Debra. 2005. "The War on Judges." *Newsweek,* 25 April, 23–27.

Rosenberg, Gerald N. 1991. *The Hollow Hope: Can Courts Bring About Social Change?* Chicago: University of Chicago Press.

———. 1992. "Judicial Independence and the Reality of Political Power." *Review of Politics,* 54:369–98.

———. 2005. "The Impact of Courts on American Public Life." In *The Institutions of American Democracy: The Judicial Branch,* edited by Kermit L. Hall and Kevin T. McGuire. New York: Oxford University Press.

Ross, William G. 1994. *A Muted Fury: Populists, Progressives, and Labor Unions Confront the Courts, 1890–1937.* Princeton, NJ: Princeton University Press.

Rozell, Mark J. 2002. "The Christian Right in the 2000 GOP Presidential Campaign." In *Piety, Politics, and Pluralism: Religion, the Courts, and the 2000 Election,* edited by Mary C. Segers. Lanham, MD: Rowman & Littlefield.

Rubin, Edward L. 2002. "Independence as a Governance Mechanism." In Burbank and Friedman, *Judicial Independence at the Crossroads.*

Sager, Lawrence Gene. 1981. "The Supreme Court, 1980 Term—Foreword: Constitutional Limitations on Congress' Authority to Regulate the Jurisdiction of the Federal Courts." *Harvard Law Review* 95:17–345.

Salisbury, Robert H., and Kenneth A. Shepsle. 1981. "U.S. Congressman as Enterprise." *Legislative Studies Quarterly* 6:559–76.

Salmon, Jacqueline L. 2007. "Romney Aims to Prove His Christianity." *Washington Post,* 6 December, A10.

Sammon, Bill. 2002. "Bush Seeks Relaxing of Logging Rules; Urges Exemption Daschle Got." *Washington Times,* 23 August, A1.

Savage, David G. 2008. "Two Visions of the Supreme Court: McCain Wants to End 'Judicial Activism.' Obama Favors Justices with 'Empathy' for Ordinary People." *Los Angeles Times,* 19 May, 8.

Schaeffer, Eric. 2006. "Junketing Judges: A Case of Bad Science." *Washington Post,* 4 June, B2.

Schauer, Frederick. 2004. "Judicial Supremacy and the Modest Constitution." *California Law Review* 92:1045–67.

Scherer, Nancy. 2005. *Scoring Points: Politicians, Activists, and the Lower Court Appointment Process.* Palo Alto, CA: Stanford University Press.

Schlafly, Phyllis. 2006. *The Supremacists: The Tyranny of Judges and How to Stop It.* Rev. and expanded ed. Dallas: Spence.

Schlesinger, Arthur M., Jr. 1953. *The Age of Jackson.* Boston: Little, Brown.

Schmidhauser, John R., and Larry L. Berg. 1972. *The Supreme Court and Congress: Conflict and Interaction, 1945–1968.* New York: Free Press.

Scholl, Michael. 2006. "Alito: Threat to Judicial Independence at Historic High." *Law.com,* 4 October.

Schubert, Glendon A. 1960. *Constitutional Politics: The Political Behavior of Supreme*

Court Justices and the Constitutional Policies They Make. New York: Holt, Rinehart, & Winston.

Schumer, Charles E. 2007. "Under Attack: Congressional Power in the Twenty-first Century." *Harvard Law and Policy Review* 1:3–40.

Schwartz, Herman. 2004. *Right Wing Justice: The Conservative Campaign to Take Over the Courts.* New York: Nation Books.

Sears, Alan, and Craig Osten. 2005. *The ACLU vs. America: Exposing the Agenda to Redefine Moral Values.* Nashville: Broadman & Holman.

Segal, Jeffrey A., and Harold J. Spaeth. 2002. *The Supreme Court and the Attitudinal Model Revisited.* New York: Cambridge University Press.

Segal, Jeffrey A., Harold J. Spaeth, and Sara C. Benesh. 2005. *The Supreme Court in the American Legal System.* New York: Cambridge University Press.

Sekulow, Jay Alan. 2006. *Witnessing Their Faith: Religious Influence on Supreme Court Justices and Their Opinions.* Lanham, MD: Rowman & Littlefield.

Sensenbrenner, F. James, Jr. 2005. "Robust Congressional Oversight Will Improve Federal Judiciary." *Human Events,* 23 May.

———. 2006. "Sensenbrenner, Grassley Introduce Legislation Establishing an Inspector General for the Judicial Branch." Press release from U.S. House Judiciary Committee, 27 April. http://www.judiciary.house.gov/media/pdfs/judgeintro42706.pdf.

Shamir, Ronen. 1995. *Managing Legal Uncertainty: Elite Lawyers in the New Deal.* Durham, NC: Duke University Press.

Shapiro, Martin. 1964a. *Law and Politics in the Supreme Court: New Approaches to Political Jurisprudence.* New York: Free Press.

———. 1964b. "Political Jurisprudence." *Kentucky Law Journal* 52:294–345.

———. 1968. *The Supreme Court and Administrative Agencies.* New York: Free Press.

Silverstein, Mark. 1994. *Judicious Choices: The New Politics of Supreme Court Confirmations.* New York: W. W. Norton.

Simon, James F. 1973. *In His Own Image: The Supreme Court in Richard Nixon's America.* New York: David McKay.

Smith, Christopher. 2003. "Battle Looms on Forest Thinning: Initiative Seeks to Thin Forests." *Salt Lake Tribune,* 27 May, C1.

Smith, Christopher E. 1993. *Courts, Politics and the Judicial Process.* Chicago: Nelson Hall.

Smith, Lamar. 2003. "Smith & Chabot Form Judicial Accountability Group." Press release from U.S. House of Representatives, 23 July. http://www.lamarsmith.house.gov/Read.aspx?ID=28.

Smith, Mark W. 2006. *Disrobed: The New Battle Plan to Break the Left's Stranglehold on the Courts.* New York: Crown Forum.

Smith, Neal. 1996. *Mr. Smith Went to Washington: From Eisenhower to Clinton.* Ames: Iowa State University Press.

Smith, Rogers. 1988. "Political Jurisprudence: The New Institutionalism and the Future of Public Law." *American Political Science Review* 82:89–108.

Smith, William French. 1982. Letter of Attorney General William French Smith to

Senate Judiciary Chairman Strom Thurmond on S. 1742, 6 May. 97th Cong., 2nd sess. *Congressional Record* 128, daily ed. (6 May), S 4727–30.

Songer, Donald R., Reginald S. Sheehan, and Susan B. Haire. 2000. *Continuity and Change on the United States Courts of Appeals.* Ann Arbor: University of Michigan Press.

Sprigg, Peter. 2004. *Outrage: How Gay Activists and Liberal Judges Are Trashing Democracy to Redefine Marriage.* Washington, D.C.: Regnery.

Steigerwalt, Amy. 2007. "Religious Conservatives and the Courts." Paper presented at the annual meeting of the Midwest Political Science Association, Chicago, 12–15 April.

Stephens, Joe. 2006. "Ethics Lapses by Federal Judges Persist, Review Finds." *Washington Post,* 18 April, A17.

Stephenson, Donald Grier, Jr. 1999. *Campaigns and the Court: The U.S. Supreme Court in Presidential Elections.* New York: Columbia University Press.

Stern, Seth. 2002. "A Career as a Federal Judge Isn't What It Used to Be." *Christian Science Monitor,* 22 January, 1.

———. 2005. "Hearings Unlikely to Pin Roberts Down." *Congressional Quarterly Weekly Report,* 5 September, 2334–35.

Stern, Seth, and Keith Perine. 2005. "Beyond the Roberts Confirmation." *Congressional Quarterly Weekly Report,* 3 October, 2650–52.

———. 2006. "Alito Confirmed after Filibuster Fails." *Congressional Quarterly Weekly Report,* 6 February, 340–41.

Stolberg, Sheryl Gay. 2005a. "Nominee Is Pressed on End-of-Life Care." *New York Times,* 10 August, A18.

———. 2005b. "Panel Chairman to Press Roberts on Cases." *New York Times,* 9 August, A16.

———. 2006. "In Supreme Court Confirmation Hearings, Test for Democrats as Well as Alito." *New York Times,* 8 January, A18.

Sunstein, Cass. 1998. *Legal Reasoning and Political Conflict.* New York: Oxford University Press.

Tarr, G. Alan. 2006. *Judicial Process and Judicial Policymaking.* 4th ed. Belmont, CA: Thomson Wadsworth.

———. 2007. "Rethinking Judicial Independence and Judicial Accountability." Paper presented at the annual meeting of the Midwest Political Science Association, Chicago, 12–15 April.

Taylor, Andrew J. 2005. *Elephant's Edge: The Republicans as a Ruling Party.* Westport, CT: Praeger.

Teles, Steven M. 2008. *The Rise of the Conservative Legal Movement: The Battle for Control of the Law.* Princeton, NJ: Princeton University Press.

Thomas, Kenneth R. 2005. *Limiting Court Jurisdiction over Federal Constitutional Issues: "Court-Stripping."* CRS Report RL32171. 24 January.

Tiefer, Charles. 2004. *Veering Right: How the Bush Administration Subverts the Law for Conservative Causes.* Berkeley and Los Angeles: University of California Press.

Tobias, Carl. 2005. "Should the Ninth Circuit Be Split? Congress Considers Dividing the Appellate Court." *Washington Times,* 30 December, A23.

———. 2008. "GOP Strategy on Judicial Selection." *Richmond Times Dispatch,* 12 February, A13.

Tolley, Michael C. 2006. "Legal Controversies over Federal Judicial Selection in the United States: Breaking the Cycle of Obstruction and Retribution over Judicial Appointments." In *Appointing Judges in an Age of Judicial Power: Critical Perspectives from Around the World,* edited by Kate Malleson and Peter H. Russell. Toronto: University of Toronto Press.

Toma, Eugenia Froedge. 1991. "Congressional Influence and the Supreme Court: The Budget as a Signaling Device." *Journal of Legal Studies* 20:131–46.

Toobin, Jeffrey. 2007. *The Nine: Inside the Secret World of the Supreme Court.* New York: Doubleday.

———. 2008. "In McCain's Court." *New Yorker,* 26 May.

Tribe, Lawrence H. 2000. *American Constitutional Law.* 3rd ed. Vol. 1. New York: Foundation Press.

Trippet, Frank. 1981. "Trying to Trim the Courts." *Time,* 28 September, 93.

Tushnet, Mark V. 1999. *Taking the Constitution Away from the Courts.* Princeton, NJ: Princeton University Press.

———. 2003. *The New Constitutional Order.* Princeton, NJ: Princeton University Press.

———, ed. 2005. *Arguing Marbury v. Madison.* Stanford, CA: Stanford University Press.

———. 2006a. *A Court Divided: The Rehnquist Court and the Future of Constitutional Law.* New York: W. W. Norton.

———. 2006b. "Referring to Foreign Law in Constitutional Interpretation: An Episode in the Culture Wars." *University of Baltimore Law Review* 35:299–313.

———. 2008. *Weak Courts, Strong Rights: Judicial Review and Social Welfare Rights in Comparative Constitutional Law.* Princeton, NJ: Princeton University Press.

USA Today. 2006. "How to Influence Judges." 3 May, A10.

U.S. House. Committee on the Judiciary. 2005a. Subcommittee on the Constitution. *House Resolution on the Appropriate Role of Foreign Judgments in the Interpretation of the Constitution of the United States: Hearing before the Subcommittee on the Constitution of the House Judiciary Committee.* 109th Cong., 1st sess., 19 July.

———. 2005b. Subcommittee on the Constitution. *Supreme Court's Kelo Decision and Potential Congressional Responses: Hearing before the Subcommittee on the Constitution of the House Judiciary Committee.* 109th Cong., 1st sess., 22 September.

———. 2006a. Subcommittee on the Constitution. *Public Expression of Religion Act of 2005: Hearing before the Subcommittee on the Constitution of the House Committee of the Judiciary.* 109th Cong., 2nd sess., 22 June.

———. 2006b. Subcommittee on Crime, Terrorism, and Homeland Security.

Judicial Transparency and Ethics Enhancement Act of 2006: Hearings before the Subcommittee on Crime, Terrorism, and Homeland Security of the House Judiciary Committee. 109th Cong., 2nd sess., 29 June.

U.S. Senate. 2007. Committee on the Judiciary. *Hearings before the Senate Judiciary Committee on Judicial Security and Independence.* 110th Cong., 1st sess., 14 February.

Valis, Wayne, ed. 1981. *The Future under President Reagan.* Westport, CT: Arlington House.

Van den Brook, Tom. 2002. "Critics Say Court was 'California Dreaming.'" *USA Today,* 27 June.

Vegh, Steven G. 2007. "For Law School, Unwanted Fame: Justice Dept. Scandal Brings Scrutiny to Aide's Alma Mater." *Washington Post,* 8 July, A8.

Volcansek, Mary L. 2001. "Separation of Powers and Judicial Impeachment." In Campbell and Stack, *Congress Confronts the Court.*

Volcansek, Mary L., and Jacqueline Lucienne Lafon. 1988. *Judicial Selection: The Cross-Evolution of French and American Practices.* New York: Greenwood.

Wald, Kenneth. 1997. *Religion and Politics in the United States.* 3rd ed. Washington, D.C.: CQ Press.

Wald, Patricia, and Neil Kinkopf. 2007. "Putting Separation of Powers into Practice: Reflections on Senator Schumer's Essay." *Harvard Law and Policy Review* 1:41–74.

Walker, John M., Jr. 2004. "Politics and the Confirmation Process: The Importance of Congressional Restraint in Safeguarding Judicial Independence." *Syracuse Law Review* 55:1–14.

———. 2007. "Politics and the Confirmation Process: Thoughts on the Roberts and Alito Hearings." In *Bench Press: The Collision of Courts, Politics, and the Media,* edited by Keith J. Bybee. Palo Alto, CA: Stanford University Press.

Walker, Thomas G., and Deborah J. Barrow. 1985. "Funding the Federal Judiciary: The Congressional Connection." *Judicature* 69:43–50.

Wallance, Gregory J. 2003. "A Judiciary in Peril." *Recorder,* 7 November, 4.

Walter, Donna. 2006. "ABA Opposes Proposed Inspector General for Federal Judges." *St. Louis Daily Record,* 17 August.

Warren, Charles. 1926. *The Supreme Court in United States History.* Rev. ed. Vol. 2. Boston: Little, Brown.

Wasby, Stephen L. 1993. *The Supreme Court in the Federal Judicial System.* 4th ed. Chicago: Nelson-Hall.

Washington Post. 2005. "Real ID, Real Problems." Editorial. 10 February, A22.

———. 2006. "An Inspector General?" Editorial. 9 October, A16.

———. 2008. "The Justices' Refrain." Editorial. 13 June, A22.

Weinstein, Henry. 2006a. "Complaint against Judge Has Broader Ramifications." *Los Angeles Times,* 7 May, B3.

———. 2006b. "Plan to Break Up 9th Circuit Court Faces Opposition: Judges, Politicians, and Law Professors Line Up against the Move That Some Conservatives Seek." *Los Angeles Times,* 21 September, B4.

Weinstein, Henry, and Moises Mendoza. 2006. "Ethics Charges a Bid for Revenge, U.S. Judge Says." *Los Angeles Times,* 22 September, B1.

Weisman, Jonathan. 2007. "GOP Blocks Bid on Rights of Detainees." *Washington Post,* 20 September, A5.

Wells, Michael. 1991. "Congress's Paramount Role in Setting the Scope of Federal Jurisdiction." *Northwestern University Law Review* 85:465–77.

Westin, Alan F. 1953. "The Supreme Court, the Populist Movement, and the Campaign of 1896." *Journal of Politics* 15:3–41.

Whiteman, David. 1995. *Communication in Congress: Members, Staff, and the Search for Information.* Lawrence: University Press of Kansas.

Whittington, Keith E. 2000. "Once More unto the Breach: Post-Behavioralist Approaches to Judicial Politics." *Law and Social Inquiry* 25:601–32.

———. 2005. "Interpose Your Friendly Hand: Political Supports for the Exercise of Judicial Review by the United States Supreme Court." *American Political Science Review* 99:583–96.

———. 2007. *Political Foundations of Judicial Supremacy: The Presidency, the Supreme Court, and Constitutional Leadership in U.S. History.* Princeton, NJ: Princeton University Press.

Wilcox, Clyde. 1992. *God's Warriors: The Christian Right in Twentieth-Century America.* Baltimore: Johns Hopkins University Press.

———. 1995. *The Latest American Revolution?* New York: St. Martin's.

Wilcox, Clyde, Matthew DeBell, and Lee Sigelman. 1999. "The Second Coming of the New Christian Right: Patterns of Popular Support in 1984 and 1996." *Social Science Quarterly* 80:181–92.

Wilcox, Clyde, and Carin Larson. 2006. *Onward Christian Soldiers? The Religious Right in American Politics.* 3rd ed. Boulder: Westview.

Wittes, Benjamin. 2006. *Confirmation Wars: Preserving Independent Courts in Angry Times.* Lanham, MD: Rowman & Littlefield.

Yalof, David A. 1999. *Pursuit of Justices: Presidential Politics and the Selection of Supreme Court Nominees.* Chicago: University of Chicago Press.

Yap, Albert. 2005. "Congressman Speaks on Legislature, Judiciary." *Stanford Review,* 20 May.

Zemans, Frances Kahn. 1999. "The Accountable Judge: Guardian of Judicial Independence." *Southern California Law Review* 72:625–56.

Zernike, Kate. 2008. "McCain and Obama Split on Justices' Ruling." *New York Times,* 13 June, A21.

Zorn, Christopher. 2006. "Institutions and Independence in Models of Judicial Review." In Rogers, Flemming, and Bond, *Institutional Games and the U.S. Supreme Court.*

Cases

Barenblatt v. United States, 360 U.S. 109 (1959).

Boumediene v. Bush, 128 S.Ct. 2229 (2008).

Brown v. Board of Education, 347 U.S. 483 (1954).

Bush v. Gore, 531 U.S. 98 (2000).
Chisholm v. Georgia, 2 U.S. 419 (1793).
City of Boerne v. Archbishop Flores, 521 U.S 507 (1997).
Cummings v. Missouri, 71 U.S. 277 (1866).
Dickerson v. United States, 530 U.S. 428 (2000).
Dred Scott v. Sandford, 60 U.S. 393 (1857).
Employment Division v. Smith, 494 U.S. 872 (1990).
Ex Parte Garland, 71 U.S. 333 (1866).
Ex Parte McCardle, 74 U.S. 506 (1869).
Ex Parte Merryman, 17 F. Cas. 144 (Circuit Court, D. Maryland, 1861).
Ex Parte Milligan, 71 U.S. 2 (1866).
Ex Parte Vallandigham, 68 U.S. 243 (1864).
Ex Parte Yerger, 75 U.S 85 (1869)
Glidden Co. v. Zdanok, 370 U.S. 530 (1962).
Gonzales v. Raich, 545 U.S. 1 (2005).
Goodridge v. Department of Public Health, 440 Mass. 309, 798 N.E. 2d 941 (2003).
Griswold v. Connecticut, 381 U.S. 479 (1965).
Hamdan v. Rumsfeld, 126 S.Ct. 2749 (2006).
Hamdi v. Rumsfeld, 542 U.S. 507 (2004).
Hepburn v. Griswold, 75 U.S. 603 (1870).
Immigration and Naturalization Service v. Chadha, 462 U.S. 919 (1983).
In re Debs, 158 U.S. 1 (1895).
Jencks v. United States, 353 U.S. 657 (1957).
Kelo v. City of New London, 545 U.S. 469 (2005).
Knox v. Lee, 79 U.S. 457 (1871).
Lawrence v. Texas, 539 U.S. 558 (2003).
Ledbetter v. Goodyear Tire and Rubber, 127 S. Ct. 2162 (2007).
Lochner v. New York, 198 U.S. 45 (1905).
Marbury v. Madison, 5 U.S. 137 (1803).
Martin v. Hunter's Lessee, 14 U.S. 304 (1816).
McCulloch v. Maryland, 17 U.S. 315 (1819).
Miranda v. Arizona, 384 U.S. 436 (1966).
National Mutual Insurance v. Tidewater Transfer Co., 337 U.S. 582 (1949).
Pollock v. Farmers Loan and Trust Co., 157 U.S. 429 (1895).
Rasul v. Bush, 542 U.S. 466 (2004).
Roper v. Simmons, 543 U.S. 551 (2005).
Roosevelt v. Meyer, 68 U.S. 512 (1863).
Stuart v. Laird, 5 U.S. 298 (1803).
Texas v. Johnson, 491 U.S. 397 (1989).
The Prize Cases, 67 U.S. 635 (1863).
United States v. Bitty, 208 U.S. 393 (1908).
United States v. Booker, 543 U.S. 220 (2005).
United States v. Carolene Products Co., 304 U.S. 144 (1938).
United States v. E. C. Knight, 156 U.S. 1 (1895).

United States v. Eichman, 496 U.S. 310 (1990).
United States v. Klein, 80 U.S. 128 (1872).
United States v. Lopez, 514 U.S. 549 (1995).
United States v. Nixon, 418 U.S. 683 (1974).
United States v. Will, 449 U.S. 200 (1980).
Watkins v. United States, 354 U.S. 178 (1957).
West Coast Hotel Co. v. Parrish, 300 U.S. 379 (1937).
West Virginia State Board of Education v. Barnette, 319 U.S. 624 (1943).
Worcester v. Georgia, 31 U.S. 515 (1832).
Yates v. United States, 354 U.S. 298 (1957).

INDEX

Constitutionalism and Democracy

KEVIN T. MCGUIRE
The Supreme Court Bar: Legal Elites in the Washington Community

MARK TUSHNET, ED.
The Warren Court in Historical and Political Perspective

DAVID N. MAYER
The Constitutional Thought of Thomas Jefferson

F. THORNTON MILLER
Juries and Judges versus the Law: Virginia's Provincial Legal Perspective, 1783–1828

MARTIN EDELMAN
Courts, Politics, and Culture in Israel

TONY FREYER
Producers versus Capitalists: Constitutional Conflict in Antebellum America

AMITAI ETZIONI, ED.
New Communitarian Thinking: Persons, Virtues, Institutions, and Communities

GREGG IVERS
To Build a Wall: American Jews and the Separation of Church and State

ERIC W. RISE
The Martinsville Seven: Race, Rape, and Capital Punishment

STEPHEN L. WASBY
Race Relations Litigation in an Age of Complexity

PETER H. RUSSELL AND DAVID M. O'BRIEN, EDS.
Judicial Independence in the Age of Democracy: Critical Perspectives from around the World

GREGG IVERS AND KEVIN T. MCGUIRE, EDS.
Creating Constitutional Change

STUART STREICHLER
Justice Curtis in the Civil War Era: At the Crossroads of American Constitutionalism

VIRGINIA A. HETTINGER, STEFANIE A. LINDQUIST, AND WENDY L. MARTINEK
Judging on a Collegial Court: Influences on Federal Appellate Decision Making

JAMES R. ROGERS, ROY B. FLEMMING, JON R. BOND, EDS.
Institutional Games and the U.S. Supreme Court

VANESSA A. BAIRD
Answering the Call of the Court: How Justices and Litigants Set the Supreme Court Agenda

CHRISTINE L. NEMACHECK
Strategic Selection: Presidential Selection of Supreme Court Justices from Herbert Hoover through George W. Bush

BARRY ALAN SHAIN, ED.
The Nature of Rights at the American Founding and Beyond

MARK C. MILLER
The View of the Courts from the Hill: Interactions between Congress and the Federal Judiciary